1959

Augustine,

philosopher of freedom

AUGUSTINE

Philosopher of Freedom

A STUDY IN COMPARATIVE PHILOSOPHY

by

MARY T. CLARK, R.S.C.J.

DESCLÉE COMPANY

NEW YORK — TOURNAI — ROME — PARIS

NIHIL OBSTAT

John A. Goodwine, J. C. D.

Censor Librorum

IMPRIMATUR June 30, 1958

✠ Francis Cardinal Spellman

ARCHBISHOP OF NEW YORK

The nihil obstat and imprimatur are official declarations that a book or pamphlet is free of doctrinal or moral error. No implication is contained therein that those who have granted the nihil obstat and imprimatur agree with the contents, opinions or statements expressed.

Printed in Belgium

To

my Mother

FOREWORD

That we live our lives in dependence on a heritage of cultural traditions stemming from the remote past, is evident to all who read history. Without a past, the race of men would lack a great dimension. Of course, modern people are tremendously indebted to Greece and Rome for the seeds of western civilization. One writer has asserted that nothing moves in our world today which is not Greek in origin. Another has claimed that we owe it all to Plato. It does not really matter who these historians are, for they are wrong. There are obvious values in our society which came from Judaeo-Christian sources and not from the classic thinkers of Greece and Rome.

Perhaps no reader's equanimity will be disturbed at learning that the sages of pre-Christian philosophy knew little of the Will of God. What may disconcert some who look at this book is the judgment that these classic thinkers knew almost as little about the will of man. Mother Clark draws her conclusions with scholarly caution : she is prepared to admit that Plato and the Stoics made certain obscure overtures toward a theory of human volition. I should incline toward a more sweeping generalization : there seems to me to be no real awareness of the importance of will in any pagan thinker of antiquity. If Plotinus be an exception, it must be remembered that he lived centuries after Christ, may have studied under a Christian master, and certainly had students who knew Christianity.

*Indeed, I do not know what word in classic Greek fully conveys the present meaning of the English word, will. They had terms for appetitive consent, for decision, for choice, for desire — but they were all different words. If we look for a Greek noun with the full connotation of will, we are driven to the conclusion that the Greeks did not have it. Even Aristotle, that busy coiner of scientific and philosophic terminology, hesitated here. In a famous passage (*Nicomachean Ethics, VI, 2*) he is forced to circumlocution, saying that choice is either an understanding-which-desires or a desire-which-understands. Here we see a great mind straining to break the bonds of Greek necessitarianism and not quite achieving the freedom of a personal will.*

However this may be, it is clear that will as a power of self-commitment, of free choice, of turning toward or away from the good, is fully appreciated in early Christian writings and particularly in the works of St. Augustine of Hippo. He saw this capacity as one of the most essential attributes of the human person. For Augustine, man is understanding, is memory, is will. It was apparent to him that, without will, man's political, social, cultural freedom would be but an empty negation. Liberty cannot mean merely the absence of external restraint, for there must be some positive ability to act when constraining bonds have been removed.

This is the important message of the present book. Of late years, many studies have been made and published on the role of freedom in modern society. Great impetus was given these investigations by a program initiated by Dwight D. Eisenhower while he was at Columbia University. What many of these studies overlooked is what Mother Clark's book makes clear. You cannot have a free Society unless its citizens be free men. You cannot have free men unless you have free choice within each person. You may spend millions on learned studies of the origins of western democracy and its free institutions — but if you have a psychology which gives no place to the will in the human person, you end with citizen robots automatically stamping out business machine decisions, in complete conformity with the data that they are fed.

That we should be reminded of this practical truth, in a book which takes us back to the very origins of our modern concepts of will and human freedom, is now most opportune. The struggle for the hearts and minds of men today is basically an ideological one. And since all human wills are but the shadow of the divine Will, and all man's freedoms but images of the transcendent Freedom, it may be that only one who meditates upon the prototype can describe the copy.

VERNON J. BOURKE

Saint Louis University.

PREFACE

This book makes no pretence to be anything more than a listening post. Within these pages can be heard many voices uplifted to share with us their insights into freedom. Freedom is important to every man, and for our times it has a special significance. Freedom, however, is that kind of reality that people do not merely want to know about but to experience. Freedom is somehow bound up with the dialectic between man and God Who chose to communicate with free men. That is why the thinker who was the first to see history as evolving from the tension between nature and supernature is strategically situated to report on freedom. Augustine was interested, moreover, not only in teaching the meaning of freedom, but in showing how freedom can be personalized.

The novelty and the permanence of the Augustinian contribution are of interest, and discoverable only by textual studies which reveal how free will was treated by predecessors and successors. Since such studies have more of a philosophical purpose than an historical one, the principle of the comparative critique has been allowed to modify the principle of the immanent critique. Since knowledge is ever advancing, we should expect the notion of freedom to be fuller in modern times, but it seems that not only time but Christianity has made the difference. If we measure the contributions to the notion of freedom offered by the ancients against subsequent elucidations, this is not done in a spirit of censure but in an effort at clarification.

I hope that it is unnecessary to insist that there is no intention on the author's part to speak definitively upon the profound and limitless subject of freedom. There is only a hope that this work may be a point of departure for a deeper penetration into the Augustinian doctrine of freedom through the combined explorations of philosophers and theologians.

With sincere appreciation for their kind encouragement, I wish to thank Reverend Mother Gertrude Bodkin, without whom this work would never have been undertaken, Mother Eleanor O'Byrne, formerly Dean and now President of Manhattanville, Reverend Denis Kavanagh, O.S.A., and my brothers, Reverend James D. Clark, O.S.A. and Mr. George A. Clark.

To Mother Louise Keyes, Dr. Robert C. Pollock and the Philosophy Faculty of Fordham University's Graduate School, I am indebted for numerous insights that could not have been gained from libraries.

I have profited likewise from the suggestions of my kind critics. I wish to thank Reverend John Courtney Murray, S.J., editor of *Theological Studies*, and Reverend Norris Clarke, S.J., of Fordham University for their valued comments. I especially thank Mr. Jacques Maritain for his courteous criticism of the pages devoted to his position, Dr. Elizabeth Salmon for her criticism of the chapter on St. Thomas, Dr. James Collins for his very valuable help with the chapter on modern thought.

There is one to whom I am particularly indebted for his inspiring lectures on the Philosophy of Plotinus, for his guidance in tutorial courses on Augustine, and for the wealth of his own deep scholarship so willingly shared with others. It is a great pleasure for me to acknowledge the generous help that Reverend Paul Henry, S.J. of the Institut Catholique in Paris and now Visiting Professor in Philosophy at the University of Pennsylvania, has given me. My work owes very much to Father Henry's counsel and I thank him sincerely for his illuminating comments and criticisms. If the present book is not better than it is, the responsibility does not rest with any of these kind critics, but with the author.

Finally, I should like to thank Reverend Mario Zicarelli for his generosity in carefully proof-reading the text and for the many valuable suggestions that he offered. I am grateful also to Miss Judith Garson for her kind assistance with proof-reading.

Mary T. Clark, R.S.C.J., Ph.D.

Manhattanville College of the Sacred Heart
Purchase, New York
March 25, 1957.

TABLE OF CONTENTS

TABLE OF CONTENTS

INTRODUCTION

There is a hunger in the human heart for freedom. Struggles for freedom fill the pages of history. Since the state is the individual " writ large, " is not the ceaseless quest for political freedom a reflection of the deep longing of every man for personal freedom? But the freedom so ardently desired by men cannot be merely a power of free choice that is as universal as human nature itself. It would seem that the freedom men deeply desire is even more than a *freedom from* external or internal constraint, though this is not unimportant. Is there not a more profound meaning of freedom : the *freedom to be* all that one can and should be, the freedom to fulfill the true human vocation? There is little common agreement today on the character of this freedom in the broad sense of the word, and still less agreement upon how it is to be attained. The admiration, the discussion, the praise expended on freedom today cannot supply for a true understanding of it. Confusion about the meaning of freedom can be the cause or can be the effect of a confusion about the meaning of man. And yet there can be no dynamic conception of man if the notion of freedom is neglected. Of speculative interest, its import for the practical life is immense. Thinkers of all ages, philosophers as well as theologians, have pondered the reality of freedom. Some have attacked freedom as a problem to be solved; others have approached freedom as a mystery awakening wonder. Just as all the philosophical analyses have not succeeded in eliminating the mystery of man, so there will ever remain something mysterious about human freedom. Yet as long as man has the experience of free will and the longing for freedom in the broad sense, he will seek to understand it.

This book is concerned chiefly with Saint Augustine's teaching on free choice in relation to the larger liberty that comes from loving God. We know that it is quite impossible to exhaust the theological aspects of the topic of freedom in Augustine, and we shall not attempt to do so. Yet, as long as grace builds upon nature, there will be philosophical dimensions to any theological reality. There is no intent to state what should be thought about freedom, but only to set forth what Augustine said about it, and to compare his doctrine with certain characteristic philosophical positions before and after him. Despite the treasury of literature on every phase of Augustine's doctrine, his teaching on freedom has not hitherto been extensively presented to the English reading public. Because of the importance of the topic of freedom in the Augustinian outlook, this notion is objectively studied within the texts and the context of Augustine's writings. We shall try as thoroughly as we can to set forth Augustine's doctrine in itself, to compare and contrast it with the doctrines of Plotinus, of St. Anselm and of St. Thomas Aquinas. If Augustine's teaching on freedom in seen to differ considerably from that of Plotinus, may one not conclude that Augustine's independence of Plotinus is greater than some have thought? If there prove to be numerous points of contact between the Augustinian and the Anselmian and the Thomistic doctrines of freedom, can we not see in Augustine a pioneer philosopher of freedom?

After a preliminary investigation of how the subject of freedom was handled by non-Christian philosophers, and especially by Plotinus, Augustine's own teaching on freedom is presented. Chronologically, the philosophical dialogues were written before the *Confessions*, yet Augustine's experience with free will as revealed in the *Confessions* of 400 A.D. preceded his writing of the Dialogues of 386 A.D. and after. Following the chronological order of the writings, the teaching in the dialogues has been placed first, that is, before the *Confessions*. But Augustine's own experience had posed for him the problem of freedom even before he began to compose the dialogues. [1] So, those dialogues — especially the *De Libero Arbitrio* — present a theoretical treatment of free choice as well as a concrete description of its former state and present state in man.

[1] Augustine, *Confess.*, VII, 3, 5; PL 32, 735.

Accordingly, we have distinguished in them what Augustine said of will or choice as such, and what he said of the freedom or slavery of the human will in accordance with the use made of it. His statements about the freedom or the slavery of the will seem to have originated with the experience of his free will that he reveals in the *Confessions*, as well as from the notion of freedom as efficacy in the direction of the good, a notion that he discovered in the epistles of St. Paul. There have been attempts by critics to bring Augustine's statements concerning free will and concerning freedom into contradiction. Yet in Augustine's own experience, when that experience is viewed in its full theological dimensions, the realities of free choice and of freedom are reconciled. He learned that for the slavery of doing evil the human will sufficed, but for the freedom of doing good both man's consent and God's grace are needed. Augustine's defence of free will as a reality and as a source of responsibility is more than a polemical answer to Manichaeans — it is a recall to the sense of sin. Augustine's doctrine of theological freedom through grace is more than a polemical answer to the Pelagians — it is a recall to the sense of the dignity of man and of the greatness of God. So it is that in this work we shall keep distinct what Augustine's vocabulary has first distinguished,[1] free choice as a capacity for good or evil, a capacity found in every man, and freedom as an actuality that is the fruit of an engraced will. After the textual analyses, the doctrine of freedom is envisaged within the total Augustinian framework and is illuminated by the interpretations of outstanding Augustinian scholars.

Having been thought out by a Christian convert, a thinker steeped in classical culture, reacting forcefully against the natu-

[1] St. Augustine's own language is the key to understanding his statements about freedom. He considers that *arbitrium voluntatis* or *liberum arbitrium* is a *capacity* to do good or evil and is always present. But *libertas*, the good use of free choice, of *liberum arbitrium*, is not always present and is found in different degrees. *Contra duas epistolas Pelagianorum*, II, 5; PL 44, 552: Quis autem nostrum dicat, quod primi hominis peccato perierit *liberum arbitrium* de humano genere? *Libertas* quidem periit per peccatum, sed illa quæ in paradiso fuit, habendi plenam cum immortalitate justitiam; propter quod natura humana divina indiget gratia, dicente Domino, *Si vos Filius liberaverit, tunc vere liberi eritis* (Joan. VIII, 36): utique liberi ad bene justeque vivendum.

ralistic mental clime of his day, this doctrine is necessarily related to its intellectual and to its religious milieu. These relations have served to hasten the formation of the Augustinian doctrine of freedom but they have not, as some have suggested, jeopardized its integrity. Thus, Augustine's evaluation of free choice in the *De Libero Arbitrio* cannot be dismissed as the undeveloped thought of an early work, and Augustine's conception of freedom as the simultaneous work of God and man cannot be treated as an ecclesiastic's answer to the momentary challenge of Pelagianism. For, three years before his death, in the *Retractations*,[1] Augustine reiterates his teaching that free will is a power that can be badly used but without which we can do no good, a teaching that he had fully expounded in the early dialogue; and in this last expression of his mind he insists just as strongly as he had insisted against the Pelagians that the good use of free will comes from God. So it is that the *Retractations* provide certainty that all Augustine's statements with regard to free will, whether he is trying to show philosophically to the Manichaeans that God is not the cause of evil or whether he is trying to show scripturally to the Pelagians that God is the cause of the good will, are equally representative of his mature thought on the topic of freedom.

Through his genius and his versatility, as well as his happy facility for striking a sympathetic chord in the human heart, Augustine has been the contemporary of every age; he is of kindred spirit with our own. He will always remain a modern man. Hence, Augustinism has exerted a vital influence on every age, and Augustine's teaching on freedom is both of historical interest and of present-day value. A thorough investigation of the Augustinian influence would take us far beyond the scope of this present work. But just as the originality of Augustine is highlighted by the doctrinal comparison with Plotinus, so the permanence of his contribution to our understanding of freedom can be spotlighted by the comparison of his teaching with that of two great philosophers, St. Anselm and

[1] Augustine, *Retract.* I, 9, 6; PL 32, 598.

St. Thomas Aquinas. Through their works the notion of freedom has been widely disseminated, while in the works of modern philosophers like Jacques Maritain and Maurice Blondel the notion of freedom developed by the great Christian philosophers of the past has been preserved intact, and is being presented today through their writings and their disciples with the dynamism that is demanded by the impact of the present crisis of freedom in our modern world. Yet there are some today who do not admit the existence of free will; still others do not agree on the purpose of free will. And so two basic questions remain with us : Is freedom possible? In what does freedom consist? Explicitly or implicitly, materialists and rationalists will deny the possibility of freedom. Christian realists will disagree with atheistic existentialists and totalitarians of all kinds upon the meaning of freedom. Yet in the twentieth century the yearning for freedom on the part of all is accompanied by an appreciation of its value on the part of many. This bespeaks a growing understanding of the relation of freedom to personality, to which the statements of many modern thinkers bear witness. The chapter on the twentieth century will reveal the wide variety of views on freedom, among which can be detected the authentic voice of Augustine.

So it is that after a close doctrinal study of freedom in the writings of Augustine, it will be of interest to see how this notion of freedom, after being submitted to the precision of Anselm, and to the metaphysical analysis of Thomas Aquinas, can be fruitful today :

> ... whereas in classical culture man reached an understanding of the power and value of thought, through Christianity there is added a new dimension, that of freedom, and out of the fusion of thought and freedom has come a higher and more potent form of intellectuality.[1]

[1] Robert C. Pollock, "Freedom and History," *Thought*, XXVII (1952), p. 414.

PART ONE

THE NOTION OF FREEDOM IN THE PAGAN PHILOSOPHERS

CHAPTER I

FREE WILL IN GREEK PHILOSOPHY

Freedom to mould one's world within and without, freedom to find fulfillment in communal living — was such freedom explored by the ancient philosophers? It seems that only slowly, very slowly, did human personality emerge and extricate itself from social structures. It was not that the potency for freedom did not reside within the ancient man. It was there, a power belonging to human nature, but because it was not fully evaluated, it seems to have been unappreciated. The man of antiquity was aware of novelty, of contingency, but he seems to have feared it and to have preferred necessity. He recognized necessity as the law of his mental life, knew the inexorable static security of the changeless idea, felt certainty in conclusions that inevitably followed from valid premises. He had not witnessed that great moment that was to come to change the face of the earth, when the Roman world had worn out and ideas could not revive it nor long preserve it from interior collapse — that second peak-moment in the history of freedom when Christ, without any necessity, entered history. Nor had he heard of that first peak-moment in the history of freedom, the moment of its birth, when God, without any necessity, created the world of free men. Outside the influence of divine revelation, the Greek was not outside the influence of religion. All religion is a belief in the dependence of man, and the Greek felt himself under the power of the gods. Because his gods were divinized forces of nature, the foremost Greek thinkers concluded that all is done by necessity. This teaching is attributed by Cicero [1] to Democritus, Heraclitus and Empedocles, as well as to Aristotle; it is attributed by Plutarch to Thales, Pythagoras and Parmenides.[2]

[1] Marcus T. Cicero, *De Fato*, (Loeb edition), Cambridge, Harvard University Press, 1942, p. 235.

[2] Plutarch, *De Placitis Philosophorum* (Loeb edition) Cambridge, Harvard University Press, 1949, Vol. XI, I, 25.

The early Hellenic philosophers concentrated on accounting for "nature." They were concerned with the certain causes of things, with science as such. They were cosmologists. When Plato, inspired by Socrates, became interested in the psychological aspect of reality, we might expect to hear him mention choice and desire. We are not disappointed in that expectation. The place accorded to *Goodness* and to *eros* by Plato is significant. It is a forward step in the appreciation of the affective aspects of man. But Goodness in the Platonic universe does not cease to be the *Idea* of Goodness, and *eros* remains a necessary *élan*. The Platonic ethic, therefore, is on the speculative level and its end is eudaimonistic. The will is not speculatively distinguished from free will, and the truth of the practical judgment is not recognized as dependent upon free will. The words Plato uses, such as "to choose" and "to will," must not deceive us as to the true Platonic position on this point. Like Socrates who thought that if we do evil it is by ignorance, Plato does not seem to admit that man is free to choose either the general end of his acts, or the means when he knows the end clearly. According to Plato,[1] one is never unjust voluntarily, although the unjust act can be accomplished voluntarily. In an unjust action one is merely mistaken in the choice of means. This power of free choice belongs in the realm of opinion, the region of the undetermined. It is a lack of power, a lack of perfection. Perfection flows rather from the determinism of the Good. Plato would be consistent if he eliminated praise or blame, but he does not do this. In the *Republic*[2] we are shown judges who command the just to "ascend by the heavenly way" and the unjust "to descend by the lower way; these also bore the symbols of their deeds, but fastened on their backs. ...Even for the last comer, if he chooses wisely and lives diligently, there is appointed a happy and not undesirable existence." But Plato should stipulate greater punishments for voluntary than for involuntary crimes, a distinction recognized by all

[1] Plato, *Laws* (trans. B. Jowett), New York, Random House, 1938, II, 861.
[2] Plato, *Republic*, X, 872-879.

peoples. Because he will not admit that anyone does injustice willingly, [1] he finds another basis for the division of punishments, that of the kind of offence.

Although Plato does not defend a robust freedom of will, his keen awareness of the profound place of intellect in the human being prevents him from making of man a victim of physical forces. He would have this to say to the materialistic determinist of today:

> There is surely a strange confusion of causes and conditions in all this [materialist way of reasoning]. It may be said, indeed, that without bones and muscles and the other parts of the body I cannot execute my purposes. But to say that I do as I do because of them, and this is the way in which mind acts, and not from the choice of the best, is a very careless and idle mode of speaking. I wonder that they cannot distinguish the cause from the condition. [2]

This choice of the best occurs when "the better elements of the mind which lead to order and philosophy prevail." [3] One can see that for Plato the fairest jewel in the philosopher-king's crown is wisdom, the companion inseparable and, he would seem to suggest, the *raison d'être* of virtue. [4]

Aristotle likewise grapples with the meaning of the voluntary and discusses the position that Plato had inherited from his predecessors.

> The saying that 'no one is voluntarily wicked nor involuntarily happy' seems to be partly false and partly true; for no one is involuntarily happy, but wickedness *is* voluntary. Or else we shall have to dispute what has just been said, at any rate, and deny that man is a moving principle or begetter of his actions as of children. [5]

[1] Plato, *Laws*, II, 860-861. Cf. A. E. Taylor, *Plato*, London, Methuen, 1949, p. 37 : "In Plato, the voluntary, as Proclus says, means regularly what we really wish to have. Now no man wishes to have what he knows or believes to be bad for him. (Of course he may know or believe that he will be sent to prison or to hell for choosing as he does, but at heart he thinks that it will be 'worth his while' to take these consequences, he will be 'better off' even after paying this price for what he desires.)"

[2] Plato, *Phaedo*, 483.

[3] Plato, *Phaedrus*, 259.

[4] Plato, *Phaedo*, 452.

[5] Aristotle, *Ethica Nicomachea* (trans. W. D. Ross), London, Oxford University Press, 1925, III, 5; 1113 b.

That man is the master of his acts is, according to Aristotle, the implication of all punishment whether private or public. Such punishment is withheld if it can be proved that one acted under compulsion or through invincible ignorance. It is also the implication of all rewards for virtuous conduct, rewards which seek to encourage others to be likewise virtuous. If certain acts inevitably spring from certain characters, it must be remembered that "it is activities exercised on particular objects that make the corresponding character." [1] Aristotle realizes that "each man is somehow responsible for his state of mind," and therefore "he will also be himself somehow responsible for the appearance," that is, for what appears good to him. [2] Aristotle states that "the origin of action... its efficient, not its final cause... is choice, and that of choice is desire and reasoning with a view to an end." [3] Aristotle here implies psychological liberty, but does he say that the free choice comes from the will determining itself? Does he explain the reciprocal causality of desire and reasoning in the act of choice? Has he ever decided whether the will is appetitive intellect or intellectual appetite? Gilson states that "it remains a fact that Aristotle spoke neither of liberty nor of free will." [4] As for will itself, could it be properly understood apart from a transcendent object? If will is not an infinite capacity, can the radical indetermination of free will be grasped? Is there any mention of that freedom born of man's efficacious choice of the good, by which he is free for attaining his end? Or, if virtue rather than God is for Aristotle the end of man, when he evaluates free choice in relation to this end, does he not implicitly agree with the Stoics that liberty is conformity to the laws of nature? There are some who point to the frequent use that Aristotle makes of the word freedom in the *Politics*. The text shows that he equates freedom with the political asset of independence, freedom from external constraint. He defined the free man by

[1] Aristotle, *Eth. Nic.*, III, 5, 1114 a.
[2] Aristotle, *Eth. Nic.*, III, 5, 1114 b.
[3] Aristotle, *Eth. Nic.*, VI, 2, 1139 a.
[4] E. Gilson, *The Spirit of Medieval Philosophy*, (trans. A.H.C. Downes), New York, Scribner's, 1940, p. 307.

opposition to a slave. [1] Even in the *Metaphysics* where the free man is referred to, it is clear that the notion has a political origin. [2] The political ideal, the aesthetic ideal, not the formally moral ideal, is offered. [3] But if psychological freedom has not a purpose that raises the individual above the purposes of the state, the way is open to refuse to man the freedoms which flow from his psychological liberty whenever the well-being of the state may seem more important.

To note that Aristotle did not give us an explicit notion of the meaning and grandeur of freedom is to recognize that he has not fully elaborated the notion of person, although he faithfully describes some aspects of its functioning. He points to the reality of free will and gropes towards an appreciation of freedom — it is a case of deficiency, not denial. [4]

What are one's reasons for questioning the adequacy of the Aristotelian treatment of the will? It seems that for Aristotle as for Plato the indetermination of the will is not something of which we can be proud. It signifies a contingency that is not proper to the spirit world. It does belong to human nature, (Aristotle is too scientific to refuse the evidence of free choice), as matter belongs to human nature, and possibly belongs to human nature because matter is a co-principle of that nature. Obviously, Aristotle does not reduce the will to the sensible appetite, for he often describes the will in its struggle against sensitive appetite. [5] But if he has not reduced the will to sensibility, has he not reduced its role to that of controlling sensibility, [6] is not this his reason for distinguishing the human intellect from the will? The human will is not merely ordered

[1] Aristotle, *Politica*, (trans. W.D. Ross), London, Oxford University Press, 1925, I, 5; 1255 a; IV, 4; 1290 b.

[2] Aristotle, *Metaphysica*, A, 10; 1075 a.

[3] Cf. M. Wittman, *Die Ethik des Aristoteles*, Regensburg, 1920; *Aristoteles und die Willensfreiheit*, Fulda, 1921.

[4] Jacques Maritain, *Bergsonian Philosophy and Thomism* (trans. M.L. Andison), New York, Philosophical Library, 1955; p. 354: "There is a whole domain [in Aristotle] reserved for simple statements of fact, for opinion, for the probable and particularly, in the practical order, for art and prudence, — which by nature baffles the infallible certitudes of scientific demonstration and anticipation... It is the domain of our free will as well..."

[5] Aristotle, *Eth. Nic.*, III, 7, 1115 b; VII, 7, 1150 a, 1150 b.

[6] Cf. Joseph de Finance, *Etre et Agir*, Paris, Beauchesne, 1945, p. 15.

to the independence of the prudent man by its mastering of the passions. The will has a higher role without which freedom of the person is not realized — this role is the love of the good as such. [1] The limited role assigned by Aristotle to free will [2] is bound up with his conception of human happiness and the destiny of man who, at best, can enjoy the heaven of metaphysical delights insofar as the independence of the wise man, by conformity to nature and evasion of the fortuitous, can be won. For, Aristotle places happiness "in the working" of that divine principle or "most divine of all our internal principles" — the intellect — "the highest of our internal principles..." And since this happy, intellectual man "can contemplate and speculate even when quite alone... he is certainly most self-sufficient." [3]

How can man be sufficient unto himself unless the beatifying contemplation needs not the First Intelligible for object? In many places Aristotle does not conceive beatitude in relation to a transcendent being, but there are, one must admit, times when he seems to. For example, at the end of *Metaphysics* V, 1, [4] he speaks of first science and of its object, either the "universal," "one genus," or *one reality* (possibly God?). A similar attitude is taken in the *Ethics*. [5] Elsewhere, however, he seems to imply that happiness for man is found, if fortune does not prevent it, in the perfect exercise of the perfect human activity — thinking. In this view, the notion of duty would not apply, for want of a relation between human nature and the Absolute, although a certain duty to oneself is suggested. That is why

[1] Louis B. Geiger, O.P., *Le Problème de l'Amour chez Saint Thomas d'Aquin*, Paris, J. Vrin, 1952, p. 130.

[2] R. A. Gauthier, O.P., "Saint Maxime le Confesseur et la Psychologie de l'Acte Humain," *Recherches de Théologie Ancienne et Médiévale*, tome XXI, 1954, p. 58 : "Never has Aristotle elaborated the concept of the will as a faculty defined by its tendency, inscribed in its very nature and impelling it towards the good known by reason. Neither has he ever conceived the wish to be an act of this faculty, and consequently a rational desire by nature. On the contrary, from the differentiated center of this desire which gives rise to impulsive desire and possessive desire does Aristotle make also the wish to spring forth. Desire finds its revenge in the primordial place Aristotle assigns to the wish in the genesis of action."

[3] Aristotle, *Eth. Nic.*, X, 7; 1177 a.

[4] Aristotle, *Metaphysica*, 1026 a, 24.

[5] Aristotle, *Eth. Nic.*, X, 8; 1178 b, 20-32; VIII, 7; 1159 a, 2-5.

some consider the Aristotelian ethic to be solely a Eudaemonism, and not an ethic of obligation. Man can prevent himself from attaining the happiness of imitating the self-contemplation of Pure Act, and when he does, this fault is a weakness, a folly, an inelegance, not a sin, not an offence against God. Such is Aristotelian autonomy — the ability to make oneself happy. The *lacunæ* in Aristotelian morality are consistent with the *lacunæ* in Aristotelian psychology, and these are concerned with the major issues of personality, personal immortality, human destiny, human happiness. We can leave these great questions to the greater competence of Aristotelian scholars, but it can be suggested that a full illumination of these important issues cannot be attained apart from a philosophy of the person, and that the meaning of the person who, after all, is personal being cannot be grasped apart from a theology of being. [1] If analogy signifies that there will be some things in us that cannot be understood except from above, would not a theology help us to understand ourselves, and the fuller that theology, the fuller our understanding? In one way the *lacunæ* of Aristotle led him to expect too much from man, and in another way they led him to be unaware of the full human potential; and they also led him to give an incomplete account of the misery of man. To say that Aristotle preferred the species to the individual is not, as some have thought, to ignore the fact that it was Aristotle who corrected the Platonic over-emphasis on form by insisting on the reality of the individual. But he seems to have postulated survival only for the species [2] in and through the individual,

[1] If willing is a perfection, why does Aristotle say never a word about the will or omnipotence of the Unmoved First Mover, why is there no place for willing in Pure Act? Cf. Anton C. Pegis, " Matter, Beatitude, and Liberty " in *The Thomist*, 6 (1943), 265-289.

[2] Cf. Jacques Maritain, " Marginal Notes on Aristotle, " in *Bergsonian Philosophy and Thomism*, pp. 361-367, against those who claim that Aristotle denied immortality. Maritain concludes : " That Aristotle, as John of Saint Thomas expressed it, suffered perplexity on this question of immortality (especially because of his theory of the eternity of the world, from which it must have followed that separate souls are infinite in number, *unde valde opprimebatur*), we grant without hesitation. Therefore, the principal question here is not to know whether he explicitly defined and set forth the thesis of the personal immortality of the human soul. Abiding by the exactitude of Saint Thomas' interpretation it is enough to say that, urged on by the internal logic of his principles, Aristotle (as we have already shown), taught in an implicit and virtual way, — positing the reasons which establish it, — and several times clearly hinted at that immortality. "

a position that, whether truly Aristotelian or not, has influenced the political naturalism of our day. The lack of an explicit doctrine of personal immortality affected his concept of human happiness. It does seem that St. Thomas himself readily recognized these omissions of Aristotle when in the *Contra Gentiles* [1] he expressed compassion for the great minds of pagan antiquity who were with splendid vigour and marvelous achievement seeking the truth. How else should one understand such a passage as: "We shall be freed from the suffering imposed by these errors if we hold, in accord with the proofs given above, that man can reach true happiness after this life, *since it is true that the soul is immortal.*"

But these are great questions and we do not intend to close them or to speak definitively upon them. They are only mentioned because they have very much bearing on the fact which has been noted: Aristotle does not give to the human will its full role in the attainment of the good of the person. [2]

CONCLUSION

Plato exempts human acts from physical determinism, and he does see the proper role of free choice in the moral life. His statements about knowledge being virtue have led some to consider him as one who teaches a moral intellectualism, through the determinism of the Good as an intelligible. Since sense knowledge can only confuse man, the ideal of human liberty would be freedom from the body, from the world of shadows. Aristotle in his discussion of free choice in the *Nicomachean Ethics* seems to assert psychological liberty, but he also seems to limit the role of free choice. Knowledge is gained through sense knowledge, but human free will has the negative role of keeping man free from sensible affectivity so that man may contemplate. The freedom honored by Aristotle is

[1] St. Thomas, *Summa Contra Gentiles*, III, 37; II, 44; II, 48; cf. Pegis, *op. cit.*

[2] Etienne Gilson, *The Spirit of Medieval Philosophy*, New York, Scribners, 1940, p. 307: "However elaborate was the Aristotelian theory of choice conceived as a decision of will following upon a rational deliberation, yet it remains a fact that Aristotle spoke neither of liberty nor of free will."

a " freedom from. " For these reasons some have claimed that Aristotle sees mental perfection as the end of man, and they consider him as one who teaches an intellectual naturalism.

Plato has scarcely done justice to the nature of free choice, while Aristotle has not recognized the role of free choice. After Aristotle there is the confusion of free choice with spontaneity by Epicurus and then the establishment of a rigorous doctrine of universal determinism by the Stoics. It would seem true then that the early Greeks, while understanding the power and the value of thought, did not understand freedom.

CHAPTER II

THE TREATISE *ON FREE WILL* OF PLOTINUS

Plotinus discusses the ideal of human freedom as an intellectual self-determination, a freedom from all that is below leading to a freedom of absolute absorption in a higher unity. To become free is to become self-aware by transcending one's present status. The way is by meditative effort, with the use of free choice as a necessary evil, almost as necessary as matter. When acts are born of Reason-Principle, they are voluntary, and because they come from a principle unmingled with matter, they are free. After describing the attainment of human freedom, Plotinus portrays the Absolute Liberty of the One, and we realize that this is the freedom he honors, this the freedom that he holds out to man.

The Eighth Tractate of the Sixth *Ennead* is entitled :
On Free Will and the Will of the One. Closely following this text, we listen to Plotinus as he develops his teaching on freedom.

WHAT IS FREE WILL?

If we look at men and if we examine ourselves we shall see that free will, which gives rise to voluntary action, is a " blend of power and impotence. "[1]

WHAT IS FREEDOM?

Freedom is the exercise of power; but what is meant by power? Power here means " our power, " that is, the power of our wills. This in no way rules out knowledge but greatly implies it. A voluntary act may be defined as one produced —

[1] Plotinus, *Enneads* (trans. Stephen MacKenna and B.S. Page), Chicago, Encyclopaedia Britannica, Inc., 1952, VI, 8, 1.

1) under no compulsion (adverse fortunes, compulsions, violent assaults of passion);

2) with full knowledge of all circumstances, above all, of the rightness of the act. Plotinus here maintains that, ignorance being involuntary, any act done in ignorance must be involuntary.[1]

WHENCE COMES FREEDOM?

Freedom of action in man does not come from passion, nor from a false deliberate desire, but from a *right* deliberate desire.[2] But which comes first: the deliberation or the desire? If the desire comes first, it could only be " dictated by its very nature. "[3] If so dictated, it would come: 1) either from the conjoint of soul and body; then the soul is under physical compulsions; 2) or from the nature of the soul alone; but this would be metaphysical necessity. Therefore, desire must follow upon reasoning. But can we be sure that the act following upon the desire is not brought about by imagination and emotion? Then man would be living and acting according to a preestablished natural functioning, no freer than the animals who so act. Moreover, if this is the freedom of man, that he lives " as he has been moulded, "[4] then even soulless things are free: as " fire acts in accordance with its characteristic being. "[5] No, Plotinus assures us that desire following upon deliberation is not left unprotected by knowledge. In this, the power of knowledge to bring deliberate desire to fruition in act, we see how essential Plotinus considers knowledge to free action. In man, knowledge has a more active role than merely to accompany desire and act. In animals there is this awareness, and this in no way constitutes freedom. In man, knowledge is a controlling factor, not only giving rise to deliberate desire, but repressing opposing appetites and acts.

[1] *Enn.* VI, 8, 1. ἑκούσιον μὲν γὰρ πᾶν, ὃ μὴ βίᾳ μετὰ τοῦ εἰδέναι, ἐφ' ἡμῖν δέ, ὃ καὶ κύριοι πρᾶξαι·...

[2] *Enn.* VI, 8, 3.

[3] *Enn.* VI, 8, 2.

[4] *Enn.* VI, 8, 2.

[5] *Enn.* VI, 8, 2.

HOW FREEDOM COMES

Plotinus asks: how does knowledge confer freedom? Does it set up an opposing desire; if so, how? or does it merely still the appetite? He does not clarify this question, but he concludes: in either case, freedom would seem to be "a thing of the mind." [1]

Self-disposal has been traced "...to will, will to reasoning, and, next step, to right reasoning," [2] plus "...knowledge of the foundations of that rightness." [3] This last notation would seem to imply that knowledge of the end, that is, of the One, is needed to be the norm of choice and to provide security. In other words, the spirituality and the unity and aseity of the One would require that the way to Him be similar.

PROGRAM FOR HUMAN FREEDOM

Thus, Plotinus would indicate that a separation in man must take place if freedom is to be attained. The free life will be lived on condition that reason gives rise to desire for the spiritual life and protects man's acts from passion's influence. The enslaved life will be lived if the instincts of hunger, thirst, sex give rise to images from which acts spring.

Thus the Plotinian proposal for freedom in man is to simplify his complex state by a rigid program of splendid isolation of the states of the soul from the states of the body.

Self-disposal, to us, belongs to those who, through the activities of the Intellectual Principle, live above the states of the body. The spring of freedom is the activity of Intellectual Principle, the highest in our being; the proposals emanating thence are freedom; such desires as are formed in the exercise of the Intellectual act cannot be classed as involuntary. [4]

[1] *Enn.* VI, 8, 2.
[2] *Enn.* VI, 8, 3.
[3] *Enn.* VI, 8, 3.
[4] *Enn.* VI, 8, 3.

CHARACTERISTICS OF HUMAN FREEDOM

In man a free act is reconcilable with need, since a movement towards a fully recognized good is not involuntary. [1] The need in man somehow or other contributes towards human freedom. Since freedom in man is characterized by movement towards a right good, without such a need there would be no movement; "...servitude lies in being powerless to move towards one's good." [2]

Plotinus gradually reveals that human freedom is characterized by the transcending of one's present conditions. The Stoics had held to the necessity of following one's nature. Plotinus seems to say that to have to act according to nature would be slavery. He also counts as slavery the having to yield one's good "in favor of another's." [3] Two new notes have thus been added to the notion of human freedom: not only must the free act proceed from oneself after complete knowledge, but it must take one beyond one's limits while being for oneself, that is, for the sake of oneself.

The act thus described seems to be, according to Plotinus, the intellectual one. We have seen that the free act cannot be of the bodily state. Above the acts of the bodily state there are two kinds of acts. There is the act of knowing — and since this act is directed towards the Principle by which it proceeds, it is "self-centered and must entail its very greatest good." [4] Then there is the virtuous act, the exercise of control over the obstacles to contemplation. But in such an act there is little freedom; it is exercised only because there are external factors not of one's own making. [5] Moreover, if virtue "heightens the soul to Intellectual quality, then once more, our freedom is found to lie not in act but in Intellectual Principle immune from act." [6] So, not only must there be made the separation

[1] *Enn.* VI, 8, 4.
[2] *Enn.* VI, 8, 4.
[3] *Enn.* VI, 8, 4.
[4] *Enn.* VI, 8, 4.
[5] *Enn.* VI, 8, 5.
[6] *Enn.* VI, 8, 5.

of the reasonable from the imaginative state in order that liberty may flourish in the life of the thinking subject, but the life of virtue has as its *raison d'être* the deliverance of the soul from all passion or external event. [1]

Although freedom was first spoken of in connection with will, we have come to see that " Virtue and Intellectual-Principle are sovran and must be held the sole foundation of our self-disposal... "; and hence " virtue is a mode of Intellectual Principle. " [2] As long as man relies on Intellectual Principle, safeguarded by virtue, man is as free as he can be at any moment. " This makes it all the more evident that the unembodied is the free... " [3]

For a time only there is in man a will striving " ...towards the good which the act of Intellectual Principle realizes. Thus that Principle holds what will seeks, that good whose attainment makes will identical with Intellection. " [4] Because there is in man a " ...will aiming at the good, " [5] man should eagerly go the way of Intellectual Principle already in possession of the good. We may, loosely speaking, call an act free that is done in the spirit of " aiming at the good, " but while one is aiming, we cannot in the strict sense speak of freedom of soul, only of soul becoming free. " Soul becomes free when it moves without hindrance, through Intellectual-Principle, towards The Good... " [6] When the soul finally attains to that " principle of Good, " " the sole object of desire, " the soul can be called free. [7]

Therefore, free will, signifying deliberate desire, made possible by Intellectual Principle and virtue, is characterized as long as it is in the state of becoming free, by autonomy with regard to itself and all that is lower than self, and characterized by dependence on that which is beyond itself, the Good. This observation of the relation of transcendence to the achievement

[1] *Enn.* VI, 8, 5.
[2] *Enn.* VI, 8, 6.
[3] *Enn.* VI, 8, 6.
[4] *Eun.* VI, 8, 6.
[5] *Enn.* VI, 8, 6.
[6] *Enn.* VI, 8, 7.
[7] *Enn.* VI, 8, 7.

of human freedom is a great advance over Aristotelian thought.

Having said that a man by reason of his body is far from reality and that by his soul man participates in reality, Plotinus concludes that in our compound state we are not masters of our being : " ...in some sense the reality in us is one thing and we another. " [1] This difficulty can be eliminated only by identifying the " I " with the real in us, namely, the soul : then we can be considered self-disposing; but this division would make it impossible to claim that the human individual is " sovran over itself. " [2] Self-mastery in men is not perfect, but the setting for it is there : the essence as the principle of action. If freedom denotes self-mastery, and the possibility of it in man is because of his duality, freedom likewise denotes self-determination, and the possibility of it in man is by reason of his imperfection, i.e., his limited being. In their being, irrational animals, plants, and minerals are determined from without. Man is free to become other than he is if he allows himself to be determined from within. In other words, all being is the partaking of good, and every being seeks to become the good which it pursues; hence, it seeks to be something else than what it is : " ...it judges itself most truly to be when it partakes of its good : in so far as it thus draws on its good its being is its choice. " [3]

Here we have just touched upon what could be the essence of human freedom in its state of becoming : self-determination; man, not moulded by chance, nor by external force, nor by nature, nor by passion, but by deliberate desire, inspired by Intellectual Principle, safeguarded by virtue. How much freedom the Intellectual-Principle leaves the will is the doubtful point.

When will man accept himself as he is? Only when he attains his good. Only then will he be fully determined. But self-determination in the human sphere seems to be a misleading expression. It really turns out to mean that the true self, that is, the unembodied in man, is determined by the good, intellectually

[1] *Enn.* VI, 8, 12.
[2] *Enn.* VI, 8, 12.
[3] *Enn.* VI, 8, 13.

presented. Only when man possesses his good, will the self be complete and man free. At that point there will be no question of self-determination, but freedom will signify self-possession. Our moral necessity, the need for the pursuit of the good, turns out to be a metaphysical necessity that lifts us out of subjection to our essence. By our absorption in thinking, self-mastery gives way to unity.

But it is no less characteristic of man that he is free in this sense too, that he can make himself otherwise than he would be if he continually chose the good. He can become absorbed in the organization of the material world. This is autonomy but it is also impotence. That is why true liberty in man becoming free can be identified as a blend of autonomy and dependence, while free will as we see it operating in man is a "blend of power and impotence."[1] Without recollecting himself into intellectual activity, man will not arrive at self-possession, the holding of his good, perfect freedom. For, man has the ability to depart from unity, the unity between what he should be and what he could be: and that ability is a powerlessness, an impotence and, of course, a lack of liberty — since true liberty is power. Only through recollection can man become himself. As we begin life, we are not aware of our greatness. We feel this lack. Our poverty, our need — this is the backdrop of our liberty.

SUMMARY OF HUMAN FREEDOM

Actions in man are voluntary when they proceed from a so-called will, implying an intellectual principle.

All actions in man do not proceed from the will alone:

three possibilities:	1. knowledge, will:	act.
	2. knowledge, will, image, passion:	act.
	3. instincts, image, appetite:	act.

Only acts which proceed from the so-called will-alone are free acts. Such acts proceed from power; other acts proceed

[1] *Enn.* VI, 8, 1.

from impotence. But with Plotinus the will-alone seems to mean, adherence to Intellectual-Principle; and this is itself an aspiration towards the Good.

Capable of contemplation, man here and now is not free. Plotinus does not make clear whether this state is one that must be or whether it is the result of a fault. Man becomes free by moving towards a good, something that seems distant, a movement more negative than positive, accomplished by withdrawal through greater interiority.

A free human individual is one not limited by matter and acting for his own sake. This seems to be made possible by a certain infinity in the subject acting.

Only by complete disembodiment can freedom be won, and this victory will be simultaneous with the possession of the good : intellect and will are then identified, in the utter unity of self-possession, liberty.

CONCLUSION

In conclusion we may note three striking aspects of the Plotinian doctrine of free will in man :

1. a certain alliance of liberty with necessity;
2. a certain emphasis upon the Intellectual Principle as so-called liberator (actually, more of a determinator);
3. a certain attribution to man of divine qualities : aseity, infinity, self-satisfaction.

This brief conclusion may be amplified by the following considerations. For Plotinus, freedom is self-determination in a very Plotinian sense. He contrasts self-determination with chance. Now necessity is opposed to chance. The higher you go in the realm of being the more necessity you find. The lower you go in the realm of being the more chance you find. But, the higher you go in the realm of being the more independence of others you find, and this implies a self-determination. Therefore, in the mind of Plotinus self-determination does not seem opposed to a certain kind of necessity, being one's self. Thus it is that the Plotinian remarks on free will as self-determination must be placed within the larger framework of the entire Plotinian system.

Freedom then, as self-determination, signifies power to be all that one can be, to be everything; an absolute freedom is an absolute infinity. If metaphysical necessity in the One, demanded by the absurdity of its denial, does not destroy its freedom, intellectual necessity in man only assists man to exercise his power by being all he can be. The One transcends man insofar as man is becoming free; when man makes contact with the One in Whom he is immanent, man is free. Freedom for man has its positive side of self-realization, its negative side of abstraction from all that interferes with his spiritual activity. This self to be realized is infinite, containing all that is, so that the self is divinely free. But human freedom is a freedom from the finite. It takes the form of successive separations as a prelude to unity : man flies from his bodily states; then man flies from his soul as organizer to the *Nous* that he is, until man is pure subject, absolutely infinite.

> Even you are able to take contact with Something in which there is no more than That Thing itself to affirm and know, Something which lies away above all and is — it alone — veritably free, subject not even to its own law, solely and essentially That One Thing, while all else is thing and something added. [1]

In this consideration of freedom, the reader is conscious of the intense intellectualism of the Plotinian system. The intellect is itself desire of the Good, of the One. This is the intellect in its willing-phase. There is necessity here and spontaneity but, according to Plotinus, no coercion. The mind confronted with the truth would never be unwilling to adhere to it, according to Plotinus. The synthesis of the metaphysical and the moral viewpoints leaves no gap for the contingent factor of free will. Men do evil involuntarily, but voluntarily they follow their *élan* towards the good, and in this their nature becomes free. Their evil is a falling away from reason, and so from the order

[1] *Enn.* VI, 8, 21.

of Providence. If the freedom of man that comes from growth in perfection is within the order of Providence, then the causality of man was given for the sake of relating man to the Good. But this relating is done in and through the intellect; therefore, the intellectual life is the free life and decisions proceeding from intelligence are free. [1] If virtue is the freedom of the soul, this is only so that soul may be more thoroughly intellectual. Virtue allows the soul to be interior and releases it from contact with matter. Virtue participates in freedom insofar as it bears the mark of reason, that is, as an act proceeding from reason. The intellectual action is itself free because it is free from all exterior constraint. It would only be involuntary if it had to go against its good. But the good of the soul is not merely the good-in-general, but the Good, God. [2] According to Plotinus, man's most voluntary tendency is his natural tendency towards God, a religious aspiration which he identifies with freedom. The achieved desire ushers the soul into the truest liberty, union with the will of God, characterized by omnipotence or efficacy. [3] There is still freedom from any external force because the Good, principle of his freedom, is within. [4] With the One as object, intellection and volition are at peace. Plotinus has shown that the profound *raison d'être* of human liberty is to will the Good that is none other than God. Thus Plotinus has defined human liberty as a dynamic relation to God, [5] and has understood that free choice is not the perfection of liberty, but liberty in God is freedom from anything above or below.

FREEDOM IN THE ONE

When we turn to Plotinus' description of freedom in the One we recognize it as the Exemplar of the freedom he held out to man. In analyzing the nature of freedom in man, Plotinus

[1] *Enn.* VI, 8, 5.
[2] *Enn.* VI, 9, 10; VI, 7, 25; V, 5, 13.
[3] *Enn.* VI, 8, 15;
[4] *Enn.* VI, 8, 6.
[5] *Enn.* VI, 7, 35; V, 6, 5.

discussed it as it reveals itself to all of us : " a combination of powerlessness and hesitating power. " [1] If this were liberty *qua* liberty, there would be no use discussing the liberty of the One.

But if voluntary action indicates power, and there are degrees of power, we could make the following classification :

1. The One	omnipotent	most free
2. The Two Hypostases (*Nous* and World-Soul)	powerful	free
3. Man	" a blend of power and impotence "	less free
4. Irrational beings	powerless	not free

Only when we clearly understand what is signified when we say something is " in our power " shall we feel right in ascribing " freedom to the gods and still more to God... " [2] There would be four possible ways of ascribing freedom to God and to men; it could be ascribed :

1. univocally to God and men;

2. not to God but to men;

3. not to men but to God;

4. analogically to God and men; that is to say, if liberty is to be found both in God and men, it must be found in them very differently : " [we] question still, in regard both to the higher and the lower, the mode of its presence. " [3]

In posing the problem : " How can act rising from desire be voluntary since desire pulls outward and implies need? " [4] Plotinus prepares the way for linking the voluntary and the necessary in the One. If the One necessarily produces, it is not because of desire that it produces. Now if production is something occurring on account of the great wealth of perfection in the One, this production can be reduced to the One. And so if the One wills itself to be what it is, production

[1] *Enn.* VI, 8, 1.
[2] *Enn.* VI, 8, 1.
[3] *Enn.* VI, 8, 1.
[4] *Enn.* VI, 8, 4.

would be voluntary as being voluntary in its cause. Therefore the question is reduced to the voluntariness, the self-disposal to be found in the One with regard to what it is. If its nature is due to itself, then it is not subject to its nature, and there will be no such thing as acting in accordance with nature in a subservient fashion. Since a being who is the Good cannot move toward itself, [1] a being who is the Good would be free; doubly free, because there would be no question of yielding one's personal good in favor of another's, and triply free if it had no nature to which act must be conformed, that is, if it were Pure Act. [2]

Although we are treating of the liberty of the One, the freedom to be found in the *Nous* has a bearing on the liberty of the One insofar as it points to the appropriateness and the necessity of liberty in the One. Referring to the freedom of the *Nous*, Plotinus says :

> The contemplating Intellect, the first or highest, has self-disposal to the point that its operation is utterly independent; it turns wholly upon itself; its very action is itself; at rest in its good it is without need, complete, and may be said to live to its will; there the will is intellection; it is called will because it expresses the Intellectual Principle in the willing phase and, besides, what we know as will imitates this operation taking place within the Intellectual Principle. Will strives towards the good which the act of Intellectual Principle realizes. Thus that principle holds what will seeks, that good whose attainment makes will identical with Intellection. [3]

From this passage we learn that will is a sign of imperfection, a lack of liberty, belonging properly on the level where intellection is inconstant; will is a striving towards the true; when will is operating one cannot speak of independence.

Plotinus, having successively shown that the One is the good towards which souls aspire and which the Intellectual Principle knows, the source of independence for the Intellectual Principle, and the source of becoming-free for souls, inquires how the One can be " ...brought under the freedom belonging to you

[1] *Enn.* VI, 8, 4.
[2] *Enn.* VI, 8, 4.
[3] *Enn.* VI, 8, 6.

and to me." [1] For, duality is implied in the self-disposal found in the *Nous* and in souls.

Yet, if freedom is denied to the One, is the One not open to chance, control or compulsion? So Plotinus pursues the following line of argument: if chance, external control, or compulsion-through-need can be ruled out, then the One is the Master; but because of its Unity, it would be better to call it "very activity," for will in the One is not a striving after, nor an enjoyment of, but something that escapes all confinement, — "activity." Therefore, after two hypothetical statements:

1. If the One is chance-made, then free act exists nowhere;

2. If you understand the word freedom, then it must be applied to the One [2] (by freedom here is understood independence), he concludes:

> This state of freedom belongs in the absolute degree to the Eternals in right of that eternity and to other beings insofar as without hindrance they possess or pursue The Good which, standing above them all, must manifestly be the only good they can reasonably seek. [3]

Thus is it hinted that freedom for men and for the Intellectual Principle confers upon them independence of all that is "beneath them"; while freedom in the One is freedom from anything "above." The One is Master; the others are self-masters. The One is sovereign.

Plotinus then proposes and answers four objections to ascribing freedom to the One:

1. The good exists by chance.

This is false because the good is eternal, and so cannot have happened to be.

2. The One acts according to its nature.

With the One, the Act and Being are identical; "...from the two (Being and Act) it forms itself into The Good, self-springing and unspringing." [4]

[1] *Enn.* VI, 8, 7.
[2] *Enn.* VI, 8, 7.
[3] *Enn.* VI, 8, 7.
[4] *Enn.* VI, 8, 7.

3. Freedom in a unique being is meaningless.

Freedom in the One "...means only that The Good is no other than itself, is self complete and has no higher."[1]

4. Where there is most good there is least freedom.

Plotinus dismisses this as an absurd position.

Although Plotinus has met all the objections against ascribing freedom to the One, he fears a possible threat to the unity of the One, and so he explicitly states that freedom is not in the One as an attribute.[2] Exactly how liberty is to be ascribed without duality must be explained. His method of convincing us is admittedly inspired by Plato — it amounts to showing that the position of the One requires liberty, and that to deny it would be highly inappropriate.

The Principle of all could not be some chance-product; therefore it is necessitated or determined, but without compulsion; hence it is self-determined. It is "...simply what it must be..." "...and yet without a 'Must'."[3] Alert against threats to unity, Plotinus indicates that this self-determination does not imply a will in the One, — but a supra-willing :

> ... at most it is to be perceived as the total power towards things, supremely self-concentred, being what it wills to be or rather projecting into existence what it wills, itself higher than all will, will a thing beneath it.[4]

By being the Best, the Supreme Good, the One escapes not only chance but necessity. "No, what He is, He is not because He could not be otherwise but because so is best."[5] In being what He is, the Best, He is exercising his power. Omnipotence is freedom, and He must be what He is, because He is necessarily free. This necessity is born of what He is, but He has willed to be what He is.

If then we are to allow Activities in the Supreme and make them depend upon will — and certainly Act cannot There be will-less —

[1] *Enn.* VI, 8, 7.
[2] *Enn.* VI, 8, 8.
[3] *Enn.* VI, 8, 9.
[4] *Enn.* VI, 8, 9.
[5] *Enn.* VI, 8, 10. Notice that here the One is referred to by a personal pronoun.

and these activities are to be the very essence, then will and essence in the Supreme must be identical... This admitted, as He willed to be so He is... [1]

Nothing is master over the One; self-mastery only begins with Being, a certain duality of act against essence. The mastery in the One is so very unique that it might better be called self-possession :

If then this Principle is the means of determination to everything else, we see at once that self-possession must belong primally to it, so that through it others in their turn may be self-belonging; what we must call its essence comports its will to possess such a manner of being; we can form no idea of it without including in it the will towards itself as it is. It must be a consistent self willing its being and being what it wills; its will and itself must be one thing, all the more one from the absence of distinction between a given nature and one which would be preferred. What could The Good have wished to be other than what it is?... The Good is what from always it wished and wishes to be. For the really existent Good is a willing towards itself, towards a good not gained by any wiles or even attracted to it by force of its nature; The Good is what it chose to be and, in fact, there was never anything outside it to which it could be drawn.

It may be added that nothing else contains in its essence the principle of its own satisfaction; there will be inner discord; but this hypostasis of the Good must necessarily have self-option, the will towards the self; if it had not, it could not bring satisfaction to the beings whose contentment demands participation in it or imagination of it. [2]

After explaining how self-possession excludes the manifold, Plotinus reiterates that the One is nonetheless self-determined, self-caused, His own Author. [3] As Principle and Exemplar of all, God is Cause of Himself. He is what He is, the first self, transcendently The Self. [4]

Lovable, very love, the Supreme is also self-love in that He is lovely not otherwise than from Himself and in Himself. [5]

[1] *Enn.* VI, 8, 13.
[2] *Enn.* VI, 8, 13.
[3] *Enn.* VI, 8, 13.
[4] *Enn.* VI, 8, 14.
[5] *Enn.* VI, 8, 15.

The greatest freedom is in the One. In Him there is act and repose, born of a " self-originating self-tendance, ...an eternal awakening. " [1]

In one last proof that chance is unthinkable in relation to the One, Plotinus states that no one would think of allying chance to reason; so, if Intellectual Principle is at every point " reason and cause, " [2] this must be so with the One in a far transcendent mode. He assures us that willing in the Supreme is " ...not apart from reason. " [3]

It seems then that the best way to state the One is to call Him " self-existent. " [4] This points to his necessity and to his freedom. The necessary aspect of the One is evidenced by the absurdity of attributing chance to the source of an ordered universe; the liberty of the One is evidenced by recognizing the absolute simplicity of the One, hence its sovereignty. "Now, assuredly an Activity not subjected to essence is utterly free; God's self-hood then, is of His own Act." [5]

To end where we began : can Liberty be ascribed to the One? Liberty can be ascribed to the One because there is nothing in Him that is not Himself, that is not in Act, that is not His work. [6] His liberty is Omnipotence, born of the fact that He is Supreme Goodness and utter unity.

SUMMARY : FREEDOM IN THE ONE

The One, source of reason and order in the world, could not be by chance.

The One, source of being, cannot be controlled by anything external.

The One, without need, cannot be compelled by desire.

Therefore the activity of the One must be wholly from itself, *a se;* but this activity is a stability, for it must be what

[1] *Enn.* VI, 8, 16.
[2] *Enn.* VI, 8, 18.
[3] *Enn.* VI, 8, 18.
[4] *Enn.* VI, 8, 19.
[5] *Enn.* VI, 8, 20.
[6] *Enn.* VI, 8, 20.

it is on account of its omnipotence, the omnipotence implied in the fact that the One is *a se*. Its position as Sovereign determines it to be free.

CONCLUSION

It would seem that Plotinus, although apparently commencing the study of freedom with the human person, has kept his vision on the One, and while the exigencies of his system lead him to place even desire in the One, but a perfectly fulfilled desire, he is led to place in the human being, at least in hope, the kind of freedom he considers worthy of the One, namely, a Divine Independence shot through with the intellectual necessity of the essential order. The human ascent to freedom is to be accomplished, moreover, without call from the One, without help from the One. This would be logical if man himself were incipiently divine. Human freedom was revealed by Plotinus as a freedom *from* the body and even from the act of willing: willing giving way completely to intellection in the higher spheres. Will becomes unnecessary in a being which is its own good, its own divinity, a divinity without society.

Although Plotinus pays scant attention to free choice because it is characterized by impotence, his discussion of freedom in man and in the One cannot conceal an admiration for what the word freedom signifies and is a glorious attempt to discover the dimensions of freedom. This attitude is not evident in Plato or Aristotle. Thus, the Plotinian notion of freedom provides some worthwhile insights:

Freedom is recognized as an accompaniment of perfection.

There is no dichotomy between truth and freedom.

Freedom comes from the heights, following one's higher tendencies.

Freedom comes from within, and is unassailable from the external side of life.

Absolute freedom implies aseity, and this is freedom not only from all that is below but from anything above. This is true of the One, but not of man nor even of the *Nous*.

In holding out this divine freedom to man, however, is not Plotinus too optimistic, expecting too much from man as he is; or does Plotinus believe that man is really other than he appears to be? To imitate this divine freedom man is asked to forsake the sensible world, to follow only the tendency to think, to ascend to truth by his own meditative efforts. Man can attain to a freedom from all that is above if there is nothing above man, and such would be the case if man became identified with the One, *causa sui*, holding his Heaven within. Only a beautiful dream, or is it an ideal form standing on the shore of Reason, awaiting realization by the power of Love, Who would satisfy the longing of man by conferring on him the favor, the grace of the "Divine Indwelling?"

CHAPTER III

RESUME OF THE PAGAN POSITION ON FREE WILL

After reviewing the attitude toward freedom on the part of the outstanding Greek philosophers before the time of Christ, and after a close doctrinal study of the treatise of Plotinus on the topic of freedom, it appears to us that freedom was not adequately understood by the great non-Christian philosophers before Augustine's time. May one suggest that a proper notion of freedom could not be attained as long as individuality is explained only through matter, [1] and as long as matter is considered an obstacle to perfection, and as long as contingency is considered to be irrational?

PLATO

Responsibility is inextricably linked with individuality; that is why there is no escape from responsibility. But responsibility is rooted in personal choice, a choice whose immediate subject is the will, since things are chosen because they seem *good.* The intellect can suggest a virtuous act, but only the will can make the virtuous act *to be*, and so *to be my own*. This understanding of free choice is absent from the Platonic explanation of virtue. Responsibility as a fact universally accepted is recognized, but it is not really made intelligible. Freedom from ignorance seems to be the only requirement for virtue. Even the Platonic *Eros*, the universal tendency of all things towards the Good, [2] is an intellectual thirst, a craving to participate in the Supreme Intelligible — the Idea of the Good. So-called Platonic love is predominantly need for fulfillment rather than the free gift of a personal preference for the beloved. It seems therefore that the moral intellectualism that is the Platonic

[1] This was a position of Aristotle, not of Plato or Plotinus.

[2] Plato, *Republic*, VI, 505-506.

ethic has not given to individuality its proper value because Plato lacked the notion of the person, which alone guarantees true notions of responsibility and of human love, — responsibility through autonomous free choice and human love through an objective love for the good.

ARISTOTLE

The minor role assigned to free choice by Aristotle, namely, that of controlling sensibility, may derive from other factors in his philosophy. Might not the tremendous role of the will in responding to the human vocation, and adding by its moral effort to man's perfection and his very being, have been slighted by Aristotle because even he had failed to grasp the ineffable grandeur of the human person? If Aristotle had properly appreciated the human person, would he not have explicitly taught personal immortality, the immortality of the individual human soul? With Aristotle as with Plato, the character of his First Principle has influenced his evaluation of the will. A Pure Act that is a thought of thought, final cause of the universe, influences man only by bringing him to imitate it by spontaneously following the natural appetite to contemplate the truths he can rationally gather and thus enter the deific state of pure contemplation.

Imitation of the First Cause is the extent of human achievement, and the efficacy of second causes in the universe is reduced to the circular causality of renewing the species. Do we not miss here the human power of re-creating the face of the earth by exercising rational choice, without determination from within or without, from the past or the present? But why this human act of contemplation? Why this human universe? These are embarrassing questions to Aristotle. We must ask only what things are. The human mind cannot explain an absolute beginning, nor can it explain the contingent. The contingent, the chance happening — Aristotle is not unaware of these things, but he finds them unintelligible, inexplicable by man with his way of knowing the essential in things. If Aristotle had known that the absolute free creative Will of God is the origin of all things, explaining why things are, and that whatever is, is known by the Divine Mind, then he would have recognized that all things are intelligible, even individual things. He would also have been able to account for some of the reality that he omitted from his explanations or investigations — namely, the free act of giving, the act of love as gift, for in the act of Creation is found the prototype of the truest love. Because there was wanting to Aristotle an adequate notion of God and of his free relations of knowledge and love with individuals in the universe, Aristotle missed the value of the human individual as a person, limited human destiny to this world, and reduced the role of human free will to the negative power of creating conditions favorable for contemplation. When free will is admitted to be at the origin of the world, this world becomes more comprehensible, not less so. Free will is distinctive of intellectual being, and hence nothing that is traceable to will-activity can be pushed aside as irrational.

PLOTINUS

When we turn to Plotinus we find that he has done a wondrous thing. He tries to suppress the problem between the religious and the rationalist conceptions of the universe, emphasized by Aristotle. He makes the discovery of the First Principle the way of salvation. [1] The *Nous* will satisfy the exigencies of Greek rationalism while the One as the principle of the *Nous*, to whom the soul must return to have contact with the Good, will be the source of the mystical experience. The neglected dimension in Greek rationalism had been the affective dimension, which at its profound depths in human nature was a natural religious desire. [2] As E. Bréhier sees it, certain longings in man found no justification in Greek philosophy. Plotinus then very remarkably united man's desire for mystical union, for salvation, for purification with the knowing

[1] *Enn.* I, 3, 1.

[2] For this interpretation of Plotinus I rely on : Emile Bréhier, *La Philosophie de Plotin*, Paris, Boivin, 1951.

of the First Principle, which knowledge at its highest is an intimate contact with the One. [1] This contact is attained more by intense recollection, a sort of deepening of sensation, a tasting, rather than by syllogistic reasoning. It is true that Plotinus adopted the Platonic triad, the Good, the *Nous*, and the Soul, but he transformed them into stages of the spiritual life, that is, of "thinking," the supreme human activity revered by Aristotle.

The One is the unity of all that is expressed separately, the true reality of spiritual life beyond all appearances. The religious problem has a philosophic solution, and the solution is that the spiritual life is the only reality. Knowing subjects are as important as the objects known; knowledge is not valuable only because of its representative role, but for its effect upon the knower. To think is to get closer to reality. The soul, organizer of the material world, is capable of recollecting itself to its higher reality of "*Nous*," the order of all things, which the world imitates, and it is capable too of enjoying the vision of the One by desire — a supra-intellective power of contact.

This spiritual journey of the soul to the One is a stationary one made possible because Plotinus has added the notion of immanence to Platonic transcendence. Things can be absorbed into superior realities by being more what they really are, as awareness gradually measures up to the reality. The being which comes from the One is not separated from it, although it is not identical to it. [2] Mystical knowledge, through identity, alone satisfies the aspiration to unity that seems to be in the depths of our intellectual life. [3] It is achieved through a greater interiority by successive acts of self-transcendence. To transcend one's limitations by becoming all things through union with universal being is to become infinite. For Plotinus, infinity is a perfection, and not the least reason for this is its

[1] René Arnou, "L'Acte de l'Intelligence en tant qu'elle n'est pas Intelligence," *Mélanges Joseph Maréchal*, Paris, Desclée de Brouwer, t. II (1950), p. 249 : "The intellect, says Plotinus, has two powers, one to act as intellect : in this way it sees what is below it; and a power not to act as intellect. The first belongs to intellect in possession of the means; the second to the intellect that loves, inebriated and outside itself; and this kind of intoxication is better than sobriety." Cf. *Enn.* VI, 7, 35.

[2] *Enn.* V, 3, 12.

[3] *Enn.* VI, 5, 1.

characteristic of absolute freedom. Such is the freedom held out to man.

"Suppose we found such a nature in ourselves;... by this new state alone we acquire self-disposal and free act, the freedom of that light which belongs to the order of the good and is good in actuality, greater than anything Intellectual-Principle has to give, an actuality whose advantage over Intellection is no adventitious superiority. When we attain to this state and become This alone, what can we say but that we are more than free, more than self-disposing? And who then could link us to chance, hazard, happening, when thus we are become veritable Life, entered into That which contains no alloy but is purely itself. [1]"

We cannot be really ourselves unless we are concentrated in the One; the pursuit of truth becomes the pursuit of self-knowledge, and through self-knowledge, of the "One" in ourselves.

Until the time of Plotinus the notion of liberty operative in Greek morality had been "acting according to nature." Plotinus sees freedom as a mode of the spiritual life of intellection without limitation, and the principle of such freedom is transcendent Goodness. The control of passions and actions by free choice is only a secondary aspect of freedom. Freedom as infinity, independence of anything above or below, *causa sui*, becomes the root of reality. Metaphysical reality is spiritual life hypostatized. The *Nous* is enriched by contemplation. Spiritual activity is not something superadded but is the profound reality of which all things are inferior copies. The One is super-intellection, but immanent to all things, and so he is discovered in the interior life, the life of recollection.

It is thus that the problem of the soul's destiny is bound up with the soul's search for knowledge. Knowledge, not action, makes one better, simply because it recalls us to ourselves; there is no real change for the better possible, or else things were not good in the first place. When knowledge is fully achieved in its principle, the One, the soul has the absolute

[1] *Enn.* VI, 8, 15.

autonomy that is the aim of its thinking, its metaphysical voyage through various spiritual levels. Plotinian idealism sees in the life of the mind a natural autonomy, and in the activity of thinking the very reality of the world. This is the enjoyment of absolute liberty, realized more and more by an interior recollection which intimately unites us with the life of the One.

Although before the time of Plotinus there were others who gave to spiritual life a meaning simultaneously cosmic and moral, Bréhier points out the particular Plotinian way of conceiving the relation of the soul with God:

1. The soul is related to the One by its own power, alone with the Alone, without the help of mediator or savior.

2. The One does not desire, draw, call or invite the soul to union; the One is the term of its aspiration.

3. The One is everywhere; there is immanence of the individual subject in the One.

When we realize that in the Plotinian world the real is identical with the possible, [1] we see why there is no place for will at the origin of things or in the moral effort. To become merely aware of one's greatness has not the dramatic quality of reform, achievement, complete conversion. The origin of the world is merely accounted for by the shining forth of the One, [2] or by its perfection giving rise to necessary emanation without loss to the One. [3]

Plotinus is as far as possible from considering the principle of things as a creative will. The system of Plotinus was born of an effort to interpret all that was real in things in terms of spiritual activity; this activity is not a reality that is superadded accidentally and in a contingent manner to a world already completely made; it is the profound reality of which all the others are only degradations. [4]

[1] *Enn.* IV, 8, 6.
[2] *Enn.* V, 1, 6.
[3] *Enn.* V, 4, 1.
[4] Bréhier, *Phil. de Plotin*, p. 44.

CONCLUSION

Although freedom was not adequately understood by the non-Christian philosophers, they contributed some valuable insights towards a fuller comprehension of that reality. The Platonic doctrine of *Eros* implies the existence of natural appetite to which the will as will is not unrelated, and the Platonic conviction that man was blameworthy and praiseworthy for his actions led Aristotle to conclude that man's free choice was in his power and that man is not the victim of his knowledge or lack of it. Plotinus shares with us a vision of freedom, not merely associated with control, but as a perfection generated by self-transcendence and productive of man's perfection, yet something achieved by spiritual activity. Thus Plotinus adopted the Aristotelian notion of the end of man as spiritual perfection, an end that makes him self-sufficient, independent. But with Plotinus the independence extended to a freedom from the object of thought because the act of thinking is itself divine. Whereas Aristotle had made man content without Heaven, Plotinus promised to man a Heaven on earth.

The inadequacy of the notion of freedom found in the ancient philosophers may be linked with certain *lacunæ* in their works on the subject of the person, of duty, of love, and of a freely creative God. Although liberty is not an invention of Christian thinkers, its elucidation by the non-Christian thinkers is not entirely satisfactory.

PART TWO

THE NOTION OF FREEDOM IN AUGUSTINE

CHAPTER IV

FREE WILL IN THE *DE LIBERO ARBITRIO* OF ST. AUGUSTINE

As we turn to Augustine's treatment of freedom in man, we find that he distinguishes two aspects of human freedom: the faculty of free choice or free will, and the freedom that qualifies man when free choice is used according to its purpose — to attain the true end of man, thereby enabling him to be all that he should be. [1] And for Augustine the drawing power of love is crucial for the perfect exercise of free choice. [2]

In the *De Libero Arbitrio* [3] Augustine is seeking an answer to the problem of evil. That is why he discusses free choice. He points out that man does evil by his own power and brings evil consequences into a world that God has made good. Yet Augustine insists that this free choice is a perfection, an asset,

[1] The quotations to follow will reveal the distinction made by Augustine between *free choice*, which he uses as a synonym for free will and which is found in all men, and *freedom* or *liberty*, which is synonymous with the good will and which is the fruit of the grace of God and the effort of man. Cf. also: Gilson, *Introd. à l'étude de St. Augustin*, Paris, Vrin, pp. 212-214.

Augustine, *De Libero Arbitrio*, I, 11, 21; PL 32, 1233: ...nulla res alia mentem cupiditatis comitem faciet, quam propria *voluntas* et *liberum arbitrium*.

Ibid., I, 16, 35; PL 32, 1240: ...facimus [malum] ex *libero* voluntatis *arbitrio*.

Ibid., II, 1, 3; PL 32, 1241: ...debuit habere *liberam voluntatem*, sine qua recte facere non posset.

Ibid., I, 12, 25; PL 32, 1234: Quid est *bona voluntas?* Voluntas qua appetimus recte honesteque vivere, et ad summam sapientiam pervenire.

De Civ. Dei, XIV, 7; PL 41, 410: *Recta* itaque *voluntas* est *bonus amor*.

De Lib. Arb., II, 13, 37; PL 32, 1261: Hæc est *libertas* nostra, cum isti subdimur veritati: et ipse est Deus noster qui nos *liberat* a morte, id est a conditione peccati. Ipsa enim Veritas etiam homo cum hominibus loquens ait credentibus sibi: 'Si manseritis in verbo meo, vere discipuli mei estis et cognoscetis veritatem, et veritas *liberabit* vos' (Joan. 8, 31, 32). Nulla enim re fruitur anima cum *libertate*, nisi qua fruitur cum securitate.

For the state of man in the absence of freedom, cf. *De Civ. Dei*, XII, 8; PL 41, 355.

For the restoration of freedom by Christ, cf. *De Lib. Arb.*, II, 20, 54; PL 32, 1270.

[2] Cf. Augustine, *Conf.*, XIII, 9, 10; PL 32, 848; *De Doct. Christ.*, I; PL 34, 19-36; *De Civ. Dei*, XV, 22; PL 41, 467; *De Lib. Arb.* II, 20, 54; PL 32, 1269-1270; Augustine, *De Lib. Arb.*, I, 12; 24-26; PL 32, 1234-1235.

[3] The English translation quoted in this chapter is *The Problem of Free Choice*, by Dom Mark Pontifex, (Ancient Christian Writers Series), Westminster, Maryland, Newman Press, 1955.

a power and not by nature an impotence. He sees the glory of personal option for the good. He senses the adventure of the pursuit of truth. He recalls from experience the almost overwhelming obstacles of ignorance and difficulty in man's use of this wondrous power of will. He recognizes that when separated from true love it is a source of disorder in a world that will only be at peace when order prevails. Yet not even for the sake of peace or order or happiness will Augustine sacrifice human free choice. A personal embrace of the good far transcends in value the attainment of the most perfect harmony by imposition from above. If there have been those who thought that it was better to deprive man of his free choice lest he misuse it, Augustine was not among them. If God was willing to take the risk of confiding to man the constructive and destructive power of free choice, we can see how He cherishes freedom. Shall we cherish it less?

WHAT IS FREE WILL?

Augustine arrives at the answer to this by first considering will in itself. He says that it cannot be denied that we have a will (voluntas)[1] : one's experience of living is the experience of willing. Everyone is conscious of wanting to be happy. That is will, not free will. Now we call that will which aims to lead a right and honest life a good will. [2] Evidently, then, it is possible for a will to be bad, a will that does not aim to live rightly. If a will can be good or bad according to its aim, it is not immutable. But if its goodness is praiseworthy and its evil is blameworthy, it must be free. Responsibility without free will is unthinkable. [3] Therefore, free will is the faculty of responsibility. It not only fashions man's acts, but it fashions man himself, for the good man is the man with a good will. [4] From what Augustine says we can conclude that human free will is a sign of imperfection, in the sense that it can be badly used and in the sense that it

[1] Augustine, *De Lib. Arb.*, I, 12; 24-26; PL 32, 1234-1235.
For a modern discussion of this, cf. Yves Simon, *Traité du Libre Arbitre*, Liège, Sciences et Lettres, 1951; especially the chapter: " Un cas privilégié de nécessité naturelle " (pp. 38-53).

[2] Augustine, *De Lib. Arb.*, I, 12, 25; PL 32, 1234.

[3] Augustine, *De Lib. Arb.*, I, 1, 1; PL 32, 1223.

[4] Augustine, *De Civ. Dei*, XII, 6; PL 41, 353, 354.

belongs to one who is metaphysically incomplete, who is not all that he can be, who lacks something, whose end is beyond him. But Augustine does affirm that free will is a perfection in this sense : by it man can live rightly, and this possibility of free adherence to the good is worth the risk of exposing man to error. It is not possible for animals to live rightly. They share in reason through instinct, but they have no faculty of control. The faculty by which man can live rightly raises him above the animal level and denotes a radical difference in his end. We know that living rightly implies conforming one's thoughts and desires to truth and goodness, truth being related to mind, goodness to will. Thus, he who lives rightly has no static object as end, such as the material object of animal desires. Man is in dynamic relationship with his end through intellectual and voluntary activity, and it is commonly felt today that in achieving a certain harmony of thought and will, man achieves the unity of his personality.

Free will in man can be called natural inasmuch as it is proper to him. Yet it is one thing to say that man is naturally determined, [1] that is, that he acts as he does of his very nature, and it is quite another thing to say that man is by nature free. The latter statement leaves the possibility of freedom intact; the former does not. [2] There is, of course, a natural tendency of the soul to forsake things higher and devote itself to the interests of the lower; nevertheless, the soul can always check this tendency because freedom is also "natural" to it. [3] A stone

[1] Augustine, *De Lib. Arb.*, III, 1, 1; PL 32, 1270 : Quia si ita data est [voluntas] ut naturalem habeat istum motum, jam necessitate ad hæc convertitur; neque ulla culpa deprehendi potest, ubi natura necessitasque dominatur.

[2] Augustine, *De Lib. Arb.*, III, 1, 2; PL 32, 1271 : Non equidem nego motum quod ita ut dicis inclinatur, et ima petit, motum esse lapidis, sed naturalem. Si autem hoc modo etiam illum motum habet anima, profecto etiam ipse naturalis est; nec ex eo quod naturaliter movetur, recte vituperari potest : quia etiamsi ad perniciem movetur, naturæ tamen suæ necessitate compellitur. Porro quia istum motum non dubitamus esse culpabilem, omnimodo negandum est esse naturalem; et ideo non est similis illi motui quo naturaliter movetur lapis.

[3] Augustine, *De Lib. Arb.*, III, 1, 2; PL 32, 1269, 1270 : Credo ergo meminisse te, in prima disputatione satis esset compertum, nulla re fieri mentem servam libidinis, nisi propria voluntate : nam neque a superiore, neque ab aequali eam posse ad hoc dedecus cogi, quia injustum est; neque ab inferiore, quia non potest. Restat igitur ut ejus sit proprius iste motus, quo fruendi voluntatem ad creaturam a Creatore convertit : qui motus si culpae deputatur (unde qui dubitat, irrisione dignus tibi visus est), non est utique naturalis, sed voluntarius; in eoque

cannot resist its natural downward movement; so "when we prove that the soul, leaving things higher, prefers things lower for enjoyment, we charge that it is guilty of sin." [1] (Plotinus did not charge the soul with sin.)

It is essential to the human will that it be free: by this is meant that the will is "in our power." If we examine all things and actions in the universe we shall find "nothing so completely in our power as the will itself." [2] Augustine's statements allow us to hold that the will is the interior citadel of free decision that cannot be taken by storm. It is just because the will really is in our power that we are responsible for the kind of will we have, and so it would follow — for the kind of person we become.

So characteristic is it of the will to dominate human actions that one would fly in the face of universal experience by saying "we will, not by means of will." [3] So, if man's knowledge does not cause his will to act, neither does God's foreknowledge cause human free choices. In knowing what is future to us, God's knowledge is of things as they *are*, in His eternal present, which means that He knows our acts of will as *free* acts.

It would seem then that the will in man is well-nigh an omnipotent faculty, exempt from constraint of any kind. But Augustine is referring to the free will of man in the state of original justice. For he warns us: "When we speak of a will free to act rightly, we speak of the will with which man was created." [4]

similis est illi motui quo deorsum versus lapis fertur, quod sicut iste proprius est lapidis, sic ille animi; verumtamen in eo dissimilis, quod in potestate non habet lapis cohibere motum quo fertur inferius; animus vero dum non vult, non ita movetur, ut superioribus desertis inferiora deligat; et ideo lapidi naturalis est ille motus, animo vero iste voluntarius.

[1] Augustine, *De Lib. Arb.*, III, 1, 2; PL 32, 1272: ...animum vero peccati arguimus, cum eum convincimus superioribus desertis ad fruendum inferiora praeponere.

[2] Augustine, *De Lib. Arb.*, III, 3, 7; PL 32, 1274: Quapropter nihil tam in nostra potestate, quam ipsa voluntas est. Cf. *De Duab. Anim.*, I, 10, 14; PL 42, 104.

[3] Augustine, *De Lib. Arb.*, III, 3, 7; PL 32, 1274: ...non voluntate autem volumus, quis vel delirus audeat dicere?

[4] Augustine, *De Lib. Arb.*, III, 18, 52; PL 32, 1296: Sed approbare falsa pro veris, ut erret invitus, et resistente atque torquente dolore carnalis vinculi, non posse a libidinosis operibus temperare, non est natura instituti hominis, sed poena damnat. Cum autem de libera voluntate recte faciendi loquimur, de illa scilicet, in qua homo factus est loquimur Cf. *De Nat. et Grat.*, I, 67, 81; PL 44, 287; *Retract.*, I, 15, 3; PL 32, 609.

This will had not been misused, and it was moreover strengthened by grace. If we weigh well these lines we shall find that Augustine is not denying the existence of free will as a faculty in the historical man after the Fall, but he is denying in fallen man the existence of a perfect freedom to do good, the freedom of the upright will, and, of course, he is denying any freedom to do the salutary good.

WHAT IS FREEDOM?

Freedom qualifies man when man is in "the most perfect order," [1] "when reason controls the motions of the soul." [2] "When this reason, or mind, or spirit, controls the irrational motions of the soul, then that element is ruling in man which ought to rule by virtue of that law which we found to be eternal." [3] Hence the free man is the wise man, who has quelled "the risings of lust by the reign of the mind." [4] The mind of man is in such a superior position with regard to all else created that there is really nothing to prevent this rule of the mind except the will of man. The will alone has a metaphysical stature comparable to the mind, and its object is the human good. Thus, if freedom is the rule of mind, it must be accomplished and maintained by self-mastery. For Augustine distinguishes between the mind in man and the mind in control of man. The "mind is in control only in wise men." [5] But what power enables one man to bring his passions under the rule of mind, and not another? Is it not the virtuous will? Plotinus spoke of self-mastery, but it was achieved not so much by a struggle, with the will triumphing over all opposition, but by the withdrawal of mind from matter, the soul ignoring the body.

[1] *De Lib. Arb.*, I, 6, 15; PL 32, 1229 : ...omnia esse ordinatissima. Cf. I, 15, 32.
[2] *De Lib. Arb.*, I, 8, 18; PL 32, 1231 : Hisce igitur motibus animæ cum ratio dominatur...
[3] *De Lib. Arb.*, I, 8, 18; PL 32, 1231 : Ratio ista ergo, vel mens, vel spiritus cum irrationales animi motus regit, id scilicet dominatur in homine, cui dominatio lege debetur ea quam æternam esse comperimus.
[4] *De Lib. Arb.*, I, 9, 19; PL 32, 1232 : Eos enim sapientes voco, quos veritas vocari jubet, id est, qui regno mentis omni libidinis subjugatione pacati sunt.
[5] *De Lib. Arb.*, I, 9, 19; PL 32, 1232 : ...neque regnum mentis nisi sapientium esse... I, 11, 21; PL 32, 1233 : ...nulla res alia mentem cupiditatis comitem faciat, quam propria voluntas et liberum arbitrium.

WHENCE FREEDOM?

Freedom comes not from separation of mind and body, nor by separation from temporal goods. It comes from seeking only those goods which a man cannot lose against his will. [1] That man is truly free who only strives after what is "in his power." That is the way of the wise man. Now, the things within the soul's power are truth and goodness. They can be found in all things when things are thoroughly known and properly loved as images of God and as aids in man's ascent to God. To seek truth and goodness in all things would make the will good, the man wise and free. We saw that the good will was an affair of willing rightly; so, too, the wisdom of the soul, like its freedom, is not unrelated to the will.

But no one loses truth and wisdom against his will, for no one can be separated from them physically. That which we call separation from truth and wisdom is a perverted will, which loves lower things. No one wishes for something against his will. [2]

Again we see Augustine's moral trend as he views the problem : for him, wrong-mindedness is nothing other than wrong will. Truth is all about us for the taking; another's possession of the truth does not leave less for us. Without any defect of the object, it would seem that much poverty of mind, want of wisdom, is traceable to the will.

HOW FREEDOM?

He who would be free must attend to the will; for, just as reason can have reason itself as its object, so also have we will-power over our wills. [3] By using that power we can become free. In other words, at any point in time, in any circumstances, the will can be free. The will has not as its sole purpose the insuring of unrestricted mental activity, —

[1] *De Lib. Arb.*, I, 16, 34; PL 32, 1240.

[2] *De Lib. Arb.*, II, 14, 37; PL 32, 1261 : Veritatem autem atque sapientiam nemo amittit invitus : non enim locis separari ab ea quisquam potest; sed ea quæ dicitur a veritate atque sapientia separatio, perversa voluntas est, quæ inferiora diliguntur. Nemo autem vult aliquid nolens.

[3] Augustine, *De Lib. Arb.*, II, 19, 51; PL 32, 1268.

no, the will must take itself as object in order that man may act best and so become free :

... whoever wishes to live rightly and virtuously, if he wishes this in preference to the goods which are but passing, acquires this great possession with such ease, that to wish for it is the same as to possess what he wished. [1]

The freedom Augustine visualizes for man is conferred not by the mind, but by the will. If only a purified soul can contemplate inward truth, its purity comes not from the fact that mind has removed itself from the realm of matter by withdrawal, but from the fact that will is not clinging to things of lower value and thereby disregarding higher values : " And therefore he is not attached to them by love, does not make them, as it were, members of his own soul, as would happen if he loved them. " [2] Early in his analysis of will we get a glimpse of the role that Augustine will give to love. Free will gives to love its precious value, and right love gives will its freedom.

Now, some may say that only virtues are necessary for freedom, because in them " right reason reigns. " [3] Yet, virtue is acquired by the will which must love enough to acquire it, and the purpose of virtue is to free the will for the good, since " virtue is the good use of those things which we are capable of using wrongly. " [4] To acquire all virtues is merely to adhere by means of the will to the changeless good. [5] Virtues are ordered to a more powerful and more ardent love of superior values, [6] and insofar as such love lifts man above the passions, the reign of reason is also increased.

[1] *De Lib. Arb.*, I, 13, 29; PL 32, 1236, 1237 : Ex quo conficitur ut quisquis recte honesteque vult vivere, si id se velle præ fugacibus bonis velit, assequatur tantam rem tanta facilitate, ut nihil aliud ei quam ipsum velle sit habere quod voluit.

[2] *De Lib. Arb.*, I, 15, 33; PL 32, 1239 : ...et ideo non eis amore agglutinetur, neque, velut membra qui animi faciat, quod fit amando...

[3] *De Lib. Arb.*, II, 18, 50; PL 32, 1267 : ...recta ratio viget...

[4] *De Lib. Arb.*, II, 19, 50; PL 32, 1268 : ...opus virtutis est bonus usus istorum, quibus etiam non bene uti possumus.

[5] Augustine, *De Lib. Arb.*, II, 19, 53; PL 32, 1269.

[6] Augustine, unlike Aristotle, values virtues only in relation to the love of God.

PROGRAM FOR HUMAN FREEDOM

The program for the freedom of the essential man would be : let the will be guided by the intellect. Then it would be a good will because it would be perfectly docile to the truth, free to do right. Yet such a program is only for the " will with which man was created. " [1] The program for the freedom of the historical man, the existential man, is somewhat different. Man has not always much learning by which to abide. Yet even in its present state the soul is still superior to all bodies and it is a fact that " it is capable, with the help of the Creator, of developing itself, and if it does its duty earnestly, of acquiring and possessing the virtues which will free it from painful difficulty and blind ignorance. " [2]

> If this is so, ignorance and difficulty will not be a punishment for sin to souls at their birth, but an encouragement to progress and a beginning of perfection...
>
> Only Almighty God, and no one else, could create such souls. For, though not loved by them He gives them being, and because He loves them He repairs their being, and when loved by them He perfects their being. He who gives being to what has no being, gives happiness to those who love the author of their being. [3]

We see that even when professedly treating of free will and freedom from the standpoint of reason alone, Augustine is mindful of the chains of ignorance and concupiscence by which man is at present bound.

CHARACTERISTICS OF HUMAN FREEDOM

The chief characteristic of human freedom is the happiness it brings with it. The truly free man is as happy as man can be in this life.

[1] Augustine, *De Lib. Arb.*, III, 18, 52; PL 32, 1296.

[2] *De Lib. Arb.*, III, 20, 56; PL 32, 1298 : ...sed etiam quod facultatem habet, ut adjuvante creatore seipsam excolat, et pio studio possit omnes acquirere et capere virtutes, per quas et a difficultate cruciante, et ab ignorantia caecante liberetur.

[3] *Ibid.;* Quod si ita est non erit nascentibus animis ignorantia et difficultas supplicium peccati, sed proficiendi admonitio, et perfectionis exordium... neque omnino potuit nisi Deus

We hold, then, that a man is happy who loves his own good will, and who despises in comparison with this whatever else is called good and can be lost, while the desire to keep it remains. [1]

Augustine came to realize that contact with God is open to all, a contact not achieved, however, without man's will. Joy is revealed not so much as the concomitant of the intellectual act, but as communion with Divine Love. As the Beatific Vision, above man's natural powers, will ultimately be given by God, so this communication with Divine Love on earth is the daily gift of God. Augustine gives a place to the will in bringing man to the truth. In his discussion of freedom we find that happiness, liberty and security are more and more synonymous. [2]

HOW FREEDOM IS LOST

"...The mind is not cast down from its position of control, and from its right order, except by the will." [3] The right order in man that brings freedom to man is lost by the will; and this destruction of God's order is sin. Upon sin there follows separation, the usual effect of disorder, a lack of harmony between God and man, mind and will, soul and body. Augustine shows that the body is not powerful enough to bring about sin; one mind has not more power than another, so that it cannot force anyone to succumb to lower desires; a superior mind, if wise, would not wish for such a condition. [4] Therefore, if sin occurs, with disorder and disquiet announcing its presence, it is man himself who has allowed it: "...the argument has shown that we do wrong through the free choice of our will." [5]

omnipotens esse etiam talium creator animarum, quas et non dilectus ipse faciat, et diligens eas reficiat, et dilectus ipse perficiat; qui et non existentibus praestat ut sint, et amantibus eum a quo sunt præstat ut beatæ sint.

[1] Augustine, *De Lib. Arb.*, I, 13, 28; PL 32, 1236: Placet igitur beatum esse hominem dilectorem bonæ voluntatis suæ, et præ illa contemnentem quodcumque aliud bonum dicitur, cujus amissio potest accidere etiam cum voluntas tenendi manet.

[2] De *Lib. Arb.*, II, 14; PL 32, 1261; III, 22, 63, 64; PL 32, 1302; III, 25, 74; PL 32, 1307.

[3] *De Lib. Arb.*, I, 16, 34; PL 32, 1239: ...nullaque re de arce dominandi, rectoque ordine mentem deponi, nisi voluntate...

[4] Augustine, *De Lib. Arb.*, I, 10, 20; PL 32, 1232.

[5] *De lib. Arb.*, I, 16, 35; PL 32, 1240: ...ratio tractata monstravit, id [malum] facimus ex libero voluntatis arbitrio.

FREE WILL AN ASSET OR A LIABILITY?

"But I want to know whether that very free choice itself, by which we have concluded that we have power of sinning, ought to have been given us by Him who created us."[1] After much consideration, for it was a problem which disturbed him, Augustine answered in the affirmative. When Augustine represents the freedom of the will as a contributory cause of the harmony of the universe, he is not unaware of the fact that sin — which follows in the wake of that freedom — is the prime source of disorder in the universe. But he sees that a being who can be not only metaphysically good but morally good, while uniting in himself the intellectual and material elements of the universe, can by love restore all things to God in a way that mind alone cannot.

If man were uncertain about how he should use his will, then it could be a cause of consternation to him to have it in his power; but he knows that God has given it to him so that he may live rightly. And all right living commences with right loving. Without free will, man merits no reward, for if the intellect simply determined him to live above the sensible, he would be necessitated, as it were, to an angelic life. He would not be humanly free; in fact, he would not be man. As it is, by his will man can use the sensible — sense-knowledge, sense-affections, sensible things — for spiritual ends, making them into acts that accord with a spiritual *esse*, by which they exist and operate. This is human life, human activity. It is the will that determines the intellect to consider a particular truth, and the will is called upon to be loyal to that truth and to draw upon all man's energies, spiritual and physical, to assure his abiding in truth. The program for human freedom, according to Augustine, is not separation of soul from body, but an ever closer union of soul and body, body becoming more and more not merely the servant of the soul, but its friend and spouse,

[1] *De Lib. Arb.*, I, 16, 35; PL 32, 1240: Sed quæro utrum ipsum liberum arbitrium, quo peccandi facultatem habere convincimur, oportuerit nobis dari ab eo qui nos fecit.

so that the spiritualized body of the resurrection will be a fitting climax to a life of ever closer penetration of body by spirit.

Augustine's conviction as to the value of free will is as real as his former perplexity about it :

> So too free will, without which no one can live rightly, must be a God-given good, and you must admit rather that those who use this good wrongly are to be condemned than that He who gave it ought not to have given it. [1]

CONCLUSION

In his discussion of free choice, Augustine has underscored some important points :

The human will is essentially free. Man has an absolute power over it, an autonomous control. No one, unwelcomed, can usurp man's power over his own will. [2]

The human will is the immediate source of all man's options for the good as well as his descent to evil; neither human knowledge nor divine fore-knowledge necessitates human choice.

In his treatment of freedom as a quality of the will doing what it was meant to do, Augustine provides some helpful insights :

A really free human will is one that is free to do right.

In this sense a human will is free when man's actions follow the law of reason which participates in the eternal law. Whether reason is to be master, that is, whether man is to enjoy personal freedom, is decided by the will. [3]

Reason will be the master if man's will is used in quest of man's true good, the total good of the person. Then all man's

[1] Augustine, *De Lib. Arb.*, II, 18, 48; PL 32, 1267 : ...sic liberam voluntatem sine qua nemo potest recte vivere, oportet et bonum, et divinitus datum, et potius eos damnandos qui hoc bono mala utuntur, quam eum qui dederit dare non debuisse fatearis.

[2] Augustine, *De Lib. Arb.*, III, 1, 3; PL 32, 1272 : Motus autem quo huc aut illuc voluntas convertitur, nisi esset voluntarius, atque in nostra positus potestate, neque laudandus cum ad superiora, neque culpandus homo esset cum ad inferiora detorquet quasi quemdam cardinem voluntatis; neque omnino monendus esset ut istis neglectis æterna vellet adipisci, atque ut male nollet vivere, vellet autem bene.

[3] Augustine, *De Lib. Arb.*, III, 24, 72; PL 32, 1306.

powers, material and spiritual, will be engaged in the love of God.[1]

The way of freedom is entered upon by willing to live rightly. Each new illumination of truth will increase one's freedom, if one submits to it.[2]

Although to abide in truth is to abide in freedom, man's present state as an heir to the losses of Adam leaves him only an initial free will that is radically impotent with regard to any meritorious good, and very weak with regard to any good at all. With his free choice, however, man can ask God for the help that He willingly extends to man, and when God helps him to do the truth that he knows, he begins to grow in freedom.[3] This is the condition and not the sufficient cause of the help that is given.

Since no one else can separate us from truth and goodness, freedom can only be lost by using the will badly. Since neither people nor external events nor force can deprive man of his end as man, no loss of physical, social or political liberty can deprive man of spiritual liberty, which is his freedom to choose the good.[4]

Freedom is characterized by happiness and security, and is accessible to all men.[5]

The danger of man's possession of free choice would be too great if its purpose were concealed from him. But man's knowledge of the glorious purpose of free will in relation to God, himself, and the world, as well as the knowledge of the horrors of its misuse, should lead man not to abuse this power.[6]

Above all, true freedom must be distinguished from apparent freedom.

[1] *De Lib. Arb.*, III, 24, 72-74; PL 32, 1306-1307.
[2] *De Lib. Arb.*, I, 13, 29; PL 32, 1236-1237; II, 10, 29; PL 32, 1256-1257.
[3] *De Lib. Arb.*, III, 19, 53; PL 32, 1296-1297; *Retract.*, I, 9, 4; PL 32, 596-597.
[4] *De Lib. Arb.*, I, 11, 21; PL 32, 1233.
[5] *De Lib. Arb.*, II, 13, 35-37; PL 32, 1260-1261.
[6] *De Lib. Arb.*, II, 18, 47-50; II, 19, 50-53; PL 32, 1266-1269.

Then there is freedom, though indeed there is no true freedom except for those who are happy and cling to the eternal law; but here I speak of that freedom by which men think they are free, when they do not have other men as their masters, and which is desired by those who wish to be released from any human masters. [1]

[1] *De Lib. Arb.*, I, 15, 32; PL 32, 1238. Deinde, libertas, quæ quidem nulla vera est, nisi beatorum, et legi æternæ adhærentium. Sed eam nunc libertatem commemoro, qua se liberos putant, qui dominos homines non habent, et quam desiderant ii, qui a dominis hominibus manumitti volunt.

CHAPTER V

FREEDOM IN THE EARLY DIALOGUES OF ST. AUGUSTINE

Although in the *De Libero Arbitrio* Augustine provided some insights into the quality of freedom that should characterize the mature and integrated person, he there gave more attention to establishing the reality, the conditions, the misuse, and the greatness of God's natural gift to man — free will or free choice. In the other dialogues Augustine gives us a greater understanding of that freedom in truth and goodness which comes when man is free to love God, a freedom that is not possessed by man without Divine assistance and without human consent. To say that he discusses freedom is not to say that he ignores free choice, for these two are so related that to speak truly of one is to shed light upon the other. The notion of freedom is clarified by linking it to wisdom and happiness. The origin of happiness is indicated by analysing the subjective and objective reasons why it is a gift from God rather than a conquest by man.

In the first work of Augustine, the *Contra Academicos*, we find a semi-Plotinian concept of what liberty is, namely, a person being " himself, " a maintenance of that being which is proper to man, the being of the mind with its proper activity. But in the very same context Augustine presents his conception of how the liberty that makes a man " to be himself " is obtained, namely, by dependence upon God. Since God is the author of freedom as well as of free will, just as we cannot have free will without Him, so we cannot have freedom, the perfect functioning of free will, without Him. So it is that Augustine assures Romanianus :

> ... Nothing remains for us in your behalf except to pray to God, who has these things in His care — to the end that, if it is possible, we may obtain from Him that He restore you to yourself. For in

doing that, He will readily restore you to us also. We pray that He permit your mind — which has long been gasping for breath — to emerge at length into the pure air of liberty. [1]

In the *De Beata Vita*, Augustine evinces his own lack of confidence in man's free will and even a lack of conviction with regard to the scope of free will in the running of human affairs. Having first said : Since the voyage "...to the port of philosophy is accomplished only by rational choice of will, few will attain it," [2] he says :

For, since God or nature, or necessity, or our will, or a combination of some or all of these would have us founder in this world heedlessly and by chance as in a stormy sea, — and how few would perceive whither to strive or where to return, unless, at some time, a tempest, against our will and way, a tempest that to fools would appear adverse, should thrust us, all unaware, off our faulty course upon the land so dearly wished for. [3]

Very early indeed Augustine is aware not only that God is needed to restore man to himself, but that even for men who are living according to their high nature, willing to be happy, the happiness so ardently sought must be received from God. Happiness cannot be attained directly. It can be desired by man; but it is not one of the things directly in our power. Of happiness Augustine says : "I do not see what else could better be called a gift of God." [4] The desire for happiness found in all men evinces the existence in men of a natural tendency, and this is a mark of the imperfection of human nature. But the fact that happiness cannot be secured by the will alone is a mark of man's dependence.

[1] Augustine, *Contra Academicos*, I, 1, 1; PL 32, 905 : ...nihil pro te nobis aliud quam vota restant, quibus ab illo cui hæc curæ sunt Deo, si possumus, impetremus ut te tibi reddat; ita enim facile reddet et nobis; sinatque mentem illam tuam, quæ respirationem jamdiu parturit, aliquando in auras veræ libertatis emergere.

[2] Augustine, *De Beata Vita*, I, 1; PL 32, 959 : Si ad philosophiæ portum... ratione institutus cursus, et voluntas ipsa perduceret... paucique perveniant.

[3] *De Beata Vita*, I, 1; PL 32, 959 : Cum enim in hunc mundum, sive Deus, sive natura, sive necessitas, sive voluntas nostra, sive conjuncta horum aliqua, sive simul omnia... veluti in quoddam procellosum salum nos quasi temere passimque projecerit; quotusquisque cognosceret quo sibi nitendum esset, quave redeundum, nisi aliquando et invitos contraque obnitentes aliqua tempestas, quæ stultis videtur adversa, in optatissimam terram nescientes errantesque compingeret.

[4] *De Beata Vita*, I, 5; PL 32, 962 : ...nihilque aliud video quod magis Dei donum vocandum sit.

If happiness were wholly in the power of man, all men would be happy, for certainly all desire it. That people cannot give happiness to themselves becomes all the clearer when we remember that people can give themselves other things they want — pleasure, money, honor; but these do not bring happiness. Some think that to have whatever they want or to do whatever they please is the gauge of being happy. About this pseudo-liberty, Augustine says :

Behold, not the philosophers, but only people who like to argue, state that all are happy who live according to their own desires. This, of course is not true, for to desire what is not fitting is the worst of wretchedness. But it is not so deplorable to fail in attaining what we desire as it is to wish to attain what is not proper. For more evil is brought about through one's wicked will than happiness through fortune. [1]

Exactly why happiness is out of man's grasp is revealed when Augustine concludes that communication with God is the cause of happiness to man. How could man win God, so to speak? And yet " ...it is He, through His steady presence in man, who makes man happy. " [2]

The happy man may have many needs but he does not lack what is best and what he wants. This happiness is given to man when he is in the right relation to things that are in his power, setting " ...his will only on very definite things, so that, whatever he undertakes, he acts either in conformity with virtuous duty or the divine law of wisdom; those things can by no means be taken away from him. " [3] In the *Retractations* Augustine blames himself for having given the impression here that man could be perfectly happy in this world, whereas man on earth is happy only potentially. [4]

[1] Augustine, *De Beata Vita*, II, 10; PL 32, 964 : Ecce autem... non philosophi quidem, sed prompti tamen ad disputandum, omnes aiunt esse beatos qui vivant ut ipsi velint. Falsum id quidem : Velle enim quod non deceat, idem ipsum miserrimum. Nec tam miserum est non adipisci quod velis, quam adipisci velle quod non oporteat. Plus enim mali pravitas voluntatis affert, quam fortuna cuiquam boni.

[2] *De Beata Vita*, III, 17; PL 32, 968 : ...quem manentem in hominibus beatos eos facere.

[3] *De Beata Vita*, IV, 25; PL 32, 971, 972 : Habet enim rerum certissimarum voluntatem, id est, ut quidquid agit, non agat nisi ex virtutis quodam præscripto et divina lege sapientiæ, quæ nullo ab eo pacto eripi possunt.

[4] Augustine, *Retract.*, I, 2; PL 32, 588.

What precisely is the relation between wisdom and happiness? The soul that lives according to the truth is wise, inasmuch as it permits itself to be formed according to its true measure, neither puffed up, nor narrowed down. [1] By being measured, that is, conforming to the truth, one communicates with the Supreme Measure, Supreme Truth, and opens as it were a passageway to one's soul from above.

Whoever attains to the supreme measure, through truth, is happy. This means to have God within the soul, that is, to enjoy God. Other beings do not have God, although they are possessed by God. [2]

Already in this first work of Augustine the import of truth for the enjoyment of liberty is underlined.

Augustine's distance from Plotinus is once more shown by the difference between the Plotinian concept of free will as power over the lower world, with the Intellectual-Principle, attained by human efforts alone, as the Liberator of man from impotence, and the Augustinian concept of the will's freedom as submission to the moral measurement of the soul, and this through the power of God.

This, then is the full satisfaction of souls, this the happy life: to recognize piously and completely the One through whom you are led into the truth, the nature of the truth you enjoy, and the bond that connects you with the supreme measure. These three show to the intelligent man the one God, the one substance. [3]

Then comes Monica's interruption that Faith, Hope and Charity are prerequisites for the attainment of truth and of the happy life, so we can be certain that Augustine is indeed treating of the historical man whose supernatural end is an historical fact. Augustine's own conclusion is a fitting crown to his mother's thought:

[1] Augustine, *De Beata Vita*, IV, 33; PL 32, 975.

[2] *De Beata Vita*, IV, 34; PL 32, 976: Quisquis igitur ad summum modum per veritatem venerit, beatus est. Hoc est animo Deum habere, id est Deo frui. Cætera enim quamvis a Deo habeantur, non habent Deum.

[3] *De Beata Vita*, IV, 35; PL 32, 976: Illa est igitur plena satietas animorum, hæc est beata vita, pie perfecteque cognoscere a quo inducaris in veritatem, qua veritate perfruaris, per quid connectaris summo modo. Quæ tria unum Deum intelligentibus unamque substantiam, exclusis vanitatibus variæ superstitionis, ostendunt.

I give my deepest thanks to the supreme and true God, the Father and Master, the Liberator of souls. [1]

And so Augustine has drawn to the actual scale of man a blueprint for Christian morality in which the dimension of freedom is adequately recognized. By participation man receives his being, an imperfect, unachieved being, and it always remains received being. By communication we receive the perfection of being, and it always remains a received light and love. The coming forth of man is by participation; the return to God is by communication. For communication there must be a certain equality. Divine Love offers man this equality. The consent that henceforth makes possible man's communication with God is a response to a Divine desire for communication. Consent or dissent, the yes-no power, is the prerogative of will.

So the return to God, the vocation of man, cannot be accomplished without either God or man. It is begun in heaven by God's free decision to communicate with man, and it awaits man's free choice of response to Divine Love. This communication is the meeting of two desires. Love on the part of men is a loving submission to the Truth before the Truth is contemplated. One of the effects of submission is a certain restoration of natural perfections to the soul. The spiritual soul becomes self-possessed without forsaking its legitimate relation to the body; it is the master, the mover, so that in all the acts of the body the will is in control. Instead of the soul being contaminated by its association with body, the body is spiritualized, charged more and more with spirit-power, made a supple instrument of the will without the power to distract. Thus, the soul becomes the master it should be, the body becomes the instrument of spirit it should be; man becomes truly himself — but by dependence. This is evidenced in man's actions by their submission to the rule of reason : obedience to the order of nature, human nature, is a response to the dialogue that God

[1] Augustine, *De Beata Vita*, IV, 36; PL 32, 976 : ...gratias ago summo et vero Deo Patri, Domino liberatori animarum.

has initiated with man; it is a test of the sincerity of one's love for God.

The order of nature is God's order of love. In obeying the law of nature, acting according to nature one does not like a Stoic submit to the lower, but like the creature of God that one is, one submits to a higher Person, a Creator whose law is His love. When nature and supernature, creation and salvation, are seen for what they are — manifestations of the love of a God Who is Love, — then man is willing to embrace the will of God. In showing His Love for man to man, God opens the human heart. The power of making mountains, of releasing waterfalls, of providing all peoples with air and food and clothing and shelter is nothing in comparison with this power of entering human hearts. God is omnipotent more because He is Love than because of His might. Thus, when Augustine concludes the dialogue he has had with the young friends whom he wishes to bring closer to Christ, he warns :

> This measure is to be observed everywhere and everywhere to be loved, if our return to God is in your heart. [1]

Could it have been from the Plotinian *Enneads* that such understanding had come to Augustine so early in life? That Augustine was far from satisfied with what he found in Plotinus on the subject of evil and of Providence has been proposed by Régis Jolivet. [2] Augustine tells us :

> Wherefore, those who ponder these matters are seemingly forced to believe either that Divine Providence does not reach to these outer limits of things or else that all evils are surely committed by the Will of God. [3]

By the outer limits is meant matter, considered by Plotinus as the extremity of being, but nonetheless in honorable descent

[1] Augustine, *De Beata Vita*, IV, 36; PL 32, 976 : Modus, inquam, ille ubique servandus est, ubique amandus, si vobis cordi est ad Deum reditus noster.

[2] Régis Jolivet, *Essai sur les Rapports entre la Pensée Grecque et la Pensée Chrétienne*, Paris, J. Vrin, 1931.

[3] Augustine, *De Ordine*, I, 1, 1; PL 32, 978 : Quamobrem illud quasi necessarium iis quibus talia sunt curæ, credendum dimittitur; aut divinam providentiam non usque in hæc ultima et ima pertendi, aut certe mala omnia Dei voluntate committi.

from the One. Augustine is aware of the dilemma : if matter is blamed for evil, it must be outside God's control unless God is also ultimately blameworthy, since matter came forth from Him. Did Plotinus ever settle the question of evil? It is often said that Augustine found the solution to the problem of evil in Plotinus; where is the solution in Plotinus? According to him, man's primary association with matter was voluntary, inasmuch as the perfection of soul led it to overflow, giving life to body. But is there not necessity in this? Thus soul was necessarily concerned with matter, and its absorption with the partial to the despite of the whole, though careless, was within the order of its organizing activity. The needs of the body draw the soul away from its proper determination by the Intellectual-Principle. Between intellectual and material necessity the soul fluctuates through a succession of existences until Intellectual-Principle has its way, as things should be. While it is true, as Augustine admits in the *Confessions*,[1] that the *Enneads* helped to give him principles for the solution of the problem of evil by demonstrating philosophically that evil is non-being, yet was it not rather from Ambrose that Augustine learned of the negative character of evil?[2] And did not Ambrose rather than Plotinus first teach Augustine that free will was the cause of evil?[3]

[1] Augustine, *Confess.*, VII, 9 et sqq.; VIII, 2; cf., Paul Henry, S.J., *Plotin et l'Occident*, Louvain, 1934.

[2] Augustine, *Contra Julianum Pelagianum*, I, 9, 44; PL 44, 671 : Unde ille doctor... Ambrosius, in eo libro quem *De Isaac et anima* scripsit : 'Quid ergo est', inquit, 'malitia, nisi boni indigentia?' Et iterum ait : 'Ex bonis igitur mala orta sunt. Non enim sunt mala, nisi quæ privantur bonis : per mala tamen factum est ut bona eminerent. Ergo indigentia boni radix malitiæ est.'

[3] Ambrose, *De Jacob et Vita Beata*, I, 3, 10; PL 14, 632, 633 : Non est quod cuiquam nostram ascribamus ærumnam, nisi nostræ voluntati. Nemo tenetur ad culpam, nisi voluntate propria deflexerit... Affectus igitur, non caro auctor est culpæ, caro autem voluntatis ministra. Non ergo vendat nos voluntas nostra.

Hexaemeron, I, 8, 30 & 31; PL 14, 151, 152 : Quid ergo dicunt quod Deus creaverit malum, cum ex contrariis et adversis nequaquam sibi adversa generantur?... Si enim neque sine principio est, quasi increata, neque a Deo facta, unde habet natura malitiam? ...sed mentis atque animi depravatio, a tramite virtutis devia, quæ incuriosorum animis quam frequenter obrepit. Non igitur ab extraneis est nobis, quam a nobis ipsis majus periculum. Intus est adversarius, intus auctor erroris, intus, inquam, clausis in nobismetipsis... Illa cavenda quæ ex nostra voluntate prodeunt...

In a necessary universe where all emanates from the One, there are only beings whose intrinsic cause is inseparable from them. In the Christian universe where all is caused by God's Will creating "ex nihilo," the withdrawal of God's will would leave just nothing. Augustine transposed this to the moral plane. Whatever is in accord with God's will has substance, being and goodness, whereas whatever is in discord with the Divine Will is unreal, and evil. Now, a contingent being is one with the capacity not-to-be, and a rational contingent being seems to be one with the added capacity not-to-be-good. Man's being as he receives it is metaphysically good as far as it goes, but it is, as we said, incomplete. This unfinished personal universe is to be completed by moral good. Since it is quite possible even for rational animals to live without living rightly, the very notion of right living implies free choice. But since to live rightly is to will that which is superior to us, and to choose the means thereto, the human will has a distinctive being. For Plotinus, there was a will that seemed to be a mere spontaneity, and there was free choice which he looked down upon as a mere disciplinarian of passions. Augustine sees free will as a directing power of the whole man, an initiating power, a power that is not only uncompelled from without but intimately *a se*. To this will, wherein man can often experience his radical contingency, is confided the preparation for eternal life.

And what else is all this than to be, by virtue and temperance, lulled away from the overgrowth of vices, and uplifted towards himself? And what else is the face of God than the truth for which we yearn, and for which as the object of our love, we make ourselves clean and beautiful? [1].

[1] Augustine, *De Ordine*, I, 8, 23; PL 32, 988 : Aut quid est aliud converti, nisi ab immoderatione vitiorum, virtute ac temperantia in sese attolli? Quidve aliud est Dei facies, quam ipsa cui suspiramus, et cui nos amatæ mundos pulchrosque reddimus, veritas?

Cf. R. A. Gauthier, O.P., "Saint Maxime le Confesseur et la Psychologie de l'Acte Humain," *Recherches de Théologie Ancienne et Médiévale*, t. XXI, (1954), pp. 90, 91 : "...c'est en effet dans la volonté et non plus dans la raison que saint Augustin fait résider le principe de la liberté; s'il accepte donc de faire sienne l'analyse stoicienne de la συγκατάθεσις [Eng., 'assent'] c'est en attribuant cet acte privilégié, non plus à la raison, mais à la volonté, et en transformant l'*assentiment* intellectuel des Stoïciens en un *consentement* volontaire. Cf. Augustine *De Spir. et Litt.*, 31, 54 : Quid est enim credere, nisi consentire verum esse quod dicitur?

This cleansing and beautifying process implies an ordering of the whole of man; it means keeping the senses in their proper place. In speaking of his memory, Augustine once said that he was "not as yet that servant's master... And if I sometimes give commands and he perhaps obeys me and makes me think that I have gained the mastery, yet in other matters he becomes so haughty that I grovel disconsolate at his feet."[1] But the role of the will was not merely to discipline, and Augustine's wise man uses it mainly to free himself to love God.

> A wise man therefore treats that part of the soul almost like a slave so that at first he gives it repeated commands, and then, when it has become well-trained and submissive, he imposes on it this limit as a law and a command: that as long as it is using the senses for things that are necessary not to the wise man but to itself, it must not dare become insolent or haughty towards its master, and furthermore, that even the things that are its own, it must not dare to use indiscriminately or immoderately...
>
> But a wise man embraces God and finds his joy in Him Who abides forever, for Whose presence there is no waiting and of Whose absence there is no fear, because by the very fact that He truly is, He is always present. Though the wise man remains immovable, he nevertheless exercises a certain kind of care over his slave's 'property' so that like a prudent and diligent servant, he may conserve it well and use it sparingly.[2]

Only the complete man is able to love ardently and that is Augustine's desire. He sees the soul, not as the overflow of Intellectual-Principle, but as the creation of Wisdom, of Love, of Omnipotence, and so he never underestimates the soul's power of love that reflects its origin. The greatness of Augustinism

[1] Augustine, *De Ordine*, II, 2, 7; PL 32, 997: ...nondum sum illius famuli dominus;... Et si forte aliquando impero, atque obtemperat mihi facitque sæpe putare quod vicerim, in aliis rursus rebus ita sese erigit, ut ejus sub pedibus miser jaceam.

[2] *De Ordine*, II, 2, 6; PL 32, 996: Utitur ergo hac sapiens quasi servo, ut hæc ei jubeat, easque jam domito atque substrato metas legis imponat, ut dum istis sensibus utitur propter illa quæ jam non sapienti, sed sibi sunt necessaria, non se audeat extollere, nec superbire domino, nec iis ipsis quæ ad se pertinent passim atque immoderate uti. Ad illam enim vilissimam partem possunt ea pertinere quæ prætereunt. Quibus autem est memoria necessaria, nisi prætereuntibus, et quasi fugientibus rebus? Ille igitur sapiens amplectitur Deum, eoque perfruitur qui semper manet, nec exspectatur ut sit, nec metuitur ne desit, sed eo ipso quo vere est, semper est præsens. Curat autem immobilis et in se manens servi sui quodammodo peculium, ut eo tanquam frugi et diligens famulus bene utatur, parceque custodiat.

and the assurance of its survival come from its doing justice both to intellect and to will, being neither a voluntarism nor an intellectualism but a humanism that is, as humanism should be, theocentric. Augustine's perpetual reverence for the divine quality of truth was an invaluable inheritance from Plotinianism. He says : " For I think that not only he is in error who follows the wrong path, but also he who does not follow the right one. " [1] But if Truth is superior to man, as it is in Augustine's universe, man can only approach it by love, ascending to it rather than reducing it to his own proportions. An idea is not precisely a motive. Love generates love, and so Divine Love is more adapted to move the will to desire and to decision than ideas are. With Augustine it was the love of Christ for him and the example of others loving Christ that moved his will. This experience of Augustine was to find its way into the very heart of the Augustinian philosophy of the historical man, and who shall say that love is not the very heart of that philosophy? It was when the omnipotent God in His mercy sent " the authority of the divine intellect down even to a human body " that souls " enkindled not only by His words but also by His example, " were able to rid themselves of the darkness of error and the sordid appetites of the body and taste their true country. [2]

Fully appreciating the necessity of truth, Augustine sees the will as the decisive factor for destiny. When he cries :

> Now I love Thee alone; Thee alone do I follow; Thee alone do I seek; Thee alone am I ready to serve, for Thou alone hast just dominion; under Thy sway do I long to be... [3]

— we see the highest use of love. Augustine will never admit that the liberty coming from this highest love of God detracts in any way from the free choice belonging to nature : " ...to the soul indeed is given free choice which some endeavour to disprove by futile reasonings; these are so blind that they under-

[1] Augustine, *Contra Academicos*, III, 15, 34; PL 32, 951 : Non enim solum puto eum errare, qui falsam viam sequitur; sed etiam eum qui veram non sequitur.

[2] *Contra Academicos*, III, 19, 42; PL 32, 956, 957.

[3] Augustine, *Solil.*, I, 1, 5; PL 32, 872 : Jam te solum amo, te solum sequor, te solum quæro, tibi soli servire paratus sum, quia tu solus juste dominaris; tui juris esse cupio.

stand not that they are saying even those vain and impious things by their own choice." [1] Liberty is the fulfillment of free will, not its denial. The fact that it comes from God is almost an insurance that it will not destroy the natural freedom of which He also is the giver. Man's condition of weakness of will is not God's doing but man's. If man working alone brought defect to free will, it is better for him not to work alone. So it is that man can receive from the hands of God a renewed free will, made better than before, which is always the way a Divine mending takes place. Man's liberty today is a larger liberty than that received by Adam. The price of it has increased its value :

> ... since Christ after so much suffering paid with his life's blood for us, let us cling to our Savior with a love so strong, and be so dazzled by His brightness, that nothing we see down here will be able to keep us from looking up [at Him]. [2]

CONCLUSION

We can summarize Augustine's teaching on freedom as expressed in the early dialogues by stating that freedom, like happiness, is the gift of God, but that to receive this gift man's consent is indispensable at all times. Man's part in the attainment of freedom today is to pray for divine help, to obey the law of his nature, and to allow Christ to liberate him through love.

The characteristics of human nature, of the essential man, which led Augustine to say that happiness and freedom would come from above, from a truth to which man submits himself, were : human imperfection, that is, his unfinished being, and man's natural dependence on God for the being that he has. The characteristics of the historical man, or the

[1] Augustine, *De Quantitate Animæ*, I, 36, 80; PL 32, 1079 : Datum est enim animæ liberum arbitrium, quod qui nugatoriis ratiocinationibus labefactare conantur, usque adeo cæci sunt, ut ne ista ipsa quidem vana atque sacrilega propria voluntate se dicere intelligant.

[2] Augustine, *De Libero Arbitrio*, III, 25, 76; PL 32, 1308 : ...ut prærogato nobis Christi sanguine, post labores miseriasque ineffabiles tanta charitate liberatori nostro adhæreamus, et tanto ejus in eum claritate rapiamur, ut nulla nos visa ex inferioribus a conspectu superiore detorqueant.

existential man, which led Augustine to say that happiness and freedom would come through a Divine Liberator, were : the darkness and confused state of the human understanding, and a weakness in doing the good which one knows should be done. The characteristics of God that led Augustine to the belief that He would liberate man were : the Divine Goodness and Mercy manifested by man's very existence, the Divine Mercy that would take compassion on man's misery, the Divine Will or Desire that man should share in the Divine happiness which, nevertheless, is above all natural power of man to desire, still less to achieve.

In showing that happiness had an objective basis, that is, that it consists not merely in having what you want but in wanting the right thing, Augustine has illuminated that quality of freedom which accompanies spiritual maturity. The liberty that is exercised by doing what one pleases even to self-destruction was exposed as a deviation, a pseudo-form of freedom that must be unmasked in every age.

We leave the dialogues with the realization that the most valuable freedom is not the psychological freedom to do what we will, not the physical, social or political freedom which exempts us from illegitimate interference from others, not the Stoic freedom of following the law of nature nor the Kantian freedom of doing what we ought, but the Divine freedom described by Augustine of wanting to do what we ought because we love God and take delight in Him.

CHAPTER VI

FREE WILL AND FREEDOM IN THE *CONFESSIONS* OF ST. AUGUSTINE

Though Augustine has proclaimed the reality and the grandeur of free choice in the *De Libero Arbitrio*, and in all the dialogues has exalted freedom as the actuality of loving God above all things and in all things, through the liberating power of Christ, without any suggestion of disdain for things temporal or sensible, it is only in his *Confessions* that we most vividly see why the grace of God is needed to make the human free will fit to achieve its purpose : to move, without restraint and without repugnance and without struggle, to man's true and total good. In the *Confessions* Augustine describes the existential condition of that human free will that was best known to him — his own will. The universal appeal of the *Confessions* has made of it a classic, and not the least reason for this is the candid picture that it gives of the " divided will. " Another reason may be that it is one of the first " success stories, " but it is not the story of a self-made man. Augustine's will-experience brought him a healthy self-distrust that made him look to God for all that he needed. We shall see that Augustine's teaching that freedom is a divine gift which does not destroy man's initial liberty of choice but which enables man to be truly human and truly successful has not been the mere dream of an arm-chair philosopher.

If Augustine had not himself told us that he was treating in the *De Libero Arbitrio* (387-395) of " the will with which man was created, " [1] we would have cause to wonder why the statements concerning the will made in the *Confessions* (400) are so very different. In the earlier treatise Augustine says that the will is free, not merely to choose between motives, but free to do right. Of that will he can say :

[1] Augustine, *De Libero Arbitrio*, III, 18, 52; PL 32, 1296.

1) no one wills anything against his will; [1]

2) we have will-power over our wills; [2]

3) there is nothing so completely in our power as the will itself. [3]

These statements may answer the questions he raises in his treatise but they also give rise to an important psychological problem : if one always wills willingly, and the will can command itself as reason can know itself, then man ought to be able to dictate whatever the will is to do. Theoretically, that is Augustine's position in the early dialogue. Concretely, what is Augustine's experience of free will? When Augustine told himself that he would go over to God's law " where all [his] bones cried out that [he] should be, " [4] he could not get himself there.

For I had but to will to go, in order not merely to go but to arrive; I had only to will to go - but to will powerfully and wholly, not to turn and twist a will half-wounded, this way and that, with the part that would rise struggling against the part that would keep to the earth. [5]

He is exposing his experience that the divided will cannot will effectively. It must first be unified. To be unified it will have to let go of one of the things to which it is clinging. Now, according to the third of the theoretical statements listed above from the *De Libero Arbitrio*, [6] the will can command itself to let go of the object that is the cause of its division. It ought to be easier for the will to command itself than to order something which depends on another power for its execution, for example, the act of walking, which requires both will and legs. In the case

[1] Augustine, *De Libero Arbitrio*, II, 14, 37; PL 32, 1261.

[2] *Ibid.*

[3] *De Lib. Arb.*, III, 1, 1; PL 32, 1269, 1270, 1271.

[4] Augustine, *Confess.*, VIII, 8; PL 32, 758 : ...Deus meus, in quod eundum esse omni ossa mea clamabant... We use the translation of F. J. Sheed, *The Confessions of St. Augustine*, New York, Sheed and Ward, 1947.

[5] *Confess.*, VIII, 8; PL 32, 758 : Nam non solum ire, verum etiam pervenire illuc, nihil erat aliud quam velle ire, sed velle fortiter et integre; non semisauciam hac atque hac versare et jactare voluntatem, parte assurgente cum alia parte cadente luctantem.

[6] Augustine, *De Lib. Arb.*, III, 1, 1; PL 32, 1269.

of will commanding itself, " ...given that willing means willing wholly, " ... " the willing was the doing. "[1] Yet the concrete fact was that the body responded more easily to the wishes of the mind than the will, which could respond by a simple act of willing.[2] Augustine is deeply disturbed by this " monstrousness " and asks " whether perhaps the answer lies in the mysterious punishment that has come upon men and some deeply hidden damage in the sons of Adam. "[3] He does not answer this question now, but pursues the analysis begun.

If the will is torn in two, drawn by opposing attractions, it can theoretically, as we saw, be united into one will, one desire, by a command. What Augustine sees, however, in the *Confessions* over and above what he lets us see in the *De Libero Arbitrio* is that this command itself is an act of the will; and so the will must really want what it commands — that is the dilemma. To be effective, the command cannot be simply an order; it must be one's wish, one's choice; man must unreservedly be for what he commands. Yet, if he unreservedly wanted what he is commanding, he would not have to command. Does the commanding power of the will extend only to the other faculties, without including itself? So it would seem. Augustine's penetration into the psychological area of man's life has deepened since he wrote those words about the will's power of self-command. It is still true that being a spiritual power it can act upon itself, and true likewise that it has more direct access to itself. Nevertheless : 1) if the will already desires what the command imposes, a command is needless; 2) if the will does not want what the will commands, the command is given half-heartedly, and not obeyed, so that it is useless to give it.

[1] Augustine, Confess., VIII, 8; PL 32, 758 : ...quia mox ut vellem, utique vellem. ...et ipsum velle jam facere erat.

[2] Augustine, *Confess.*, VIII, 8; PL 32, 758 : Ibi enim facultas ea quæ voluntas, et ipsum velle jam facere erat; et tamen non fiebat : faciliusque obtemperabat corpus tenuissimæ voluntati animæ, ut ad nutum mentis membra moverentur, quam ipsa sibi anima ad voluntatem suam magnam in sola voluntate perficiendam.

[3] *Confess.*, VIII, 9; PL 32, 758 : Unde hoc monstrum? et quare istud? Luceat misericordia tua; et interrogem, si forte mihi respondere possint latebræ pœnarum hominum, et tenebrosissimæ contritiones filiorum Adam.

The mind, I say, commands itself to will : it would not give the command unless it willed : yet it does not do what it commands. The trouble is that it does not totally will : therefore it does not totally command. It commands insofar as it wills : and it disobeys the command insofar as it does not will. The will is commanding itself to be a will, commanding itself, not some other. But it does not in its fullness give the command, so that what it commands is not done. For if the will were so in its fullness it would not command itself to will, for it would already will. [1]

Since the divided will cannot be totalized by a simple command, further psychological analysis is called for. Why is it divided? It is divided by a tug-of-war between a speculative vision of truth and a natural tendency to the good in itself on the one hand, and the concrete will, weighed down by vices and passions, which is directing the practical intellect to judge against the vision of the good.

It is therefore no monstrousness, partly to will, partly not to will, but a sickness of the soul to be so weighted down by custom that it cannot wholly rise even with the support of truth. [2]

Or again :

... when eternity attracts the higher faculties and the pleasure of some temporal good holds the lower, it is one same soul that wills both, but not either with its whole will; and it is therefore torn both ways and deeply troubled while Truth shows the one way as the better but habit keeps it to the other. [3]

The lower condition which had grown habitual was more powerful than the better condition which I had not tried [4].

Mental life, therefore, which we know to be necessary for personal action is yet insufficient to motivate the will. The will is

[1] Augustine, *Confess.*, VIII, 9; PL 32, 758, 759 : Imperat, inquam, ut velit, qui non imperaret nisi vellet, et non fit quod imperat. Sed non ex toto vult, non ergo ex toto imperat. Nam in tantum imperat, in quantum vult, et in tantum non fit quod imperat, in quantum non vult. Quoniam voluntas imperat ut sit voluntas, nec alia, sed ipsa. Non utique plena imperat, ideo non est quod imperat. Nam si plena esset, nec imperaret ut esset, quia jam esset.

[2] *Confess.*, VIII, 9; PL 32, 759 : Non igitur monstrum partim velle, partim nolle; sed ægritudo animi est, qui non totus assurgit veritate sublevatus, consuetudine prægravatus.

[3] *Confess.*, VIII, 10; PL 32, 760 : Ita etiam cum æternitas delectat superius, et temporalis boni voluptas retentat inferius, eadem anima est non tota voluntate illud aut hoc volens; et ideo discerpitur gravi molestia, dum illud veritate præponit, hoc familiaritate non ponit.

[4] *Confess.*, VIII, 11; PL 32, 760 : ...plusque in me valebat deterius inolitum, quam melius insolitum...

pre-eminently the faculty of the person. To energize the will there must be a love that engages the personal affective faculty, and yet a spiritual love. If one's love is whole, one's will is whole; when one's will is whole the person is unified; when one's love is good, the person is good. As the will, so the person. In thinking of serving God, as Augustine long thought of doing, it was " he who willed to do it, [he] who was unwilling. " The divided will is the divided person. " Therefore I strove with myself and was distracted by myself. " [1] Augustine played with the idea that his distraction was a punishment for the sin " freely committed by Adam. " [2]

If the will known to Augustine the philosopher is that " by which we will, " [3] a will over which we have power, [4] the will experienced by Augustine the man is the " unwilling will. " [5] This will was, as we have seen, unwilling to follow truth; it was willing to follow the pull of the flesh, and two forces kept it so willing :

1) a natural tendency toward sensible pleasure; Augustine speaks of this in the *De Libero Arbitrio*, III, 1; but there he says that the will, unlike an animal's appetite, can check this tendency;

2) an acquired habit of taking sensible pleasure.

Under these conditions Augustine does not say that man has lost his free will, but his words indicate that he considers freedom to have been lost. " I was bound by this need of the flesh, and dragged with me the chain of its poisonous delight, fearing to be set free. " [6] Although his will could not follow truth because it was unwilling to, that is, it was devoted to lower things, yet in another sense Augustine at first considered that what he did by natural inclination or by force of habit or by both was not done willingly. Augustine was not easily convinced

[1] Augustine, *Confess.*, VIII, 10; PL 32, 759 : Ideo mecum contendebam, et dissipabor a me ipso.

[2] *Ibid.*

[3] Augustine, *De Lib. Arb.*, III, 3, 7; PL 32, 1274.

[4] *De Lib. Arb.*, II, 19, 51; PL 32, 1268.

[5] *De Lib. Arb.*, III, 1, 1-2; PL 32, 1269, 1270, 1271.

[6] Augustine, *Confess.*, VI, 12; PL 32, 730 : ...et deligatus morbo carnis mortifera suavitate trahebam catenam meam, solvi timens...

that the will could be the cause of the evil that he lamented doing. " But what I did *unwillingly*, it seemed to me that I rather suffered from than did, and I judged it to be not my fault but my punishment. "[1] This position, that the will was more sinned against than sinning, was not one permanently held by Augustine; it had evidently been relinquished before the conclusion of the *De Libero Arbitrio*, for there in Book II, chapter 24, he declares: " No one unwillingly wills anything. " That statement is a two-edged sword; it cuts away any possibility of effectively commanding the will without getting the will to want what is commanded; and it cuts away the possibility of shirking responsibility for acts that proceed from us but which we attempt to disclaim as being undesired by us. It introduces the interesting question which Anselm will treat at length, as to whether anyone ever wills anything against his will. Augustine pioneered in posing the problem and in suggesting the solution.[2] Anselm and others will elaborate upon the answer. Augustine came to see that if at a given moment he is in the power of " libido, " he himself has conferred upon it the power it now uses against him. Did not Augustine declare that there was nothing superior to the will, none who could claim power over another's will?

So it was that Augustine experienced the dramatic struggle of will to become one with itself and in harmony with the mind in the concentration on that Final End which could free it from the conflicting claims of all the pseudo-ends then deordinating and de-energizing the will. He met this problem of evil in himself before attempting to suggest a solution. If Plotinus enlightened him upon the nature of physical evil or metaphysical evil, this was but a clue. Augustine tells us that he pondered the problem, reflected upon the condition described above: the will not

[1] Augustine, *Confess.*, VII, 3; PL 32, 735: Quod autem invitus facerem, pati me potius quam facere videbam; et id non culpam, sed pœnam esse judicabam, qua me non injuste plecti, te justum cogitans, cito fatebar.

[2] The atheistic existentialists today feel a certain resentment against any interpretation of freedom which exonerates man from responsibility for the things he does, by blaming passion, instinct, heredity. They should take note of how squarely Augustine was to shoulder the responsibility for his acts after years of habituation.

really absorbed in what it was doing and yet not free to strive after higher and better things; and this showed him how the will could be the source of evil:

So that when I now asked what is iniquity, I realized that it was not a substance but a swerving of the will which is turned toward lower things and away from You, O God, who are the supreme substance, so that it casts away what is most inward to it and swells greedily for outward things.[1]

By this negative approach Augustine began to understand the positive principle found in the Scriptures: by servitude to God man obtains self-mastery.[2]

The knowledge that freedom is a matter of " cleaving to God " is one thing; the cleaving itself is another. At first, God seemed to be freeing Augustine through psychological laws. Honor and profit, once strong motives, delighted him no longer " in comparison with your sweetness and the beauty of your house which I loved. "[3] But there was a tie that still held Augustine down. It was something that absorbed his love, and his thoughts dwelt upon what his affections so ardently appreciated. Augustine recognizes his helplessness to love efficaciously the One he knows to be supremely lovable:

Come, Lord, work upon us, call us back, set us on fire and clasp us close, be fragrant to us, draw us to Thy Loveliness; let us love, let us run to Thee. Do not many from a deeper pit of blindness than Victorinus come back to Thee, enlightened by that light in which they receive from thee the power to be made Thy Sons?[4]

The response to this prayer was a drawing, a mysterious influence upon the will of Augustine, the influence of love, a Divine Love inspiring, awakening an answering love. All at

[1] Augustine, *Confess.*, VII, 16; PL 32, 744: Et quæsivi quid esset iniquitas, et non inveni substantiam; sed a summa substantia, te Deo, detortæ in infima voluntatis perversitatem, projicientis intima sua, et tumescentis foras.

[2] Augustine, *De Musica*, VI, 5, 13, 14; PL 32, 1170, 1171.

[3] Augustine, *Confess.*, VIII, 1; PL 32, 749: Jam enim me illa non delectabant præ dulcedine tua et decore domus tuæ quam dilexi.

[4] *Confess.*, VIII, 4; PL 32, 752: Age, Domine, fac; excita, et revoca nos; accende, et rape; flagra, dulcesce; amemus, curramus. Nonne multi ex profundiore tartaro cæcitatis quam Victorinus redeunt ad te, et accedunt, et illuminantur recipientes lumen, quod si qui recipiunt, accipiunt a te potestatem ut filii tui fiant?

once, the will was whole, able to acquiesce in this love. With his will restored to him by a unifying love, Augustine was able to recover the self-possession that is essential to self-surrender. That his own will was freed from division through personal love we learn when Augustine says : " For You converted me to Yourself... " [1]

After the garden scene, after reading the words of St. Paul : " ...make not provision for the flesh, " [2] confidence flooded his heart. There was the departure of darkness, the cessation of conflict, the wholeness of will, and repose.

> By your gift I had come totally to will not what I willed, but to will what you willed. But where in all that long time was my free will, and from what deep sunken hiding place was it suddenly summoned forth in the moment in which I bowed my neck to your easy yoke and my shoulders to your light burden. How lovely I suddenly found it to be free from the loveliness of those vanities... For you cast them out of me, O true and Supreme Loveliness. [3]

Although a psychologist cannot account for that gift nor even place the cause of it, he can register, as Augustine did, the conditions surrounding the giving. As the neck was bowed, freedom was restored. This was the attitude that Augustine discovered to be so essential for the freedom of creatures, an attitude utterly absent from the *Enneads*. " In them [the books of the Platonists] no one sings : 'Shall not my soul be submissive to God?' " [4] Such is the *sine qua non* of human freedom : " In His Will is our peace. "

Nor must we think that Augustine's desire for God summoned up God, as though God were in his power. The desire that Augustine had for God was more truly God's desire for Augustine. God draws man through His own gift.

[1] Augustine, *Confess.*, VIII, 12; PL 32, 762 : Convertisti enim me ad te...

[2] *Rom.*, XIII, 14.

[3] *Confess.*, IX, 1; PL 32, 763 : Et hoc erat totum nolle quod volebam, et velle quod volebas. Sed ubi erat tam annoso tempore, et de quo imo altoque secreto evocatum est in momento liberum arbitrium meum, quo subderem cervicem leni jugo tuo, et humeros levi sarcinæ tuæ (Matt. XI, 30), Christe Jesu, adjutor meus et redemptor meus? Quam suave mihi subito factum est carere suavitatibus nugarum... Ejiciebas enim eas a me, vera tu et summa suavitas...

[4] *Confess.*, VII, 21; PL 32, 748 : Nemo ibi cantat : Nonne Deo subdita erit anima mea?

I call Thee into my soul, which Thou didst make ready to receive Thee by the desire that Thou didst inspire in it. [1]

And again:

By your gift we are on fire and borne upwards... There our good will shall place us, so that we shall desire nothing but to remain there forever. [2]

Augustine concludes that it is always possible for the soul "*to be turned* to Him by Whom it was made, and more and more to live by the Fountain of Life, and in His Light to see the light, and to be made perfect and glorified and brought to beatitude." [3]

SUMMARY

If the *Confessions* of St. Augustine are the confessions of a person, they are also the revelation of a personality. [4] If the faculties that distinguish the person from the thing are the intellect and the free will, the pre-eminent faculty in the development and achievement of personality is the will. Although personality depends greatly upon the knowledge possessed by the person, almost everyone will agree that under God it is the will that makes the scholar, the soldier, the statesman, the saint. This creative power of the will is found when the person is captivated by the love of some good that acts both as Exemplar and Final Cause. The person is completed by personality, and we know that a person becomes what he loves; ever after, he strives after those things that are suitable to the kind of person he is. Since, likewise, all that is loved is in some way good, there is a scale of values that gives rise to a scale of personalites. There are personalities orientated towards pleasure, riches, honor, ease,

[1] Augustine, *Confess.*, XIII, 1; PL 32, 845: Invoco te in animam meam, quam præparas ad capiendum te ex desiderio quod inspiras ei...

[2] *Confess.*, XIII, 9; PL 32, 849: Dono tuo accendimur, et sursum ferimur... Ibi nos collocavit voluntas bona, ut nihil velimus aliud quam permanere illic in æternum.

[3] *Confess.*, XIII, 4; PL 32, 846, 847: ...cui restat converti ad eum a quo facta est, et magis magisque vivere apud fontem vitæ, et in lumine ejus videre lumen (Psal. xxxv, 10) et perfici, et illustrari, et beati.

[4] A person from the point of view of metaphysics is a "rational supposit," that is, a distinct, subsistent individual in a rational nature. The meaning of personality in the science of psychology is the sum total of knowledge, attitudes, habits, ways of acting and so forth, formed into one pattern. Cf. Augustine, *Sermo LXXII*, 4, 5; PL 38, 468-469; *Contra Jul.*, IV, 21; PL 44, 749.

beauty, truth, things, human persons, friendship, God. The will holds the key to personality. If a right love has the power of conferring freedom, nevertheless, free will, as the power of choice, remains the highest tribunal for the sanction or disavowal of love. In the last analysis the free will is the deciding factor in personality. In the drama of personality-making the will holds the main role. Every victory of the will in life's conflicts is a Divine Comedy; life ends happily and God assists the victory. Every defeat of the will is a human tragedy; then the ending is unhappy and it is all man's doing. The sign of defeat is division. The sign of victory is harmony. Harmony in man is not attained without cognitive and affective unity, which is only attained by a love great enough to embrace all loves. The dramatization of the will-conflict in the story of his soul was the preface to Augustine's doctrine of liberty as the love of God, a liberty that will distinguish the citizens of God's City from those of the earthly city of self-love. The City of God is the soul of Augustine " writ large. " He will wish for all citizens a reverent appreciation of the power of love in personal life.

With right love the will became a power that had something of God's power to put goodness where there is no goodness. Apart from God, free will could claim only to be the deficient cause of effecting evil. By attributing evil to man's deficiency, Augustine at last solved the problem that had most disturbed this lover of God — the problem of how evil could come if God is wholly good. The last mental hazard that prevented Augustine from fully embracing God disappeared. Subconsciously, Augustine had cherished the notion that his will was not free, and that notion could not help having an effect upon his appreciation of God. After a thorough analysis of his own will-experience, Augustine, by casting out this false notion, arrived at a truer appreciation of God. Only then was there question of " confession. " " Indeed to have the very highest esteem of God is most truly the beginning of piety. " [1]

[1] Augustine, *De Libero Arbitrio*, I, 2, 5; PL 32, 1224: Optime namque de Deo existimare verissimum est pietatis exordium...

As Augustine progressed he acquired a more profound knowledge of God both as Creator and as Redeemer. [1] This knowledge of God helped him to understand free will. He came to see that freedom is an attribute of the Divine Will penetrated with the Divine Wisdom. He revered the Divine freedom and saw that it is the archetype of human freedom. Free choice, then, had as its *raison d'être* the arrival at so close an adherence to the Supreme Good that nothing could withdraw man from it. A Divine gift, grace would yet reenforce free will. Human effort would still be necessary; but the security of going towards one's true end would release more power to unify and intensify human activity. It is in the Christian atmosphere of freedom that man is perfected and personalized. [2] But at no point may he do without the God-given power of free choice. As a person, man can commune with transcendental values and bring the universe to fulfillment. As a person, also, man can escape the universe; this he does whenever he acts sinfully, for acting as a deficient cause he thereby deviates from the order of "measure, number and weight" and enters the amorphous order of nothingness. There is, as it were, a twofold infinity: an infinity of nothingness as well as an infinity of being. Between these two orders the finite order is stretched. By his will man is capable of vice or virtue, capable of descending toward nothingness or of ascending toward God, *capax peccandi* and *capax Dei*.

CONCLUSION

In the *Confessions* Augustine unveils the powerless will bringing in its wake only confusion, shame and misery. All its fruits

[1] C. N. Cochrane, *Christianity and Classical Culture*, Oxford, Clarendon Press, 1940, p. 384: "For, in the Trinity, he discovered a principle capable of saving the reason as well as the will, and thus redeeming human personality as a whole. It saved the reason because, while denying its pretensions to omniscience and infallibility, it nevertheless affirmed the existence of an order of truth and value which, being in the world as well as beyond it, was within the power of man to apprehend. And in saving reason, at the same time it saved the will, by imparting to it that element of rationality without which it must degenerate into mere subjective wilfulness."

[2] Augustine, *De Lib. Arb.*, II, 13, 37; PL 32, 1261; *De Civ. Dei*, XIII, 20; PL 41, 393; XIV, 15; PL 41, 422-425; XXII, 30; PL 41, 801-804; *Retract.*, I, 2, 4; PL 32, 588; *De Spirit. et Litt.*, XXX; PL 44, 233. Cf. Cochrane, *op. cit.*, p. 454.

are evil, or nearly all. Augustine longs to blame his present evil-doing on original sin; but although this might be a consoling position, he rejects it as an untrue one. If ignorance and difficulty are the effects of original sin, Augustine's sins are not. They are his own doing, his own fault. How does he explain his enslaved will? There were two forms of submission open to him: submission to that which is above by "cleaving to God," and submission to that which is below by attachment to lesser things. His will wanted something less than God. Yet when Augustine realized that he himself was responsible for his own evil, he grew in esteem for God and in distrust of himself. He realized that God's Wisdom was the source of order in the world, an order of truth to which he should conform and contribute by the good use of will. He realized also that God's Love was the source of the goodness in the world, a goodness that could be shared by right love. Not sincerely desirous of God, because his will was preoccupied with other things, Augustine could at least pray for the gift of love to respond to Divine Love. [1] When he said this prayer with sincerity he found that God flooded him with the love he had asked of Him, precisely because it was what God wanted for him, too. God is always before man, inspiring man with the desire for God. [2] To want God is a great grace, but a grace that God wants to give. Only by wanting God could the divided will of Augustine be unified. This could not be achieved by Augustine alone any more than it could be achieved by God alone. God would respect the inviolable intimacy of the created free will. Although God is the only one who can touch the human will, He will only do so upon request. Augustine's prayer for the gift of love was this request.

[1] Augustine, *Confess.*, VIII, 4; PL 32, 752: Age, Domine, fac; excita, et revoca nos; accende, et rape; flagra, dulcesce: amemus, curramus.

[2] Augustine, *De Dono Pers.*, XXIII, 64; PL 45, 1032: "And they will not understand that this is also a divine gift, that we pray; that is, that we ask, seek and knock. ...And this the Blessed Ambrose also said. For he says, 'To pray to God also is the work of spiritual grace...'"

CHAPTER VII

GENESIS OF THE AUGUSTINIAN DOCTRINE OF FREEDOM

St. Augustine's unalterable conviction that men have always possessed, now possess, and on this earth will ever possess a faculty of free choice, an initial liberty, was founded on Scripture as well as on experience. In the Old Testament this was the implication of God's laws commanding and forbidding certain actions. This conviction was verified by Augustine's own departure from the law of God. From Scripture also Augustine discovered that freedom, a terminal liberty, was given with grace. This truth he found in the New Testament [1] and it was verified by his own conversion to God, which was far from being a mere psychological experience. [2] The discovery that God prompted man to ask for grace and gladly gave it never led Augustine to belittle or to rule out free choice. [3] Freedom given by God must always be received by man and to receive from God is high activity. This freedom is the fulfillment of man, and the natural foundation for it is the faculty of free choice whose object is not merely the good of the faculty but the good of man.

Augustine's insight into the significance of free will as the faculty for the perfection of the person characterizes him as a pioneer philosopher of freedom. The fact remains that throughout the centuries some have hesitated to accord a full approbation

[1] *Rom.*, VIII, 21; *Gal.*, IV, 31; 2 *Cor*, III, 17; *Gal.*, V, 13; *Gal.*, II, 4; *James*, I, 25; II, 12; *John*, VIII, 32.

[2] Augustine, *De Dono Perseverantiæ*, XX, 53; PL 45, 1026: " And, moreover, in those same books, in respect of what I have related concerning my conversion, when God converted me to that faith which, with a most miserable and prating talkativeness, I was destroying, do you not recall that I showed that it was granted to the faithful and daily tears of my mother, that I should not perish (Conf. III, 1, 12; IX, 8). Where certainly I declared that God by His grace converted to the true faith the wills of men, which were not only averse, but even adverse to it. "

[3] Augustine, *De Correptione et Gratia*, II, 4; PL 44, 918.

Having previously set forth in formal fashion Augustine's explanation of free choice and his description of his own poor use of it, let us now accompany Augustine to the dawn of human history to trace the course of human freedom. Here are found historical facts about free will to guide Augustine in his formulation of a doctrine of freedom. From revealed history he will proceed to theology, and his theology contains an implicit philosophy of freedom. But what had occasioned this concern for free will in the first place? The problem of evil had long puzzled him. The Church taught, as he heard from Ambrose, that the cause of evil was bad will. He accepts the answer but it leads to a new question : whence the bad will itself? How is it compatible with a good Creator? He would look to the first human will to discover its state, its purpose, and its way of functioning.

As Adam emerges from the hand of God, what is the state of his will — how free is it? There is no incitement from the flesh, no stimulus to disobedience. [1] Augustine is considering the will in human nature " with which at first man was created in a state of innocence. " [2] Here is an ordered hierarchy of powers, diversity in unity — the reign of harmony. Adam has not only a faculty of free will given by God, but a good will given by God. There is perfect order in his love. Such was the sublime freedom of the first man which Augustine recognized as a true perfection. With this original will, man was free to choose the true good and likewise free from any constraint, external or internal, above or below. Man had a double power : the power of choosing the good and the power of not choosing evil. He also had the possibility of choosing evil. But the first man's attitude of soul was a disposition of dependence upon God, an attitude which disposed him for unlimited growth in freedom. [3] When Augustine distinguishes the freedom of the saints in heaven

[1] Augustine, *De Nup. et Concup.*, I, 1-8; PL 44, 413-419.

[2] Augustine, *De Lib. Arb.*, III, 19, 54; PL 32, 1297 : Sic etiam ipsam naturam aliter dicimus, cum proprie loquimur, naturam hominis, in qua primum in suo genere inculpabilis factus est.

[3] Augustine, *Contra Duas Epist. Pelag.*, I, 2, 5; PL 44, 552; *Cont. Jul.* V, 61; PL 44, 818; *De Civ. Dei*, XI, 1; PL 41, 315-317.

from that of the first man, he attributes to the saints the perfection of being incapable of sinning *(non posse peccare)*, and to Adam the perfection of being able to avoid sin *(posse non peccare)*.[1] Augustine satisfies himself that in the first man there was nothing drawing him toward sin. Sin came from the soul by way of a perfectly free will. Augustine does not consider the body the source of sin. He does condemn the flesh. He uses the word flesh, however, in the Scriptural sense which, as he tells us,[2] would indicate the nature of man, but a nature ranged against God. Far from blaming the body for Adam's sin, Augustine explicitly says : "...it was not the corruptible flesh that made the soul sinful, but the sinful soul that made the flesh corruptible."[3] But the soul was not of itself sinful, since man came wholly from God and was therefore wholly good.[4] The preservation of goodness hinged upon the preservation of its place in the universe according to the order of love established by God. By sin man can destroy the divine order, but if he does he ought to remember that he is destroying what he has not created and cannot, therefore, recreate.[5] On the other hand, by submission to the divine order, man can conserve and increase his being.

But by the precept He gave, God commended obedience, which is in a way the mother and guardian of all the virtues in the rational creature, which was so created that submission is advantageous to it, while the fulfillment of its own will in preference to the Creator's is destruction.[6]

Disobedience to God is the abandonment of man's end because it is a denial of the love of God by which man attains his last end. Augustine sees the loss of this love to be also the loss of liberty. Disobedience is a deordinating act. While that-which-

[1] Augustine. *De Natura et Gratia*, XII, 33; PL 44, 936.
[2] Augustine, *De Civ. Dei*, XIV, 2; PL 41, 403, 404.
[3] Augustine, *De Civ. Dei*, XIV, 3; PL 41, 405, 406.
[4] Augustine, *Cont. Jul.*, III, 206; PL 45, 1334.
[5] Augustine, *Enarr. in Ps.* 45, 15; PL 36, 524.
[6] Augustine, *De Civ. Dei*, XIV, 12; PL 41, 420 : Sed obedientia commendata est in præcepto, quæ virtus in creatura rationali mater quodammodo est omnium custosque virtutum : quandoquidem ita facta est, ut ei subditam esse sit utile; perniciosum autem suam, non ejus a quo creata est, facere voluntatem.

is-not can be called metaphysical evil, and that-which-changes-or-corrupts can be called physical evil, that-which-forsakes-its-end is moral evil. To forsake the order of God is within the scope of human free will because as a person man is free with regard to even the end of his nature. The wrong use of free will is only an apparent freedom; it is actually a descent to slavery. Adam upset the order of love when he failed to choose God and he became the deficient cause of evil. He had a choice between a closed autonomy and an open autonomy, man without God or man with God. Adam did not see that the open kind is the only true autonomy, not only because it admits man to a share in the Divine government of the universe but because it safeguards and perfects human nature itself. Because God's Will was not only best, but best for Adam, his deficient willing left him in a state of nature less strong. Why? Because Adam had been made for something better than what he chose.

> Since rational spirits are the highest of God's creatures, He has given them this power, that they cannot be corrupted against their will; provided, that is, that they remain obedient to their Lord and hold fast to Him in His incorruptible beauty. But if they freely choose to disobey, then since they are willing to be corrupted by sin they will find themselves unwillingly corrupted by punishment. For God is so great a good that nothing can ever go well for those who abandon Him; and our rational nature is so far above other created things that no good except God will ever make us happy. [1]

The freedom of the will was the indispensable condition of insuring man a good that befitted his rational nature. What was the end intended for man? It was *free* participation, that is, communication, in the nature of God, not merely that universal participation in being by which all things analogically image God, but a spiritual, supernatural communication with God making him receptive to Divine Truth and responsive to Divine

[1] Augustine, *De Natura Boni*, VII; PL 42, 554: Creaturis autem præstantissimis, hoc est, rationalibus spiritibus, hoc præstitit Deus, ut si nolint, corrumpi non possint; id est, si obedientiam conservaverint sub Domino Deo suo, ac sic incorruptibili pulchritudini ejus adhæserint; si autem obedientiam conservare noluerint, quoniam volentes corrumpuntur in peccatis nolentes corrumpantur in pœnis. Tale quippe bonum est Deus, ut nemini eum deserenti bene sit : et in rebus a Deo factis tam magnum bonum est natura rationalis, ut nullum sit bonum quo beata sit nisi Deus.

Love. The life to which man was supernaturally called was none other than a life of friendship with God. Such was the high nature of the value to which Adam did not respond.

For St. Augustine the very source of moral goodness is to have our love follow the objective order of love, to love more that which deserves more love. In line with this thought we might add, to love more that which has a higher value. In the *De Libero Arbitrio* St. Augustine claims that the source of all moral evil is the preference of a lower good over a higher one. [1]

When at the dawn of creation Adam used his free will to respond to the intrinsic Goodness of God, he was enjoying full freedom. But he had not lost free choice. It has been said that the motivation of the will can stem " equally from values, from the subjectively satisfying, or from the objective good for the person. " [2] In Paradise how could there be question of self-satisfaction? Only if man regards himself apart from his origin and destiny, as a nature closed on both ends. If, on the other hand, he recognizes that he has come from nothing, he is disposed to be humble; if he realizes that his destiny is so divine as to be above his strength, he is again humbled, and humility keeps him in order, in the order of love. And so Augustine says :

> Our first parents fell into open disobedience because they were already secretly corrupted; for the evil act would never have been done had not an evil will preceded it. And what is the origin of our evil will but pride? For ' pride is the beginning of sin '. And what is pride but the craving for undue exaltation, when the soul abandons Him to whom it ought to cleave as its end, and becomes a kind of end to itself. This happens when it becomes its own satisfaction. And it does so when it falls away from that unchangeable good which ought to satisfy it more than itself. This falling away is voluntary; for if the will had remained steadfast in the love of that higher and changeless good by which it was illumined to knowledge and kindled into love, it would not have turned away to find satisfaction in itself, and so become frigid and benighted. [3]

[1] Dietrich von Hildebrand, *Christian Ethics,* New York, David McKay, 1953, p. 380.

[2] D. von Hildebrand, *op. cit.*, p. 214.

[3] Augustine, *De Civ. Dei*, XIV, 13; PL 41, 420, 421 : In occulto autem mali esse cœperunt, ut in apertam inobedientiam laberentur. Non enim ad malum opus perveniretur, nisi præces-

By turning away from God, man's nature did not become absolutely nothing, but his being became "more contracted than it was when it cleaved to Him who supremely is." [1]

Now, Adam departed from God by free choice, [2] his will deserting the greater for the lesser good. To choose a lower good is not in itself sinful; it is only sinful when the choice involves forsaking God. "Sin is not a cleaving to evil natures; it is a defection from a nature that is better." [3]

EFFECTS OF SIN

The first and most drastic effect of sin was that the will lost God as its end and effected a union with a perverse end. This meant the loss of liberty. Henceforth the will was radically impotent with regard to the salutary good. The moral unity of man gave way to moral disunity. Since the body belongs to the very essence of man, then if man is his own end, the instincts of the flesh will rather convincingly assert their claims to satisfaction. [4] Since the fall of Adam, the souls of men struggle against rebellious natural forces inherent in man's nature but extrinsic to the human will. This opposition does not impair the will as a faculty, but it obstructs its concrete decisions. With St. Paul, every man can truly say: "To wish is within my power, but I do not find the strength to accomplish what is good." [5] Sin has caused the loss of freedom, the power to do that which is deserving of eternal life, the freedom to love God. [6] What sin

sisset mala voluntas. Porro malæ voluntatis initium quod potuit esse nisi superbia! *Initium* enim *omnis peccati superbia* est (Ecclus. X, 15). Quid est autem superbia, nisi perversæ celsitudinis appetitus? Perversa enim celsitudo est, deserto eo cui debet animus inhærere principio, sibi quodammodo fieri atque esse principium. Hoc fit, cum sibi nimis placet. Sibi vero ita placet, cum ab illo bono immutabili deficit, quod ei magis placere debuit quam ipse sibi. Spontaneus est autem iste defectus : quoniam si voluntas in amore superioris immutabilis boni, a quo illustrabatur ut videret, et accendebatur ut amaret, stabilis permaneret, non inde ad sibi placendum averteretur, et ex hoc tenebresceret et frigesceret...

[1] Augustine, *De Civ. Dei*, XIV, 13; PL 41, 421 : ...sed ut inclinatus ad se ipsum minus esset, quam erat, cum ei qui summe est inhærebat.

[2] Augustine, *De Duabus Anim.*, X, 14; PL 42, 104.

[3] Augustine, *Retract.*, I, 9, 6; PL 32, 598; *De Natura Boni*, XXXIV; PL 42, 562; *Ad Simplic.*, 1, q. 2, n. 18; PL 40, 122.

[4] Augustine, *Contra Jul.*, VI, 18; PL 45, 1541, 1542; *De Nup. et Concup.*, I, 24, 27; PL 44, 429.

[5] *Rom.*, VII, 18.

[6] Augustine, *De Correp. et Grat.*, XII, 33; PL 44, 936.

has removed from the will in making it evil is something that it ought to have, namely, the love of God.[1] Only God can restore this, because God is Love, and who else can give it but God?[2] It cannot be too strongly emphasized that, according to Augustine, when the grace of God has been forsaken by man, man is in a condition that God never intended him to be in.

For the grace of God through Jesus Christ our Lord must be understood as that by which alone men are delivered from evil, and without which they can do absolutely nothing good, whether in thought, or will and affection, or in action; not only in order that they may know, through that Grace, what ought to be done, but in order that by its help, they may do what they know they should in a spirit of love.[3]

In the light of the above we can more easily understand what Augustine meant when he said that through sin man has lost freedom *(libertas)*, but free choice remains (liberum arbitrium). This distinction between free will and freedom is clearly and amply expounded by Augustine.[4] But some interpreters have ignored the distinction and have presented Augustine as at once an antagonist and a protagonist of free will in fallen man.[5] It is easy to distort an author's meaning by selecting and contrasting various pronouncements apart from their context; it is very easy in the case of a prolific writer like Augustine. He had to contend with that kind of misrepresentation in his own day, and his rebuke to a certain Pelagian is equally applicable today.

You think, or you wish to think that my pronouncements are opposed to one another, as if I were condemning what I have previously approved, or embracing what I have previously rejected ...[6]

[1] Augustine, *De Civ. Dei*, XII, 8; PL 41, 355.
[2] Augustine, *De Lib. Arb.*, II, 20, 54; PL 32, 1270.
[3] Augustine, *De Correp. et Grat.*, II, 3; PL 44, 918 : Intelligenda est enim gratia Dei per Jesum Christum Dominum nostrum, qua sola homines liberantur a malo, et sine qua nullum prorsus sive cogitando, sive volendo et amando, sive agendo faciunt bonum : non solum ut monstrante ipsa quid faciendum sit sciant, verum etiam ut præstante ipsa faciant cum dilectione quod sciunt.
[4] Augustine, *Enchiridion*, XXXII, PL 40, 247; *Op. Imperf. Cont. Jul.*, VI, 11; PL 45, 1521.
[5] Augustine, *Contra Duas Epist. Pelag.*, I, 2, 5; PL 44, 552 : Quis autem nostrum dicat, quod primi hominis peccato perierit liberum arbitrium de humano genere?
[6] Augustine, *Contra Jul.* V, 9, 37; PL 44, 806.

My words are not opposed to one another, although they permit you to think or say so by misunderstanding them, or by not allowing others to understand them.[1]

Without the distinction that Augustine made between human choice and human freedom *(arbitrium voluntatis* and *libertas)*, his doctrine of freedom would be incomprehensible. By ignoring or misunderstanding this distinction, some have formed and propagated a distorted notion of Augustine's doctrine. Yet that distinction is at once apt and serviceable, for it helps to focus attention on two aspects of a power that is good *in se*, but whose misuse brings evil consequences. In man free will is precisely that kind of power. It is not to be confused with freedom which is the facile engagement of all man's powers upon his true end. Augustine does not claim for free choice every perfection that he attributes to freedom, nor does he restrict freedom by the limitations he ascribes to free will. The ignoring of this capital distinction has led some to believe that Augustine denies free will to fallen man; and, because Augustine expressly states the contrary on several occasions, his teaching is represented as self-contradictory. In a letter to Boniface, he writes : " Which of us has ever said that the sin of the first man made free will disappear? "[2] And to Simplicianus he quoted from St. Paul : " To wish is within my power, but I do not find the strength to accomplish what is good " (Rom. VII, 18); and commented : " Now to those who do not rightly understand [St. Paul], he seems here to be excluding [free will]. "[3] Again in 415, writing " On Nature and Grace, " he refers back to statements made in the *De Libero Arbitrio* and holds to them :

Now we do not, when we make mention of these things, take away freedom of will, by preaching the grace of God. For to whom are those gracious gifts of use, but to the man who uses, but humbly,

[1] Augustine, *Contra Julianum*, V, 5, 19; PL 44, 795 : Non sunt ergo verba mea inter se contraria, quamvis te patiantur, vel non intelligendo, vel alios intelligere non sinendo contrarium.

[2] Augustine, *Contra Duas Epist. Pelag.*, I, 2, 5; PL 44, 552.

[3] Augustine, *Ad Simpl.*, I, 2, 1, n. 11; PL 40, 107. *Rom.* VII, 18.

his own will, and makes no boast of the power and energy thereof, as if it alone were sufficient for perfecting him in righteousness? [1]

But to approve of falsehoods as if they were true, so as to err involuntarily and to be unable, owing to the resistance and pain of carnal bondage, to refrain from deeds of lust, is not a natural thing due to his creation, but a punishment due to his fall. When, however, we speak of a will free to do what is right, we of course mean that liberty in which man was first created. (*De Libero Arbitrio*, III)... Our whole discussion with [the Pelagians] on this subject turns upon this, that we frustrate not the grace of God which is in Jesus Christ our Lord by a perverted assertion of nature. [2]

Among those who have examined the question of whether or not Augustine denied free will is M. Fonsegrive, who considers that Augustine should be ranged among the partisans of free will as philosophers understand it despite " all the extenuations he makes it undergo. " [3] Referring to the contrary opinion of M. Bersot and M. Nourrison, this historian asserts that neither of these critics was in a position to appreciate the complete doctrine of Augustine.

Continuing our examination of the historical man in Augustine, we can now see in fallen man an unwilling tendency toward evil. Contemplating this, Augustine can say that man, while possessing free choice, is not truly free. [4] With the abandonment of its end, the will receives a contrary tendency. Without special help from God, it can no longer choose the salutary good. [5] But as long as God is willing and free choice

[1] Augustine, *De Nat. et Grat.*, 32, 36; PL 44, 265 : Non enim, cum iste commemoramus, arbitrium voluntatis tollimus, sed Dei gratiam prædicamus. Cui enim prosunt ista nisi volenti, sed humiliter volenti, non sede voluntatis viribus tanquam ad perfectionem justitiæ sola sufficiat, extollenti?

[2] Augustine, *De Nat. et Grat.*, 67, 81; PL 44, 287, 288 : Sed approbare falsa pro veris ut erret invitus, et resistente atque torquente dolore carnalis vinculi non posse a libidinosi operibus temperare, non est natura instituti hominis, sed pœna damnati. Cum autem de libera voluntate recte faciendi loquimur, de illa scilicet in qua homo factus est loquimur *(De Lib. Arb.)*... De qua re cum istis tota vertitur quæstio, ne gratiam Dei quæ est in Christo Jesu Domino nostro, perversa naturæ defensione frustremur.

[3] George L. Fonsegrive, *Essai sur le Libre Arbitre*, Paris, Alcan, 1887, p. 112.

[4] Augustine, *Contra Duas Epist. Pelag.*, I, 2, 5; PL 44, 552 : Libertas quidem periit per peccatum, sed illa quæ in paradiso fuit, habendi plenam cum immortalitate justitiam;... utique liberi ad bene justeque vivendum...

[5] Council of Orange, II. Denzinger, n. 180 ff.

exists, the lost freedom can be regained, and the way is *by prayer*.

Therefore, in this mortal life it remains for man, not to fulfill justice by his free choice whenever he wishes to fulfill it, but to turn with pious supplication toward Him through whose gift he may be able to fulfill it. [1]

And so " ...after the fall of man, God willed it to be due only to His grace that man should approach Him; nor did He will it to be due to aught but His grace that man should not depart from Him. " [2] The ability to love God which alone opens the way to eternal life becomes man's not by the power of free choice but by the power of God. The grace to will the salutary good and the strength to accomplish it are united in the supernatural reality of *Libertas*. Although this is over and above the natural power of the will, it is perfective and not destructive of the will. God assists man to will and does not exempt him from willing. [3] He inclines man to do the just thing by substituting delight in the good for delight in evil. [4] That man always retains a robust free choice by which he can act or not act even under grace is witnessed to by Augustine when he quotes St. Paul as saying: " We beseech you that you receive not the grace of God in vain. " (2 Cor., VI, 1).

Now how could he so enjoin them, if they received God's grace in such a manner as to lose their own will? Nevertheless, lest the will itself should be deemed capable of doing any good thing without the grace of God, after saying, ' His grace in me was not in vain, but I have laboured more abundantly than them all, ' he immediately added the qualifying clause, 'Yet not I but the grace of God which was

[1] Augustine, *Ad Simplic.*, I, q. 1, 14; PL 40, 108 : Hoc enim restat in ista mortali vita libero arbitrio, non ut impleat homo justitiam, cum voluerit, sed ut se supplici pietate convertat ad eum cujus dono eam possit implere.

[2] Augustine, *De Dono Per.*, VII, 13; PL 45, 1001 : Post casum autem hominis, nonnisi ad gratiam suam Deus voluit pertinere, ut homo accedat ad eum; neque nisi ad gratiam suam voluit pertinere, ut homo non recedat ab eo.

[3] Augustine, *De Correp. et Grat.*, II, 4; PL 44, 918.

[4] Augustine, *De Grat. et Lib. Arb.*, XX; PL 44, 905; cf. *idem*, II; PL 44, 881.

Augustine, *De Perfect. Justitiæ Hominis*, IV, 9; PL 44, 296 : Quia vero peccavit voluntas, secuta est peccantem peccatum habendi *dura* necessitas, donec tota sanetur infirmitas et accipiatur tanta *libertas* in qua sicut necesse est permaneat beate vivendi voluntas, ita ut sit etiam bene vivendi et nunquam peccandi voluntaria *felixque necessitas*.

with me.' In other words, not I alone, but the grace of God with me. And thus, neither was it the grace of God alone, not was it himself alone, but it was the grace of God with him. [1]

Augustine was peculiarly conscious of human warfare within and of its reflection without. No one could delude him concerning God's necessary part in the resolution of his own conflict; the Pauline description [2] of internal struggle helped him to understand how universal his own experience was; the Old Testament enabled him to see this same truth "writ large" in the record of the successes of the chosen people, achieved only when God the Warrior was on their side.

But if Augustine would allow no denial of God's necessary part in man's perfection, neither would he permit the dismissal of man's prerogative of free consent. God who made us without ourselves will not save us without ourselves. [3] Nature remains a very substantial foundation supporting grace. Not even the Divine foreknowledge can make void a free nature.

Moreover, if He who foreknew what would be in the power of our wills, did not foreknow nothing, but something, assuredly even though He did foreknow, there is something in the power of our wills. Therefore we are by no means compelled, either retaining the prescience of God, to take away the freedom of the will, or retaining the freedom of the will, to deny that He is prescient of future things, which is impious. But we embrace both. [4]

And so through his reflection upon free will and the conditions of human freedom in the first man, Augustine was led, not to

[1] Augustine, *De Grat. et Lib. Arb.*, I, 5, 12; PL 44, 888, 889: Hoc enim liberum arbitrium hominis exhortatur et in aliis, quibus dicit, *Rogamus ne in vacuum gratiam Dei suscipiatis* (*II Cor.*, VI, 1). Quid enim eos rogat, si gratiam sic susceperunt, ut propriam perderent voluntatem? Tamen ne ipsa voluntas sine gratia Dei putetur boni aliquid posse, continuo cum dixisset, *Gratia ejus in me vacua non fuit, sed plus omnibus illis laboravi;* subjunxit atque ait, *Non ego autem, sed gratia Dei mecum* (*I Cor.*, XV, 10); id est, non solus, sed gratia Dei mecum: ac per hoc nec gratia Dei sola, nec ipse solus, sed gratia Dei cum illo.

[2] *Rom.*, VI, 3; VI, 20; VI, 7; VI, 18; VII, 15-25; IX, 20, 21; IX, 16; XI, 6; *Hebrews* II, 16; *Philip.* II, 13; IV, 3.

[3] Augustine, *Sermo* 169, XI, 13; PL 38, 923: Qui ergo fecit te sine te, non te justificat sine te.

[4] Augustine, *De Civitate Dei*, V, 10; PL 41, 153: Porro si ille, qui præscivit quid futurum esset in nostra voluntate, non utique nihil, sed aliquid præscivit; profecto et illo præsciente est aliquid in nostra voluntate. Quocirca nullo modo cogimur, aut retenta præscientia Dei tollere voluntatis arbitrium, aut retento voluntatis arbitrio Deum (quod nefas est) negare præscium futurorum; sed utrumque amplectimur...

undervalue the present will in man, but to restore to free will its primordial sublimity as the power that can open man up to the transcendent God. The role he assigns to free will indicates the radically new character of Christian thought. [1] As heir of the Hellenistic tradition, he recognized two aspects under which the search for wisdom took place : one moral, the other intellectual. Yet unlike his Hellenistic predecessors, the wisdom that Augustine identified with happiness was "not only the fruit of culture but the effect of divine help." [2] Moralist as Augustine might appear if we looked merely at his consideration of happiness as a central problem, — yet in holding that wisdom must include "praying well," he was no mere moralistic philosopher. His thinking had the stature of the metaphysical order, nourished on the nature of God and the nature of the soul. Through the latter he came to know the former, and his enriched intellectual life was to serve his religious life, making it a dialogue of love between a finite creature and the transcendent God. The immanence of God, true as it is, never tempted him to forsake theology for a glorified anthropology. The transcendence of God, true as it is, never tempted him to give up his desire to commune with God. His would be nothing less than an integral theocentrism, very satisfying to the mind and heart of man — a prophetic tendency to proclaim the rights of God and a mystic tendency to adore Him and love Him. [3] The rights of man are not in this way jeopardized, but rather reenforced.

A certain kind of humanism, even the humanism of ideas, is not incompatible with the theocentrism under discussion; the Augustinian spirit permits us to affirm both the weakness of fallen man and the utmost elevation of man restored through grace. But this elevation is accomplished by God through a free gift and through complete submission to His guidance. Here we have a Christian humanism in the strong sense of that term, and not — as it is frequently regarded — merely a Christianized humanism... At any rate, there can be no hesitation to speak about Christian optimism, in the most rigorous

[1] H. I. Marrou, *Saint Augustin et la Fin de la Culture Antique*, Paris, E. de Boccard, 1938, p. 545.
[2] Marrou, *St. Augustin et la Fin de la Culture Antique*, p. 178.
[3] F. Cayré, " L'Augustinisme " *L'Année Théologique*, (1941), p. 86.

sense of that term. As for Augustinian pessimism, it is not to be found in Augustine; it is the invention of some of his modern disciples. [1]

Augustine keeps his philosophy and theology together, man and God together, free will and freedom together, but they remain clearly distinct. The Augustinian doctrine of free will in relation to freedom neither defrauds nature nor denies the real dependence of man upon God. The initiative in sanctification, as in creation, is with God, but man's response of gratitude to God for grace draws man closer to God. [2] Of all earthly creatures only man is able to recognize that the final cause of his tendency toward the Good is a living desire proceeding from the Trinity. By understanding the metaphysics of creation man becomes aware of this desire. Unlike emanation, creation is a free act, born of purpose and love. God loves every man into existence. Man's return to God is sealed with the sign of this origin. For love between persons there must be a certain likeness, and man becomes like God by disposing himself to receive that likeness of God from Him, since this is the only way that a creature can become like God. And so for Augustine, man returns to God, not merely by recollection, as for Plotinus, but by the love which impels him, not to identify himself with God, but to submit to Him.

For the mind becomes like God to the extent that it subjects itself to Him for information and enlightenment. And if it obtains the greatest nearness by that subjection which produces likeness, it must be far removed from that presumption which would strive to make the likeness greater. It is this presumption which leads the mind to refuse obedience to the laws of God, in the desire to be sovereign, as God is.
The farther, then, the mind departs from God, not in space, but in affection and lust after things below Him, the more it is filled with

[1] Cayré, *op. cit.*, p. 86.

[2] F. Cayré, *Initiation à la Philosophie de Saint Augustin*, Paris, Etudes Augustiniennes, 1947, p. 83 : "Human liberty itself is profoundly reenforced by it (Grace) and if, by that, the soul is made more physically independent, it is linked only more closely to God morally. Hence the role given by Augustine to piety, which is totally ignored by Plotinus. This role of prayer is doubtless a contribution of Christian revelation, but it supposes or establishes a very special conception of the relations of the soul with God. It is necessary to take great account of this, even in philosophy."

folly and wretchedness. So by love it returns to God, — a love which places it not alongside God, but under Him. And the more ardor and eagerness there is in this, the happier and more elevated will the mind be, and with God as sole governor it will be in perfect liberty. [1]

This sublime role that Augustine gives to love as the way to liberty reveals the radical transformation that all the knowledge inherited from the ancients and from Plotinus has undergone in the mind of Augustine. [2] With Augustine it is always through love that we become conformed to God. Virtues are not the end of man but are forms of the love of God:

... temperance is love keeping itself entire and incorrupt for God; fortitude is love bearing everything readily for the sake of God; justice is love serving God only and therefore ruling well all else, as subject to man; prudence is love making a right distinction between what helps it towards God and what might hinder it. [3]

The effort of purification is the combat of the soul against itself to defeat its inclination to evil by substituting an inclination towards God. Augustine was not merely interested in discovering and defending the reality of free choice, the will in act with regard to the means, but in exploring the existence and conditions of freedom, which comes from a freely sanctioned and unimpeded affective response of man to his end. If in an uncreated universe

[1] Augustine, *De Morib. Ecc. Cathol.*, I, 12, 20, 21; PL 32, 1320: Fit enim [intellectus] Deo similis quantum datum est, dum illustrandum illi atque illuminandum se subjicit. Et si maxime ei propinquat subjectione ista qua similis fit, longe ab eo fiat necesse est audacia qua vult esse similior. Ipsa est qua legibus Dei obtemperare detrectat, dum suæ potestatis esse cupit ut Deus est.

Quanto ergo magis longe discedit a Deo, non loco, sed affectione atque cupiditate ad inferiora quam est ipse, tanto magis stultitia miseriaque completur. Dilectione igitur redit in Deum, qua se illi non componere, sed supponere affectat. Quod quanto fecerit instantius ac studiosius, tanto erit beatior atque sublimior, et illo solo dominante liberrimus.

[2] René Arnou, *Le Désir de Dieu dans la Philosophie de Plotin*, Paris, Alcan, 1921. Père Arnou calls the God of Plotinus a God who is goodness without love. On p. 50, he says: "Il n'avait pas non plus la conception d'un Dieu qui entendit les prières de la terre, non seulement principe et fin de son œuvre, mais l'aimant, intimement présent au fond des âmes, et percevant leurs soupirs, leurs élans, l'orientation même de leur volonté, désirant leur salut, conception qui peut être plus facilement déformée par les éléments anthropomorphiques, mais qui se révèle aussi plus riche de sentiment religieux, et, somme toute, plus digne de Dieu."

[3] Augustine, *De Morib. Ecc. Cath.*, I, 15, 25; PL 32, 1322: Quare definire etiam sic licet, ut temperantiam dicamus esse amorem Deo sese integrum incorruptumque servantem; fortitudinem, amorem omnia propter Deum facile perferentem; justitiam, amorem Deo tantum servientem, et ab hoc bene imperantem cæteris quæ homini subjecta sunt; prudentiam, amorem bene discernentem ea quibus adjuvetur in Deum, ab iis quibus impediri potest.

the free will would have no meaning or importance, does not this help us to see why the first philosopher "who made of the world of Aristotle a creature and of the God of Plato a true Creator" [1] should also be the pioneer philosopher of freedom? [2]

The question may still arise whether Augustine's theology of predestination and grace does or does not conflict with a metaphysic of freedom or even with his own assertions on the subject. Nor can one do justice to Augustine's doctrine on free will without some serious wrestling with the famous concept of *gratia indeclinabilis*, *irresistibilis*, as this concept emerges from his theories of predestination and election.

Calvinists and Jansenists have cited ambiguous passages from St. Augustine to make it appear that he taught their brand of predestination. The cited passages are from Augustine's comments on St. Paul's First Epistle to Timothy, II, 1-6. [3] However, there is no ambiguity in Augustine elsewhere: "God in His mercy, desiring to deliver men from this destruction, that is, from everlasting punishment, if only they be not enemies to themselves and resist not the mercy of their Creator, sent His only-begotten Son... so that... all who believe in Him might enter into eternal life." [4] Even more explicit are Augustine's words in *De Spiritu et Littera*: "For God wills that all men be saved and come to a knowledge of the truth, but not in such manner as to take away their will, for they will be most justly judged regarding the good or evil use they have made of it." [5] This passage indicates one aspect of the Divine Will — the conditional Will of God which is not realized when free choice resists it. Because Augustine attributes damnation to the

[1] Etienne Gilson, *La Philosophie au Moyen Age*, (4th edition), Paris, Payot, 1944, p. 138.

[2] For a straightforward account of Augustine's position in summary fashion, consult his Epistle 186; PL 33, 815-832, written to Paulinus in the year 417.

[3] Augustine *De Corr. et Grat.*, 15, 47; PL 44, 945. *Ench.* 27, 103; PL 40, 280.

[4] Augustine, *De Catechizandis Rudibus*, XXVI, 52; PL 40, 345: A quo interitu, hoc est, pœnis sempiternis Deus misericors volens homines liberare, si sibi ipsi non sint inimici, et non resistant misericordiæ creatoris sui, misit unigenitum Filium suum, hoc est Verbum suum æquale sibi, per quod condidit omnia ... ut ... credentes in eum omnes in æternam vitam ingrederentur (Rom. V, 12-19).

[5] Augustine, *De Spiritu et Littera*, XXXIII, 58; PL 44, 238: Vult autem Deus omnes homines salvos fieri, et in agnitionem veritatis venire; non sic tamen, ut eis adimat liberum arbitrium, quo vel bene vel male utentes justissime judicentur.

resistance of the human will, he constantly asserts that every man is offered the grace to be saved. Yet there is also an efficacious Will of God which does not extend to all men. [1]

The Canons of the second Council of Orange [2] are literally borrowed from the writings of Augustine. Let us examine how Augustine was able to assure the triumph of free choice against the Manichaeans and the triumph of grace against the Pelagians and Semi-Pelagians. Let us recall what Augustine said of free choice in the *De Libero Arbitrio* and what he says of the functioning of grace, so that we may discover how he thought he had reconciled these two truths : man is free, but without God man can do nothing.

In discussing the passage : "What have you that you have not received?" [3] Augustine says : What receives except free choice? [4] He also says that God comes to help man to act and not to dispense him from acting. [5] He adverts specifically and emphatically to the role of the will under grace when he declares that supernatural life and supernatural growth and supernatural death, unlike their natural counterparts, require the free cooperation of the one living. [6] It is the opinion of E. Portalié [7] that even in his struggle with the Pelagians, Augustine was well aware of the danger of compromising free choice. Yet the very texts that bear on the Pelagian problem witness to the fact that Augustine did not sacrifice freedom to a divine determinism which he called *libertas*. We have noted that in the *Retractations* Augustine did not reverse his early position that man had the full power of his will and self-determination.

[1] Augustine, *Enchiridion*, 28, 104; PL 40, 281.
[2] Denzinger, n. 174-200.
[3] 1 Cor. IV, 7.
[4] Augustine, *De Grat. et Lib. Arb.*, XV, 31; PL 44, 899.
[5] Augustine, *De Correp. et Grat.*, II, 4; PL 44, 918; *De Grat. et Lib.*, XX; PL 44, 905.
[6] Augustine, *In Epist. Joan.*, III, 1; PL 35, 1997-1998 : Ætas corporis non est in voluntate. Ita nullus secundum carnem crescit quando vult; sicut nullus quando vult nascitur : ubi autem nativitas in voluntate est et crementum in voluntate est. Nemo ex aqua et Spiritu nascatur nisi volens. Ergo si vult, crescit : si vult, decrescit. Quid est crescere? Proficere. Quid est decrescere? Deficere.
[7] E. Portalié, "Augustin", *Dictionnaire de Théologie Catholique*, (éd. Letouzey et Ané), Paris, I, (1902), (2268-2472). Cf. *De Pecc. Mer. et Rem.*, II, 18, 28; PL 44, 168; *De Nat. et Grat.*, LXV, 78; PL 44, 286; *De Gratia Christi et de Pecc. Orig.*, I, 47, 52; PL 44, 383.

He readily admits to the Pelagians that without free choice there would be no responsibility, and therefore no merit nor demerit. He reproaches them not for defending the existence of free choice but for exaggerating its power. Although the will now has to struggle against an inclination to evil, it still retains the power of sanctioning or disavowing the evil it does. Moreover, and more fundamentally, man by his free choice is powerless to do anything meritorious for eternal life without a special gift of Divine grace, and no man can do good without the help of God. Therefore, the free choice that remains to man is not the same as that which Adam enjoyed in original integrity. Even when free choice is reinforced by grace through Baptism, it is still very defective because it is conditioned by ignorance and difficulty. [1] Even in his last works Augustine does not cease to proclaim the power of choice to exist in man. It is interesting to note this position taken about free will in an early work and to see that it remained unchanged even during the last period when he spoke forcefully of God's direction of man's choices. In 418 he faced the difficulties surrounding the question of freedom under grace when he said :

> Inasmuch, however, as the discussion on free will and God's grace has such difficulty in its distinctions, that when free will is maintained, God's grace is apparently denied, whilst when God's grace is asserted, free will is understood to be done away with; Pelagius can so involve himself in the shades of this obscurity as to profess agreement with all that we have quoted from St. Ambrose, and declare that such is, and always has been, his opinion also; and endeavour so to explain each, that men may suppose his opinion to be in fair accord with Ambrose's. [2]

In 426 he said : " For to will or not to will is in the power of the one willing or not willing, in such a way as not to impede

[1] Augustine, *Op. Imperf. cont. Jul.*, III, 117; PL 45, 1297; III, 110; PL 45, 1294; V, 48; PL 45, 1484; VI, 11; PL 45, 1520.

[2] Augustine, *De Gratia Christi et de Peccato Originali*, 47, 52; PL 44, 383 : Sed quia ista quæstio, ubi de arbitrio voluntatis et Dei gratia disputatur, ita est ad discernendum difficilis, ut quando defenditur liberum arbitrium, negari Dei gratia videatur; quando autem asseritur Dei gratia, liberum arbitrium putetur auferri : potest Pelagius ita se latebris obscuritatis hujus involvere, ut etiam iis quæ a sancto Ambrosio conscripta posuimus, consentire se dicat; et ea se quoque sentire proclamet, semperque sensisse; atque ita singula conetur exponere, ut etiam ejus sententiæ convenire credantur.

the divine will nor overcome the divine power; for even in the case of those who do what He wills not, He Himself does what He wills." [1] In 427, in the tenth of his twelve articles of faith against the Pelagians, he said: "Whoever has received the efficacious grace of faith gives his adhesion only in the full independence of his will, *sua id facere voluntate ac libero arbitrio.*" [2] Between 428 and 429 he said: "...if anyone dare to say, 'I have faith of myself, I did not, therefore, receive it,' he directly contradicts this most manifest truth (grace), — not because it is not in the power of man's will to believe or not to believe, but because in the elect the will is prepared by the Lord." [3] We see how ample is the evidence that accounts for the fact that Catholic theologians have generally recognized that Augustine adequately safeguards the rights of freedom. [4]

Augustine maintains with equal vigour, however, that God is the unique source of all good. This position is crystallized in Canons 5 and 6 of the Council of Carthage, May 1, 418. In canon 5 it is said that the help we receive from God is not only a light which reveals the law but the love of the good, *ut etiam facere diligamus atque valeamus*. And canon 6 states that the necessity of this help is absolute. [5] What precisely did Augustine mean when he said that without God man could do nothing, literally nothing? According to E. Portalié, [6] the theologians do not say that for one single act of natural virtue Augustine exacts supernatural grace (this was the error of Baius and the Jansenists). The foundation on which Augustine builds the necessity of grace for single acts is not the supernatural character of the meritorious act, but the universal principle that God must

[1] Augustine, *De Corrept. et Grat.*, XIV, 43; PL 44, 942: Sic enim velle seu nolle in volentis aut nolentis est potestate, ut divinam voluntatem non impediat nec superet potestatem. Etiam de his enim qui faciunt quæ non vult, facit ipse quæ vult.

[2] Augustine, *Epist.* 217, 16; PL 33, 285; quoted in Portalié, *Dict. Théol. Cath., art. cit.*, I, col. 2388.

[3] Augustine, *De Prædest. Sanct.*, V, 10; PL 44, 968: ...quisquis audet dicere, Habeo ex me ipso fidem, non ergo accepi; profecto contradicit huic apertissimæ veritati: non quia credere vel non credere non est in arbitrio voluntatis humanæ, sed in electis præparatur voluntas a Domino...

[4] Portalié, *Dict. Théol. Cath.*, I, col. 2376.

[5] Portalié, *Dict. Théol. Cath.*, I, col. 2384. Denzinger, n. 105.

[6] Portalié, *Dict. Théol. Cath.*, I, col. 2386. Denzinger, n. 106.

be the unique source of every good in the universe, and so of every morally good act. [1] There is no evidence that Augustine restricted the statement: "Without Me you can do nothing" to the supernatural order. The formulas affirming that every good will comes from God, and that free choice without God works only evil, are universal and without restriction.[2] Augustine requires a gift of God even for natural virtues which produce nothing for heaven. [3]

There are, however, two kinds of gifts or graces: a gift of Divine Providence which prepares the will by efficacious motives, and the gift of Divine grace for supernatural acts and even for the beginning of Faith. Augustine himself confesses that when he first commented on the Epistle of St. Paul to the Romans, he did not understand that the beginning of Faith was a supernatural gift. But by the beginning of his episcopate when he was writing the second book to Simplicianus, he had understood by meditation upon the Pauline teaching that even Faith was a supernatural gift unmerited by man. This is the doctrine that he explicitly teaches in the *De Prædestinatione Sanctorum*: "...the capacity for faith, as the capacity for love, belongs to men's nature; but to have faith, even as to have love, belongs by grace to believers." [4] And elsewhere in the same work he says: "...our sufficiency, by which we begin to believe, is from God." [5] The fact that special graces are given to some over and above what is sufficient for them is explained when he says: "Therefore God chose us in Christ before the foundation of the world, predestinating us to the adoption of children, not because we were going to be of ourselves holy and immaculate, but He chose and predestinated

[1] Augustine, *Retract.*, I, 9, 6; PL 32, 598: Quia omnia bona, sicut dictum est et magna, et media, et minima ex Deo sunt; sequitur ut ex Deo sit etiam bonus usus liberæ voluntatis, quæ virtus est, et in magnis numeratur bonis.

[2] Council of Orange II, can. 22, Denzinger, n. 195, quoted in *Dict. Théol. Cath.*, I, col. 2387.

[3] Augustine, *De Patientia*, XXVII, 24; PL 40, 624; *Epist.*, CXLIV, 2; PL 33, 591. *Cont. Jul.*, IV, 3, 16; PL 45, 744.

[4] Augustine, *De Prædest. Sanct.*, V, 10; PL 44, 968: Proinde posse habere fidem, sicut posse habere charitatem, naturæ est hominum: habere autem fidem quemadmodum habere charitatem, gratiæ est fidelium.

[5] Augustine, *ibid.*, II, 5; PL 44, 963: ...sed sufficientia nostra qua credere incipiamus, ex Deo est.

us that we might become so. Moreover, He did this according to the good pleasure of His will, so that no one might glory concerning his own will, but about God's Will towards him." [1] In discussing the difference between the grace given to Adam and the grace given to men since the Redemption, Augustine said : " The fact is that He permitted and allowed the strong one [Adam] to do what he willed; but for the weak He reserved this, that by His gift they should invincibly will what is good, and invincibly refuse to forsake it." [2] From passages such as this one has arisen the false idea of irresistible grace possessed by Harnack, Loofs, and others. [3]

Because of the difficulty of this concept of *gratia indeclinabilis*, some have thought that Augustine denied freedom to man. Just as it is necessary to keep together all that Augustine said about free choice and freedom in order to understand his concept of *libertas*, so we must consider this concept of so-called irresistible grace in the light of Augustine's total teaching. It should first of all be said that Augustine himself did not consider efficacious grace to be irresistible. How then did he look upon it? [4]

Efficacious grace is victorious without being constraining. To see how this is so, we must turn to three Augustinian theories. The first is that the will never decides anything without a motive. [5] Although the will is free in the presence of every motive, there are undoubtedly some motives more effective than others in influencing a given individual at a particular moment. Now, suppose someone had the power of presenting the most appealing motive? [6]

The second theory is that man is not the master of his first thoughts. " Ambrose said this : 'For our hearts and our thoughts

[1] Augustine, *ibid.*, XVIII, 37; PL 44, 987, 988.

[2] Augustine, *De Corrept. et Grat.*, XII, 38; PL 44, 940 : Fortissimo quippe dimisit atque permisit facere quod vellet : infirmis servavit, ut ipso donante invictissime quod bonum est vellent, et hoc deserere invictissime nollent.

[3] Portalié, *op. cit.*, col. 2377. This article is extensively used for the interpretation of Augustine's words. Cf. Gilson, *Introduction à l'Etude de Saint Augustin,* p. 329 : " Absolument indispensable. "

[4] Since the discussion of grace belongs to theologians and not to philosophers, there is no attempt here to present an original interpretation of Augustine's meaning.

[5] Augustine, *De Lib. Arb.*, III, 25, 14; PL 32, 1307.

[6] Augustine, *De Spirit. et Litt.*, XXXIV, 60; PL 44, 240.

are not in our power;' therefore it is not from themselves but from God that men receive the power to become sons of God; they receive it from Him who suggests pious thoughts to the human heart, whence it has faith, which works by love; as for the receiving and keeping of this benefit, and carrying it on perseveringly unto the end, we are not able to think anything by ourselves, but our sufficiency is from God, in whose power are our hearts and our thoughts." [1] Such is likewise the meaning of Ambrose when he says that the will of man is prepared by God. [2] Therefore through exterior and interior means the providential action of God brings it about that certain thoughts enter into man's mind without his invitation.

The third theory is that the divine foreknowledge which is an eternal "present" enables God to know the response man will make to a given motive. Augustine does not tell us in what way God can know such a thing. But he has in many passages argued that this divine foreknowledge is indeed reconcilable with free choice. [3]

In the light of these three theories, Augustine would have us understand efficacious grace in this way: it is a grace that does not cause us to act but causes us to want to act. In this sense it does not override the freedom of the will. It inclines but does not compel the will; the will determines itself. It is an efficacious invitation based on God's perfect knowledge of the *individual* man. [4] In other words, God's providential action brings it about that we think those thoughts which will move us to act

[1] Augustine, *De Dono Pers.*, VIII, 20; PL 45, 1003, 1004: Hoc autem Ambrosius ut diceret, ...Non enim in potestate nostra cor nostrum et cogitationes nostræ... Non itaque in hominum, sed in Dei est potestate, ut habeant homines potestatem filii Dei fieri (John I, 12). Ab ipso quippe accipiunt eam, qui dat cordi humano cogitationes pias, per quas habeat fidem, quæ operetur per dilectionem : ad quod bonum sumendum et tenendum, et in eo perseveranter usque in finem proficiendum, non sumus idonei cogitare aliquid quasi ex nobismetipsis, sed sufficientia nostra ex Deo est; in cujus est potestate cor nostrum et cogitationes nostræ.

[2] Augustine, *De Dono Pers.*, XIX, 49; PL 45, 1024.

[3] Augustine, *De Civ. Dei*, V, 9, 1; PL 41, 148-152; *De Lib. Arb.*, III, 3-4; PL 32, 1273-1276; *In Joan. Evan*, 53, 4; PL 35, 1776; *Expos. quar. propos. ex Epist. ad Rom.*, 55, 60, 61; PL 35, 2076-2080; 83 *Quæst.*, 68; PL 40, 71.

[4] Augustine, *De Div. Quæst. ad Simpl.*, I, q. II, n. 11, n. 12, n. 13; PL 40, 117, 118.

well. God is the Master of our hearts and of our thoughts. His grace is a divine preparation of the will which leaves the soul master over its consent. The will can refuse but it will not. The exterior Providence of God also has its role to play in the gift of perseverance, inasmuch as God sees to it that death coincides with the state of grace in a man.

The special characteristic of this victorious grace is that it substitutes delight in the good for delight in evil. Man is not constrained to keep a law previously repugnant to him, but he spontaneously finds his joy in it. [1] This so-called *delectatio* is only love, the interior weight of the will itself, a preference of the will which retains nevertheless a capacity for free choice. [2]

And so a purely objective study of the texts, but of all the texts, especially those of the last epoch, considered in their context and their relation to the total Augustinian teaching and according to the meaning indicated by Augustine himself, (which is the true historical method), leads to a conclusion absolutely different from the conclusion arrived at by Harnack and others. [3] It is the considered opinion of E. Portalié that Augustine has bequeathed to us a perfectly true and consistent system and that in this system human liberty was until the last very clearly affirmed without trace of any irresistible or necessitating impulsion. [4] We shall, however, leave the discussion of the doctrine of grace to the greater competence of theologians,

[1] Augustine, *Cont. Duas Epist. Pel.*, I, 10, 22; PL 44, 561.

[2] E. Gilson, *Introduction à l'Etude de Saint Augustin*, 2nd edition, Paris, Vrin, 1943, p. 211, n.: " Jansen always reasons as if *delectatio* were a weight in the will different from the will itself. According to him, it seems to be as different as knowledge. By this interpretation he has introduced into the Augustinian will a determining motive, making of the action of divine grace an external determining factor which would make liberty disappear... For Jansen, *delectatio* is the cause of the volition."

[3] E. Portalié, *Dict. Théol. Cath.*, I, col. 2377.

[4] E. Portalié, " Augustin, " *Dict. Théol. Cath.*, I, 2377 : " Malgré des exagérations trop réelles sur certains points, malgré des difficultés qui expliquent, même sans parti pris, les dissentiments, nous croyons les textes assez clairs et les critiques assez impartiaux pour proposer une révision de jugements trop sévères. Et nous affirmons sans hésiter : 1) que saint Augustin s'est formé un vrai système parfaitement enchaîné, sans contradictions, et dont le fond n'a pas varié depuis son épiscopat, *à en juger par ses derniers ouvrages ;* 2) que dans ce système la liberté humaine fut jusqu'au dernier jour très nettement affirmée tandis que jamais on n'y trouve une impulsion irrésistible et nécessitante. "

and in no way consider that it is possible to exhaust this theological problem which is of very vast amplitude.

Dr. Joseph von Mausbach, although best known as a theologian, has studied the texts of Augustine in such a way as to bring to the fore the philosophical statements that are found in them, and he has said that, beginning with the *De Libero Arbitrio*, Augustine clearly champions free will throughout his life, and that there is no indication of any fundamental change in his terminology. [1] The only difference Mausbach notes is that in his early work Augustine handles the existence of *liberum arbitrium* philosophically, while later he considers *liberum arbitrium* as a precept of revelation. Augustine himself even said that if Pelagius would accept as true the *whole* book, *De Libero Arbitrio*, their differences could be settled. [2]

Never, therefore, does Augustine retract the full freedom that he has attributed to man in giving to the will a causality beyond nature, a self-direction and self-command, a total responsibility for sins, the indetermination that comes from openness to opposites; but in the Pelagian disputes "he gives progressively greater stress to the ethical conditions and limitations of freedom," [3] and to the fact that "the will alone does not suffice for good." [4] In fact, even before there is any problem of the reconciliation of grace and free will, Augustine sees between himself and the Pelagians a fundamental divergence concerning the philosophical appreciation of free will. Augustine sees free will as being by nature truly voluntary, having a necessary longing for happiness, the power of a human being who acts through reflection, comparison, and finally, decision, possessing the power of acting personally and responsibly. On the other hand, the foremost Pelagian, Julian, treats of "nature and will, necessity and freedom, being and acting as unreconciled opposites." [5] Whereas Augustine regarded the

[1] Joseph Mausbach, *Die Ethik des heiligen Augustinus*, Freiburg, Herder, 1929, vol. II, p. 26.
[2] *Ibid.*
[3] *Ibid.*, p. 29.
[4] *Ibid.* : Der Wille genügt zwar allein nicht zum Guten...
[5] Mausbach, *op. cit.*, p. 32.

interior spiritual aspiration of the will as its most profound characteristic, for Julian, " the will is intrinsically indeterminate, not a striving, but a mere choice. Without any particular participation, it decrees whether good or evil shall occur. Acts of the will have no particular origin; they are within the person. " [1]

How radically opposed such a position is to that taken by Augustine becomes clear when we recall that he was unwilling to admit a complete indeterminism or absolute liberty of indifference in a faculty which experience showed as intrinsically susceptible to the good in terms of happiness and perfection. Augustine considered Julian's conception to be an untenable distortion of freedom. Mausbach observes :

Free will as Julian conceives it would be a characterless empty phantom, for anything which has activity and existence has also a way of being, a specific reality. The above theories completely dispel the unity of human existence, in that they establish will and being as opposites and place moral activity only within the soul and not without. At the same time, actual choice becomes a complete riddle, an inexplicable accident. When good and evil seem thus to hover unattached, how can sinful mankind be damned at all? [2]

Augustine's chief criticism of Julian's evaluation of the will is that it is unreal, because it is an inadequate estimate of free will, an oversimplification of a very complex thing. It overlooks the close cooperation of will with mind, the irresolution and discord that can arise from opposition of motives, the lack of control over exterior circumstances, the inability to achieve what one wills, the necessity of deciding for a good, and of making sure that it is a true good. While Augustine holds that the will is free insofar as it is healthy, he thinks that it can " through tension and seeming power" become " spiritually unfree, ill and suffering as a body ruled by fever. " [3]

The basic divergence between Augustine and Julian comes down to their different understanding of the nature of the will. Julian considers that independence is its proper characteristic.

[1] *Ibid.*
[2] Mausbach, *Die Ethik des heilg. Aug.*, II, p. 32.
[3] Mausbach, *Die Ethik des heilg. Aug.*, II, p. 33.

For Augustine, the "principal feature of the will is not its independence but love, a joyous assent to all reality and perfection." [1] It would follow that the good will is the true and natural will.

Julian has no rightful understanding of freedom, since he not merely equates good and evil, but deliberately represents the choice of evil as the test of freedom's strength. In sin is found specifically what Julian previously called the heart of freedom — the will is detached from its vital basis in nature, with no attachments or restrictions, and without any emphasis on personal act and responsibility. [2]

In addition to the differences between the Pelagians and Augustine on the nature of free will is their divergence on the topic of grace in relation to the will. Because Augustine considers that the only true freedom is that which includes willing and accomplishing the good, he thinks that grace increases the freedom of the will, while not eliminating independent choice of the good. And yet some scholars maintain that Augustine attributed a *gratia irresistibilis* to the predestined. Critics who follow Harnack and Rottmanner might consider the following elucidation.

"In Rottmanner's collection of quotations, there is only one which apparently attributes irresistible efficacy to grace: *Subventum est igitur infirmitati voluntatis humanæ, ut divina gratia indeclinabiliter et insuperabiliter ageretur, et ideo quamvis infirma non tamen deficeret neque adversitate aliqua vinceretur.* [3] One asks: is grace really here indicated as *indeclinabilis* and *insuperabilis*, so that free will could not withstand it nor turn away? Is it not much more the will which through grace learns to act firmly and invincibly — not in opposition to grace but to temptations and difficulties. *Indeclinabiliter* is in open opposition to *deficere, insuperabiliter, neque adversitate,* etc. Grace and free will do not

[1] Mausbach, *Die Ethik des heilg. Aug.*, II, p. 34.

[2] Mausbach, *op. cit.*, II, p. 34.

[3] Augustine, *De Corrept. et Grat.*, XII, 28; PL 44, 940: "Therefore an aid was given to the weakness of the human will, with the result that it is unwaveringly and invincibly influenced by divine grace, and consequently, whatever its weakness, it does not fail, and is not overcome by any difficulty."

appear as opposites, but will and the danger of sin, and here the will, aided by grace, is sure of victory.

Other collected passages help clarify this. An *adjutorium sine qua non* like that of Adam in paradise, says Augustine, is not suitable for contemporary mankind. Today man needs an *adjutorium quo*, a sure and effective grace so that his weakened will under such great temptations need not fall in defeat. For that reason the human will has been helped on its way, that it may be constantly accompanied by irresistible and invincible divine grace and so, though weak, be not besieged by adverse power nor go down to defeat.

That grace which leads unfailingly to success need not be irresistible is clear for Augustine. With regard to grace he never used the expressions *irresistibilis*, *insuperabilis*. This is clear in Rottmanner's collection : *Voluntas quippe humana... consequitur insuperabilem fortitudinem...* and also : *Quando rogavit ergo, ne fides eius (Petri) deficeret, quid aliud rogavit, nisi ut haberet in fide liberrimam, fortissimam, invictissimam, perseverantissimam voluntatem.* " [1]

Dr. Mausbach further states that in the same work, *De Correptione et Gratia,* Augustine positively affirms that there exist along with the grace of predestination the capacity for evil and real freedom of choice. Augustine, moreover, does not cease to repeat that God is not only unfailingly powerful, but irresistible and invincible; yet this is with respect to God and does not give Him absolute sovereignty over the human will. Dr. Mausbach asserts that Rottmanner's criticism of Augustine's *datur totum Deo* by which Augustine meant to show that the beginning of belief and the completion of salvation come from grace is a misinterpretation. In his last writings Augustine most clearly shows the living interpenetration of Divine and human factors, the dynamic dialectic between man and God. The notions of supernatural effectiveness and of merit are thus

[1] Mausbach, *Die Ethik des heilg. Aug.*, II, pp. 35, 36.

"The fact is that the human will achieves... invincible strength to persevere..." *De Corrept. et Grat.*, VIII, 17; PL 44, 926.

"When therefore Christ prayed that Peter's faith might not fail (Luke XXII, 32), what else did He pray for, except that Peter might have an entirely free, strong, unconquerable, and persevering will to believe?" *Idem.*

justified. " In this respect we hear the familiar expressions of his sermons, according to which we 'associate with God,' and in which 'God is our Helper and we His collaborators'; they do not need, as Rottmanner implies, a *Retractation.* "[1]

The nature of freedom which lies in the inner, self-powerful will, choosing freely, remains intact, when grace enters in as a more lofty principle. There is no doubt that for Augustine freedom of the will is in man's make-up, and that in normal circumstances in the life of the reborn, it is a fact. Only with regard to the position of sin, certain obscurities remain. [2]

Today, many interpretations of Augustine's texts are being re-evaluated according to the historical method of interpretation, which seeks to understand the statements made by Augustine in the light of the question that was actually posed to him rather than as answers to questions that have since been raised. A case in point is the interpretation of *De Correptione et Gratia.* [3] In studying this text one's attitude should be : what is the problematic to which this treatise seeks an answer? Only when this problematic is faced, will the solution be meaningful. We have seen that it is upon a sentence from this text that the Jansenists largely base their system. [4] Yet, is it correct for the Jansenists to interpret a fifth century text of Augustine in the light of concepts and problems bequeathed to them by scholasticism? The Jansenist problematic was : how does one reconcile free choice, which seems to condition the responsibility of man, with the primacy of predestination and the order of grace? They do not seem to have asked themselves this question : was Augustine offering the theory of such a reconciliation? But they sought in the *De Correptione et Gratia*, which did not treat this problem, the Augustinian solution. As a result, they

[1] Mausbach, *Die Ethik des heilg. Aug.*, II, pp. 36-39. Cf. Augustine, *In Epist. Joan.*, IV, 7; PL 35, 200; *Sermo* 156, 11, 13; PL 38, 855, 856; *De Pecc. Mer. et Rem.*, II, 6; PL 44, 154, 155.

[2] Mausbach, *op. cit.*, II, p. 39 : " Die Natur der Freiheit, die im innerlichen, selbstmächtigen, wahlfreien Wollen liegt, bleibt intakt, wenn die Gnade als höheres Prinzip hinzutritt. Dass die Willensfreiheit nach Augustin zur Anlage des Menschen gehört, dass sie im normalen Zustande, im Leben des Wiedergebornen Tatsache ist, unterliegt keinem Zweifel. Gewisse Unklarheiten bleiben nur bezüglich des Standes der Sünde. "

[3] Guy de Broglie, " Le 'De Correptione et Gratia' ", *Augustinus Magister*, III, pp. 317-337.

[4] Augustine, *De Correptione et Gratia*, XII, 38; PL 44, 940 : Subventum est igitur infirmitati voluntatis humanæ ut divina gratia indeclinabiliter et insuperabiliter ageretur.

arrived at what G. de Broglie calls a simplistic solution: the free choice of man and the primacy of divine predestination can be reconciled by proclaiming that man before the Fall enjoyed a freedom of choice which removed from God His freedom to choose His elect; and, inversely, it is the abolition of all free choice in man now which permits God freely to exercise divine predestination.[1]

This is the type of erroneous conclusion reached by setting up problems other than those historically faced by Augustine. For scholastic and modern theologians, the problem of the responsibility for individual acts is identified with their "*libertas a necessitate*," that is, with the personal autonomy exercised by the human agent. According to the Jansenists, if Augustine is to establish that sinners should be reproved, he must prove that the free choice of the sinner could not be eliminated by the general theory of the primacy of divine causality nor by the doctrine of the original fall and the consequent perversion of the will. But Augustine did not do this: instead, he explained the responsibility for a man's sinful actions even in the present by reference to the sin of Adam. The Jansenists interpret this as signifying that Augustine considers free choice to have been abolished. Is such an interpretation justified historically?

To say that Augustine is not proving the existence of free choice in these works against the Pelagians is not to say that he either ignored or misunderstood free choice. We have already quoted many texts widely scattered throughout his works which either imply or affirm the existence of free choice in all the historical periods of human life. Augustine considered it a common sense truth and there is no indication that he ever felt the need for demonstrating metaphysically that man was by nature free.[2] He utilizes moral and historical arguments

[1] G. de Broglie, "Le 'De Correptione et Gratia,'" pp. 321, 322.

[2] Augustine, *De Duab. Anim. contra Man.*, XI, 15; PL 42, 105; *Op. Imp. contra Jul.*, I, 47; PL 45, 1068.

For a more detailed study of the difference between the Augustinian and the scholastic notion of liberty and of their respective importance, consult Guy de Broglie, S. J., *De Fine Ultimo*, Paris, Beauchesne, 1947, pp. 83-90.

to uphold free will and fully accepts the fact of freedom as the supreme implication of all God's demands upon His chosen and His Christian peoples. The concepts and the techniques for establishing the metaphysical conditions of the will's freedom were eventually to be formulated by the scholastics and we shall see that St. Thomas develops the Augustinian philosophy of freedom from the side of its foundation in nature. But the fact that Augustine admitted free choice even when he was most forcefully teaching the power of grace is witnessed to by his frequent reference to the difficulty of reconciling grace with free will. [1] If he had eliminated free will, as the Jansenists would have it, there would be no difficulty.

Even against the Manichaeans Augustine is not directly intent upon proving the freedom of the will, but upon showing that moral evil resulted from a defect of willing as from a deficient cause, and that ignorance and difficulty have increased the will's deficiency. In arguing against the Manichaeans, however, the freedom of the will to do right or wrong was a constant presupposition.

Why did not the anti-Pelagian struggle lead Augustine to elaborate a precise metaphysical theory of "*libertas a necessitate*"? Augustine was not opposing people who maintained the existence of free choice as it exists in man but rather people who were holding up a caricature of free choice. Augustine had to argue against the pretentious greatness and power that the Pelagians attributed to the will, a will that they claimed to be absolutely independent of God's grace in its functioning, without damaging effects from an original transgression of God's law. Augustine's purpose then was to demonstrate not the will's "*immunitas a necessitate*" but rather its subjection to the flesh, from which only the grace of God could now deliver it. To this Augustinian position the reaction of the Pelagians was: if all is due to the grace of God, why reproach sinners?

[1] Augustine, *De Gratia Christi et de Peccato Originali*, 47, 52; PL 44, 383: Sed quia ista quæstio ubi de arbitrio voluntatis et Dei gratia disputatur, ita est ad discernendum difficilis, ut quando defenditur liberum arbitrium, negari Dei gratia videatur; quando autem asseritur Dei gratia, liberum arbitrium putetur auferri. Cf. *Epist.*, 214, 7; PL 33, 970-971.

Thus, it was the purpose of the *De Correptione et Gratia* to bring out the responsibility of sinners for transgressions both before and after Baptism. Augustine seeks to reveal why the culpable use we now make of free will deserves all the indignation of God and of men, despite the weight of original sin upon us and our powerlessness to free ourselves from it. To do this he explains the responsibility of our own culpable actions by reference to the sin of Adam. When we realize why he is having recourse to a sin already committed by our First Parent to explain why the actual sinner today should be admonished, we shall have a key to the *De Correptione et Gratia* which really unlocks its meaning, because it fits historically.

Augustine seems to hold that if the strictly individual responsibility of the sinner were alone taken into account, it would be impossible fully to justify the terrible reprimands and chastisements that God prepares for transgressors of His law. [1] He comes to the conclusion that it is the sin of Adam which calls forth the just indignation of God, and when man by personal sin renews his solidarity with Adam, God's indignation reaches out to both sins. By a willing concession to his evil tendencies, man today has the power of renewing this solidarity with Adam. [2] If original sin has brought a lessening of strictly personal responsibility, there is still nevertheless the weight of hereditary and collective responsibility. Just as our personal merits depend on free choice and yet the Heaven we merit is due to our incorporation with Christ, so our personal demerits, which likewise depend on free choice, bring us a punishment which is due to our incorporation with Adam. It is by free choice that we give way to evil tendencies and become one with Adam, who realized all the conditions of a responsibility rigorously and exclusively personal.

We are likewise well warned by G. de Broglie not to try to discover in those pages of the *De Correptione et Gratia* consecrated

[1] Augustine, *De Lib. Arb.*, III, 18, 51; PL 32, 1295, 1296. Cf. *Epist.*, 190; PL 33,857-867.
[2] Augustine, *De Corrept. et Grat.*, VII, 16; PL 44, 925; VII, 12; PL 44, 923; IX, 25. PL 44, 931.

to the "*auxilium quo*" and the "*auxilium sine qua non*" any general theory of sufficient and efficacious grace. We cannot assume that sufficient grace can exist only with innocent man, efficacious grace with fallen man. Augustine is not trying to formulate a theory of sufficient and efficacious grace any more than he is trying to establish the metaphysical conditions for the free act. Such a theory will be evolved only after the techniques for philosophical analysis are matured. Just as in speaking of true nature, Augustine is referring to a particular type of man in an historical and concrete setting, so his *auxilium sine qua non* and his *auxilium quo* are definite historical and concrete varieties of sufficient and efficacious grace. His particular *auxilium sine qua non* pacified the sensible appetite and conferred on the human subject an integral responsibility, adequately and exclusively personal. His particular *auxilium quo*, grace victoriously efficacious, had as its proper effect the strengthening of the will against powerful temptations. It is only a Jansenist assumption that no form of efficacious grace existed in the primitive state of man. Was this not because they missed the true antithesis that Augustine was making between the primitive and the present state of man? Reading the sentence, "*Subventum est igitur infirmitati voluntatis humanæ ut divina gratia indeclinabiliter et insuperabiliter ageretur,*" [1] they are fascinated by the adverbs *indeclinabiliter et insuperabiliter* and are utterly convinced that the antithesis bears directly on them. But as one scholar has recently brought out, [2] if we interpret this sentence in conformity with the total Augustinian theology whose precise meaning we seek, it is assuredly the word "*ageretur*" that constitutes the capital word and that bears all the weight of the antithesis affirmed between Adam's condition and our own. [3] In the primitive state the

[1] Augustine, *De Correp. et Grat.*, XII, 38; PL 44, 940.

[2] G. de Broglie, "Le ' De Correptione et Gratia,' " p. 334.

[3] *Ibid.*, p. 335: "Cette nouveauté ne consiste pas en ce que l'action intérieure de Dieu sur le vouloir deviendrait ainsi ' plus invincible ' qu'elle n'était auparavant. ' Invincible ' elle l'est par essence, quoique sans péril pour la liberté de nos choix, du seul fait qu'elle appartient à la Toute-Puissance créatrice, de qui toutes les libertés procèdent, avec tous les choix libres en lesquels elles s'achèvent. Mais le prodige, c'est que cette action s'accommode désormais à la condition propre de notre nature déchue, de notre intelligence aveugle, de notre volonté divisée, débile, inconstante : en sorte que ces misérables organes d'action, dont on serait fondé

justified will of Adam acted in the fullness of its God-given power; in the present state, man's will is acted upon intimately by God without loss to its freedom, and with great gain for its strength. This is the Augustinian antithesis of the grace of Adam and the grace of the Redeemer.

In his work entitled *De Correptione et Gratia,* therefore, Augustine is not seeking to establish the generic conditions of free choice, nor is he trying to prove that the fall of the first man made us wholly lose free choice. He is simply trying to bring to light two great Christian truths :

1) After the Fall, demerit and merit, wholly personal as they continue to be, must never be considered in an individualistic atmosphere, but as being the fruit of our solidarity with the first Adam or with the Second Adam, Christ;

2) The grace of Christ makes us tend freely towards eternal life by taking us in hand as living instruments of the Holy Spirit.

Although this interpretation of the text does not answer the questions raised by the Jansenists, it does answer the questions that were uppermost in the climate of thought breathed by Augustine. The questions of the metaphysical nature of the freedom of the will, the reconciliation of human freedom with divine predestination and with the congenital infirmity of our wounded wills are questions left open. These are questions for the post-Augustinian generations to ponder. Augustine's anti-Manichaean and anti-Pelagian works faced other problems.

CONCLUSION

We can, therefore, summarize the following steps in the genesis of the Augustinian notion of freedom :

Augustine wonders concerning the cause of moral evil.

à n'attendre plus rien de solidement bon, se voient pris en main par le Créateur et maintenus par Lui dans la voie du bien, avec une puissance, une constance et une sûreté sans égale : *De Corrept. et Grat.*, XII, 38; PL 44, 940 : " Subventum est igitur infirmitati voluntatis humanæ, ut divina gratia indeclinabiter et insuperabiliter ageretur; et ideo, quamvis infirma, non tamen deficeret, neque adversitate aliqua vinceretur. Ita factum est ut voluntas hominis invalida et imbecilla in bono adhuc parvo perseveraret per virtutem Dei; cum voluntas primi hominis, fortis et sana, in bono ampliore non perseveraverit, habens virtutem liberi arbitrii. "

A sermon of Ambrose informs him that the human will contains the explanation of moral evil.

A reading of the *Enneads* gives him a philosophical understanding of evil as a negation in the universe.

A consideration of the compatibility of a good Creator with man's created capacity for evil leads Augustine to investigate free will as it existed in Adam; from this comes the insight that free will was given as a power for good, not as a disability.

Augustine envisages freedom in the first man as the perfection of free will when man freely adhered to the "order of love."

The reading of St. Paul shows Augustine the cause of the divided will he had experienced *(Confessions)*; and from the Old Testament Augustine begins to recognize God as warring for the freedom of His people against Satan's enslaving power.

Meditation on the words of Scripture shows Christ as the Liberator of man.

Augustine concludes that man is most free when he participates in the Divine freedom through the reception of grace. This results from God's free gift and man's free consent. For man to enjoy this freedom there must be added to his natural power of will the supernatural virtue of charity, and as man, with God's help, does the truth in charity, he becomes free.

CHAPTER VIII

THEOLOGICAL FREEDOM AND ITS PHILOSOPHICAL IMPLICATIONS

After an over-all survey of the historical events, the personal experiences, and the Pauline explanations that let to Augustine's high evaluation of a freedom that would insure to man his spontaneous tending towards the true good, we shall now turn to the texts of Augustine where this "freedom" given by God to free the human will for God, is more profoundly elaborated. We shall see how strong, sure and swift to respond to the good is the human will that God elevates. By seeing the natural will thus perfected by grace, we can glimpse how God intended man's will to operate when He gave him this capacity for free spiritual activity as the directive force of all human actions, whether purely psychic or psychosomatic. For, not only did God want man to have free choice, a faculty of doing good or evil, but he also wanted man to have a perfectly free will, a power of doing good with the calm and the peace that characterize spiritual liberty. But there will arise today, as there arose in Augustine's day, the question of how much free choice remains to man when he enjoys freedom under grace. Augustine will maintain that just as the tendency to evil in the sons of Adam did not eliminate nor denature man's power of free choice, so the tendency to the good that has been reinforced by grace in the sons of God by Baptism does not subvert the reality of free choice.

In exploring any topic in Augustine one finds that he discusses it in relation to the destiny of man. With human destiny as his focal point, therefore, Augustine explains freedom existentially.[1]

[1] A word should be said here about the existential character of Augustine's doctrine in relation to his concern for destiny. The two are inseparable, as can be noted in the following statement of P. Cayré, *Initiation à la Philosophie de S. Augustin*, pp. 59-60 : " La philosophie de S. Thomas considère l'être en soi-même, l'être participé ou reçu : S. Augustin étudie

As we examined the genesis of his doctrine of freedom we were introduced to the various phases of the history of voluntary human behavior. Out of this concrete study of the will there emerges the Augustinian doctrine of theological freedom, that is, the liberty of man to love God as His Divine Son loved Him, with joy and exultation, with a delight that is victorious over all contrary tendencies. This freedom grows as man uses free will and the infused virtue of charity to embrace the will of God, to choose God in all that he does. For this reality that has been described by Augustine it seems fitting to use the name " theological freedom, " because this expression can best indicate : 1) that human free will is for the purpose of loving God; 2) that human free will is secured to its true end under the influx of grace, that is, by a share in divine freedom; 3) that this freedom belonged to the Old Testament " faithful " who, while perhaps beginning with fear of violating the commands of Yahweh, became filially dependent upon God their Father. Of course, like all acts availing to eternal life and done before or after Christ, this freedom was achieved through the merits of Jesus Christ.

Theological freedom, like the theological virtues to which (as we shall see) it is structurally related, presupposes the ontological basis of sanctifying grace by which man participates directly in divine life. Because grace, far from destroying

l'être participé en tant que participé, ou reçu de Dieu, et cette tendance imprime déjà à toutes les recherches qu'elle inspire une certaine orientation vers Dieu. "

Also, F. J. Thonnard, " Caractères Platoniciens de l'Ontologie Augustinienne ", in *Augustinus Magister*, Communications, Congrès International Augustinien, Paris, 1954, p. 319 : " D'où un nouveau caractère de cette ontologie; elle est, peut-on dire, *existentielle* quant à l'être et à ses propriétés, en ce sens qu'elle considère ces éminentes perfections comme étant par elles-mêmes d'abord en premier lieu, des *réalités*, des choses existantes, synthétisées d'ailleurs en une seule essence simple, vivante et personnelle, qui est Dieu... " (St. Augustine noted the various facets of created reality when he said to Nebridius in Letter XI : One can pose many questions concerning one thing : An sit? Quid sit? Quale sit? PL 33, 76.)

Thonnard, *op. cit.*, p. 320 : " Sans doute, il n'a pas traité à part des questions d'ontologie, mais il en a établi les éléments... Il apparaît alors que, pour saint Augustin, l'être et ses propriétés, qui se réalisent d'abord en Dieu, conviennent encore à toutes les créatures, mais à chacune selon l'ordre et en vertu du Principe de participation. *L'ordre* et la *participation*, par ces deux notions maîtresses, l'ontologie Augustinienne se retrouve à sa place normale, au sommet de la philosophie des créatures avant d'atteindre la théodicée. " Cf. *De Trin.*, V, 10, 11; *De Civ. Dei*, VIII, 4; *Confess.*, VII, 15; *Sermo*, VIII, 7; *De Mor. Manich.*, VII, 7.

nature, builds upon it, there is embedded in Augustine's explanation of theological freedom a philosophy of freedom that exposes the nature of the free human will, its purpose, and its relation with other human faculties, as well as insight into the conditions for attaining the perfection of man. To set up such a philosophy separately would do violence to the Augustinian method. Nevertheless, the natural structure is there, a structure of spiritual freedom, virtually present within the doctrine of theological freedom that Augustine formally treats. [1] We can, as it were, explore the constituents of spiritual freedom, but the question : how does man actually possess such freedom? brings the constant answer: by grace. This is Augustine's answer. He is unshakably insistent in giving it, and its inevitability flows from his realism, his existentialism. The question of what constitutes spiritual freedom can be raised in philosophy, and a philosophical answer can be framed, but the means of becoming free is announced only in theology. The author of natural truth is likewise the author of grace. Reason and faith belong together.

If we examine the human subject we see a being of a certain nature, that is, human, with all the assets and liabilities this entails — really and actually, not metaphorically, called by a being of a higher nature, divine, to communicate with Him in a manner that is most satisfying and most fulfilling to human powers. This is the real order. Why? Not because there is in man a natural desire for God in Himself — but because there is a real desire for man in God. [2] There is a divine intention that man should be united with God (" That they all may be one as Thou, Father in Me, and I in Thee, that they all may be one in us. " John XVII, 21), and God has given man the

[1] The special characteristic of the Augustinian doctrine is that it is *integral.* It conforms both to experience and the exigencies of thought, to the orientations of nature and to religious teaching.

[2] M. Blondel, " L'Unité Originale et la Pensée Permanente de la Doctrine Philosophique de saint Augustin ", *Revue de Métaphysique et de Morale,* (1930), p. 45. " Augustin avait vu au principe même de l'intelligence un dynamisme qui fait surgir des problèmes spéculatifs à la fois inévitables et incomplètement résolubles pour toute raison finie; semblablement, il découvre, aux racines de la volonté et de la liberté, un élan qui, tout en étant indestructible et effectif, n'aboutit point naturellement au terme entrevu et convoité. "

transcendental readiness to satisfy the divine desire. This might be called the ontological basis of the possibility of man's attainment of God, a basis that is found more in God than in man. That is why nothing less than a combination of faith and reason can enable man to take in all his possibilities, and why some questions that are raised in philosophy can be answered only in theology. For man is more than what he is by nature; — he is also what God intends him to be. To see himself as he can be in God's vision, man must share God's vision — by faith. With this vision let us glance at the kind of freedom God desires for man.

Experience, the reality of the moral order, [1] and Scripture [2] witness to the fact that man has free choice. But what is the work of free choice? The action of the will may be responsive or productive. Under its productive aspect, man acts and makes things. As responsive, the will engenders all responses whether volitional or affective, love, veneration, esteem. Now, the productive and the volitional aspects of will are sufficient for free choice, but Augustine would seem to teach that the full affective response of love for God is necessary for freedom. [3] This love is nourished by knowledge and increases the efficacy of man's efficient causality. [4] But knowledge itself is increased by man's entrance by faith into God's knowledge. It is above all a knowledge of God's extraordinary love for each human person that awakens in man a tender love, an affective response to God. Lively faith in divine love [5] is then the prelude to freedom, whereas ignorance of this love diminishes freedom.

[1] Augustine, *De Duab. Anim.*, XI, 15; PL 42, 105.

[2] Augustine, *De Gratia et Lib. Arb.*, II, 2; PL 44, 882.

[3] D. von Hildebrand, *Christian Ethics*, p. 205. He quotes Augustine, *In Joan. Evan.* XXVI, 4: " Some may censure me, and ask: ' How can I believe with the will if I am drawn?' I reply: ' it is not sufficient to be drawn by the will: you are drawn also by delight. ' What is it to be drawn by delight? *Delight in the Lord, and he will give thee the requests of thy heart*. (Ps. 36, 4). " PL 35, 1608.

[4] Augustine, *De Civ. Dei*, V, 9; PL 41, 151.

[5] This is why St. Augustine wrote a commentary on the Gospel of St. John and the Epistle of St. John, for St. John's words are a symphony with one theme: God is Love. This is also the reason for the Revelations of the Sacred Heart (natural symbol of infinite love) to St. Margaret Mary in the 17th century, and to Sister Josefa Menendez, R.S.C.J. in the 20th century. Cf. *Way of Divine Love*, Westminster, Md., Newman Press, 1950.

The truth that can be found contained within Augustine's doctrine of theological freedom is this: God never planned that man should be constrained to obey God. In making man in His own image, God intended that man should image God's own love, the love uniting the Divine Persons, and thereby love the Divine Will. That would be freedom. For there is no constraint, no law, when we love what we ought to do. If then free will depends both on willing according to truth and on loving what we will, there can be no freedom apart from God. To be free by ourselves is an impossible metaphysical wish in any order — before or after Adam's sin. An understanding of freedom demands an understanding of man's metaphysical status.

Adam, informed of his creature condition, was asked to keep his freedom by way of humility, which is an abiding in the truth. When Adam's will withdrew from the truth, it defied its metaphysical status of participated being, participated freedom. On his own he sought an absolute independence. Slavery by way of pride, which is untruth, became the lot of his heirs, with free will a diminished power. The will continued to desire the good, able to choose sin, unable of itself to act righteously for eternal life. [1] To free man for loving God there would come one who humbled himself and became obedient even unto death. Just as creation was a Trinitarian act, so was salvation. "It is only from God the Father, through Jesus Christ, with

[1] One often hears that St. Augustine denied virtue to the pagans. He merely refused them true virtues without Christ. An explanation of this is given by Joseph Wang Tch'ang-tche, S.J., *Saint Augustin et les Vertus des Païens*, Paris, Beauchesne, 1938, pp. 183, 184: "When the Pelagians suggested to St. Augustine the virtues of the pagans, which they identified with infidels properly so-called, he could only deny true virtue to infidels. These affirmations seem severe, but if we understand them correctly in their original meaning, they express simply the fundamental truth of Christianity: salvation can come only from Christ; consequently, true virtue presupposes faith in Christ. Therefore, should a pagan who ignores or despises this faith in Christ possess nevertheless some appearance of virtue, we can be sure beforehand that it is not true virtue he possesses. This is St. Augustine's only argument. As for the possibility of true virtues in pagans who are not infidels, he did not directly examine that question.

Can pagans be true followers of Christ, while remaining outside the visible Church? We find in St. Augustine no explicit answer concerning pagans contemporary with the preaching of the Gospel. However, despite his tendency to emphasize the evil consequences of original sin, he never taught that salvation is refused to every pagan, or that faith in Christ is impossible for him. On the contrary, his profound Christian sense and his penetrating insight have enriched us with truly beautiful views on the place of Christ at the center

the Holy Spirit, that men have the love of God through which they come to God." [1] And that is why true personal freedom, theological freedom, cannot be gained without Christ Who, as Mediator, reorientates man towards God. Sin had enslaved man, and only God could free him, because far greater than the cosmic consequences of sin was its offensiveness to God. One of Augustine's most comprehensive statements elucidating theological freedom is the following:

In defending free will, however, [the Pelagians] go overboard with the result that reliance is put on it, instead of on the grace of God, for the operation of justice, and each glories in himself rather than in the Lord. Now, who among us would say that because of the sin of the first man, freedom of choice was lost to the human race? True, freedom was lost through sin, that freedom, namely, which existed in paradise — the freedom of having complete justice with immortality. As a consequence, human nature needs divine aid, in accord with those words of Our Lord: 'If the Son has freed you, then truly you are free,' (John VIII, 36) free, to be sure, to live rightly and justly. For to that extent did freedom of choice not perish in sinners, that through its agency they might sin, especially all who sin with delight and love for sin. What tickles their fancy seems right to them. Thus it is that Apostle says, 'When you were slaves of sin, you were free of justice.' Now these words show that those sinners were utterly unable to serve even sin except by reason of another liberty. Free, then, from justice they are not except through free choice; free from sin, however, they do not become save through the grace of the Redeemer (Romans VI, 20-22). *Free* of justice, he says, not *freed*. Free of sin, however, he does not say, lest they attribute this to themselves, but with extreme caution he preferred to say, *freed*, linking this with that statement of Our Lord 'If the Son has freed you, then truly you are free.' So, since the sons of man do not live uprightly

of humanity, on the universality of the Christian religion, and on Christ's grace and light enveloping all individuals. According to these principles, he affirms the existence of just men among pagans, before the Incarnation. From the same principles, he also concludes that just men can be found among pagans in our times, and consequently true virtues. Moreover, he shows that above the particular economies by which Providence watches over the salvation of each individual, there is the general economy which presides over the salvation of humanity as a whole. Nothing is unforeseen: all things marvelously works together. Also one would be tempted to say that there must have been pagans in possession of true virtues since these pagan peoples have their own role in the elaboration of the total Christ."

[1] Augustine, *Contra Jul.*, IV, 3, 33; PL 44, 756: ... amor autem Dei quo pervenitur ad Deum non est nisi a Deo Patre per Jesum Christum cum Spiritu Sancto.

unless they are made sons of God, how is it that some want to attribute the power of living rightly to man's free choice, seeing that this power (of living rightly) is given only through the grace of God. [1]

And so the way to theological freedom is clearly charted by Augustine. The Father " draws " man to love Him in showing Christ as His Son, Wisdom Incarnate, the generous Redeemer of souls, the Truth that will make men free, the Life that will refresh, the Love than which there is no greater. The more conscious the human soul becomes that Christ is Incarnate Love, the more spontaneously the will responds to His attraction. Man freely consents to be drawn by love. The law of pleasure that governs the physiological phases of life is not altogether absent from the psychological plane. If grace is a participation in the divine nature, may it not bring with it divine tendencies, a delight in the Lord? It should then be easier, not more difficult, to do the things one ought to do. If the choice of evil is a deviation from the will's natural tendency, the choice of the good is the continuance of creation in harmony with the wisdom of God. For this, man must open himself to the transcendent good, love the good in itself, taking neither himself nor any created good as an absolute — this is the point of departure for spiritual liberty, a positive power in the sense of attachment to the Absolute, with a negative concomitant of detachment from the relative. If man loves God, he makes

[1] Augustine, *Contra Duas Epistulas Pelagianorum*, I, 2, 5; PL 44, 552: Liberum autem arbitrium defendendo præcipitant, ut de illo potius ad faciendam justitiam, quam de Domini adjutorio confidatur, atque ut in se quisque, non in Domino glorietur. Quis autem nostrum dicat, quod primi hominis peccato perierit liberum arbitrium de humano genere? Libertas quidem periit per peccatum, sed illa quæ in paradiso fuit, habendi plenam cum immortalitate justitiam; propter quod natura humana divina indiget gratia, dicente Domino, ' Si vos Filius liberavit, tunc vere liberi eritis, ' utique liberi ad bene justeque vivendum. Non liberum arbitrium usque adeo in peccatore non periit, ut per illud peccent, maxime omnes qui cum delectatione peccant et amore peccati, hoc eis placet quod eos libet. Unde et Apostolus ' Cum essetis ', inquit ' servi peccati, liberi fuistis justitiæ '. Ecce ostenduntur etiam peccato minime potuisse, nisi alia libertate, servire. Liberi ergo a justitia non sunt, nis arbitrio voluntatis : Liberi autem a peccato non fiunt, nisi gratia salvatoris (Rom. VI, 20-22). Liberos dixit justitiæ, non liberatos : a peccato autem non liberos, ne sibi hoc tribuerent; sed vigilantissime maluit dicere liberatos, referens hoc ad illam Domini sententiam, ' Si vos Filius liberavit, tum vere liberi eritis. ' Cum itaque non vivant bene filii hominum, nisi effecti filii Dei, quid est quod iste libero arbitrio vult bene vivendi tribuere potestatem; cum hæc potestas non detur nisi gratia Dei, per J.C.

God's will his own and, by thus doing his own will, he more easily does what he ought to do. This is what St. Augustine meant when he said: Love, and do as you please.[1] As the abandonment to one's spiritual aspirations detaches one from the materializing clutches of instincts, passions and habits, greater power of attachment to God is released. For one, however, who is in servitude to self, with a divided will, without a clear knowledge and without a love that unites him to another Person as the source of the strength and truth he needs, the beautiful ideal of spiritual freedom can scarcely be realized. That is why St. Augustine teaches that in the concrete man will not be spiritually free, will not attain unto personal liberty and the unconstrained pursuit of his true good until he becomes theologically free.

And it is out of the question for free will to realize this freedom through its own power; this it can do only through the grace of God rooted in the faith of Christ. And so the will itself, as Scripture puts it, *is made ready beforehand by the Lord* for the reception of the other gifts of God through which we come into possession of His gift everlasting.[2]

After the gift of Divine Life, in Baptism, man grows in freedom as he exercises the virtues of faith, hope and charity which are strengthened by the other Sacraments, especially the Eucharist. Faith furnishes insight into man's vocation as a spiritual creature and arouses his confidence in his supernatural call; hope provides him with the energy to organize his physical and affective acts in the quest of God; charity can transform

[1] Augustine, *In Epist. Joan.*, VII, 8; PL 35, 2033: Dilige, et quod vis fac.

[2] Augustine, *Enchirid.*, 106; PL 40, 282: Nec omnino per seipsum, sed per solam Dei gratiam, quæ in fide Christi posita est, liberatur; ut voluntas ipsa, sicut scriptum est, a Domino præparetur (Prov. VIII, 35 Greek), quæ cætera Dei munera capiantur, per quæ veniatur ad munus æternum.

The following is an interpretation of Augustine's position on the necessity of grace for good acts: Hermann Lange, *De Gratia*, Freiburg, Herder, 1929, pp. 64-65: " Opera infidelium, etiam naturaliter honestissima, vocantur *actus* mali et peccata, eo sensu quo peccatum originale est *status* malus et peccaminosus. Hoc secundum dogma definitum... vere est peccatum (habituale)... Hic status privationis Deo displicens singulis sensu *analogo* est voluntarius et proinde est *verum peccatum*, non materiale tantum, sed formale, licet nonnisi *analogum* ad peccatum personale. Eandem considerationem, utique nondum notionibus tam claris conceptam, necque terminis tam distinctis expressam, Augustinus et sequentes Patres jure transtulerunt ad *actus* quoque qui *ex culpa* originali singulis imputabili *privantur* bonitate supernaturali...

the human personality by cracking the hard shell of selfishness which closes man off from the human community in which alone he can fully develop as a child who is one of the many children of God. [1] By acts of faith, hope and charity man uses his free will to give in to God, to give up for God and to give to God more than God requires. As these efforts go forward man begins to experience the delight that comes from a concentration of all the human powers in adhesion to God. Sin no longer attracts because it goes counter to the spontaneity of a soul in love with God. Grace leads the soul with an ever greater tenderness. Here is a certain deepening of sensation to the spiritual level where the soul tastes the sweetness of the yoke, feels the lightness of the burden. Here is free will acting perfectly, theologically free. " This is what constitutes true freedom — the joy experienced in doing what is right. " [2]

> With the Holy Spirit, by whose Gift we are justified, we take delight in this, that we sin not, — and that is freedom; without the Spirit we take delight in sin, and that is slavery. [3]

This is St. Augustine's famous *frui Deo*, the delight in God that comes from the soul's communion with God by love. This is *free* will, a will powerful through love and joy, personalizing by the fulfillment of its orientation, and generating generosity. This fulfillment simplifies life whereas frustration gives birth to many complexes. Man, who from his state of indetermination often envies the security of physically determined beings, himself experiences that security by attaining " ...a permanent will to live happily, and... a voluntary and happy necessity of living virtuously, and never sinning. " [4] These are they who have " ...flown for refuge to the grace that justifies, and becoming

[1] Augustine, *De Spirit. et Litt.*, 29, 31, 32; PL 44, 232-237.

[2] Augustine, *Enchirid.*, 30; PL 40, 247 : Ipsa est vera libertas propter recti facti lætitiam,...

[3] Augustine, *De Spirit. et Litt.*, 16; PL 44, 218 : Hic autem Spiritus Dei, cujus dono justificamur, quo fit in nobis ut non peccare delectet, ubi libertas est, sicut præter hunc Spiritum peccare delectat, ubi servitus...

[4] Augustine, *De Perf. Just. Hom.*, IV, 9; PL 44, 296 : Ipsa enim sanitas est vera libertas, quæ non perisset, si bona permansisset voluntas. Quia vero peccavit voluntas, secuta est peccantem peccatum habendi dura necessitas, donec tota sanetur infirmitas et accipiatur tanta libertas, in qua sicut necesse est permaneat beate vivendi voluntas, ita ut sit etiam bene vivendi et nunquam peccandi voluntaria felixque necessitas.

delighted with the sweet pleasure of holiness, escape the penalty of the law's menacing letter through the Spirit's soothing gift." [1]

God never intended man to walk alone, to think alone, to will alone. Man's destiny was a more glorious one than a closed human autonomy. It was one born of his metaphysical condition as a living relation to God, a creature whose greatness resides more in capacity than in actuality, an image of God by his spiritual powers, a friend of God by God's free gift of Himself. God did not create the universe for aesthetic reasons or for the sake of scientific progress or out of metaphysical necessity, but for communion with man. This was to be God's glory. Love made the image which makes communion possible, and love alone can make the likeness that will make communion actual.

We, however, on our side affirm that the human will is so divinely aided in the pursuit of righteousness, that (in addition to the free choice with which man was created, and in addition to the teaching by which he is instructed how he ought to live), he receives the Holy Spirit, by whom there is formed in his mind a delight in, and a love of, that supreme and unchangeable good which is God, even now while he is still 'walking by faith' and not yet 'by sight'; in order that by this gift to him of the down-payment, as it were, of the free gift, he may conceive an ardent desire to cleave to His Maker, and may burn to enter upon the participation in that true light, that he may be approved by Him to whom he owes his existence.

A man's free will indeed avails for nothing except to sin, if he knows not the way of truth; and even after his duty and his proper aim shall begin to become known to him, unless he also take delight in and feel a love for it, he neither does his duty, nor sets about it, nor lives rightly. Now, in order that such a course may engage our affections, God's 'love is shed abroad in our hearts,' not through the free will which arises from ourselves, but 'through the Holy Spirit who is given to us.' [2]

[1] Augustine, *De Spirit. et Litt.*, X; PL 44, 210: ...confugiant per fidem ad justificantem gratiam, et per donum spiritus suavitate justitiæ delectati pœnam litteræ minantis evadant.

[2] Augustine, *De Spir. et Litt.*, III; PL 44, 203: Nos autem dicimus humanam voluntatem sic divinitus adjuvari ad faciendam justitiam, ut præter quod creatus est homo cum libero arbitrio voluntatis, præterque doctrinam qua ei præcipitur quemadmodum vivere debeat, accipiat Spiritum Sanctum, quo fiat in animo ejus delectatio dilectioque summi illius atque incommutabilis boni quod Deus est, etiam nunc cum adhuc per fidem ambulatur, nondum

When the free will, infused with charity, cooperates with grace there comes a "...delightful constancy and an insuperable fortitude which enables man to persevere." [1] This freedom, marked by a frank humility and a unifying generosity at the service of society, grows daily as men are more and more assimilated to Christ, the head of the only truly free city, the City of God.

If, in conclusion, we turn to the natural structure for spiritual freedom that is virtually present within the soul endowed with theological freedom, certain important factors emerge. One factor is the distinctive nature of human love. [2] Since the natural appetites of non-knowing beings are blind, animal love is sensibly enlightened and human love is intellectually enlightened. Whereas brute animals perceive only good things, man can know the good as such. This is the source of his free choice, because it makes him independent of every concrete realization of "good," and it is likewise the source of his freedom if he follows his natural human appetite for the Supreme Good whom he can by reason discover to be his Creator. This has important implications:

1. Man's will is ordered toward an objective good, not a subjective one.

per speciem (2 Cor. V, 7); ut hac sibi velut arrha data gratuiti muneris inardescat inhærere Creatori, atque inflammetur accedere ad participationem illius veri luminis; ut et illo ei bene sit, a quo habet ut sit.

Nam neque liberum arbitrium quidquam nisi ad peccandum valet, si lateat veritatis via: et cum id quod agendum et quo nitendum est cœperit non latere, nisi etiam delectet et ametur non agitur, non suscipitur, non bene vivitur. Ut autem diligatur, charitas Dei diffunditur in cordibus nostris, non per arbitrium liberum quod surgit ex nobis, sed per Spiritum Sanctum qui datus est nobis (Rom. V, 5).

[1] Augustine, *De Correptione et Gratia*, VIII, 17; PL 44, 926: Ecce quemadmodum secundum gratiam Dei, non contra eam, libertas defenditur voluntatis. Voluntas quippe humana non libertate consequitur gratiam, sed gratia potius libertatem, et ut perseveret delectabilem perpetuitatem, et insuperabilem fortitudinem.

[2] As Maurice Blondel has so aptly said in his masterly article, "L'Unité Originale et la Pensée Permanente de la Doctrine Philosophique de Saint Augustin" *Revue de Métaphysique et de Morale*, 1930, p. 466: "Pour rendre compte de ce qu'Augustin a dit, il a fallu suggérer des choses qu'il n'a pas dites et en une langue philosophique qui est évidemment postérieure à la sienne. Mais c'est là une condition inévitable si l'on tient à ne pas le tuer pour montrer un squelette de mort, alors que l'ossature même doit rester vivante et croître avec les chairs, par les chairs."

2. Man does not love God solely because of his own teleological trends towards self-fulfillment or in subjective pursuit of happiness.

3. Man's disinterested love of the good in itself, since it is inscribed in human nature, will have as its effect the achievement of human perfection in a unified personality.

4. This human love characterizes the world of persons, eliminates the isolation and the competition of individuals, uniting man with man.

These various features of the underlying nature of human love indicate that the characterization of Augustinian ethics as eudaemonistic is an incomplete estimate [1], unjust to the profundity of the Augustinian insights. Certainly the deep human desire for true happiness is organically linked with the love of the Good which is none other than God. But the Good is objectively loved for its value or else happiness is not attained. [2] The love of God is in reality prior to the love of self because in the " order of love " He is the Higher Good and man knows it unless he closes his eyes to the radical contingency of his own being. [3] St. Augustine links the love of God with the pursuit of perfection and happiness when he says : " Therefore He who made me is good and He is my Good. " [4] In his work " Of the Morals of the Catholic Church, " after teaching why God should be loved above all others and more intensely than

[1] Cf. Jean Rohmer, *La Finalité Morale chez les Théologiens de Saint Augustin à Duns Scot* Paris, Vrin, 1939.

[2] Th. Déman, " Héritage Antique et Innovation Chrétienne ", in *Augustinus Magister*, Communications, Congrès International Augustinien, Paris, 1954, vol. II, p. 718 : " Etre heureux n'est plus seulement avoir ce que l'on veut mais ce que l'on aime (et que l'on aime à la façon d'une personne, pour elle-même et parce qu'elle est digne d'amour). '

Cf. *De Civ. Dei*, VIII, 1 ; PL 41, 223-225 ; VIII, 8 ; PL 41, 232-233 ; *De Trin.*, XIII, 9, 12 ; PL 42, 1023 ; *De Civ. Dei*, XIX, 4 ; PL 41, 627-631 ; *De Mor. Eccles. Cath.*, VIII, 13 ; PL 32, 1316 : Audivimus quid diligere et quantum diligere debeamus : eo est omnino tendendum, ad im omnia consilia nostra referenda. Bonorum summa, Deus nobis est. Deus est nobis summud, bonum.

[3] Elizabeth G. Salmon, *The Good in Existential Metaphysics*, Milwaukee, Marquette University Press, 1953, pp. 35-36 : " But the good as good is primarily loved with a love that is in and for the good itself... Vaguely it is love of what makes a thing to be which ultimately is Existence Itself. Also vaguely Pure Existence is loved in and for itself. "

[4] Augustine, *Confess.*, I, 20, 31 ; PL 32, 676 : Bonus ergo est qui fecit me, et ipse est bonum meum...

all else, Augustine suddenly faces the question of man's natural inclinations, and says :

It may be thought that there is nothing here about man himself, the lover. But to think this shows a want of clear perception. For it is impossible for one who loves God not to love himself. For he alone has a proper love for himself who aims diligently at the attainment of the chief and true Good; and if this is nothing else but God, as has been shown, what is to prevent one who loves God from loving himself? And then among men, should there be no bond of mutual love? Yes, verily; so that we can think of no surer step towards the love of God than the love of man for man...

Now you love yourself suitably when you love God better than yourself. What then you aim at for yourself, you must aim at for your neighbor, namely, that he may love God with perfect affection. [1]

So we see Augustine emphasizing the objectivity of the operation of the human natural appetite, forging the link between the good-in-itself and the human good, [2] and identifying happiness and freedom. This, the " supreme actualization of our ontological freedom can only take place when sustained by the logos of the world of values; " [3] " this is our liberty, when we are subordinate to the truth. " [4] This is our happiness, when we do the good. [5] Such a program does not reserve freedom

[1] Augustine, *De Morib. Eccl. Cath.*, I, 26, 48-49; PL 32, 1331, 1332 : Sed cætera videamus : videtur enim de homine ipso, id est, de amatore ipso nihil actum; sed parum dilucide qui hoc arbitratur intelligit. Non enim fieri potest ut seipsum, qui Deum diligit, non diligat : imo vero solus se novit diligere, qui Deum diligit. Si quidem ille se satis diligit, qui sedulo agit, ut summo et vero perfruatur bono : quod si nihil est aliud quam Deus, sicut ea quæ dicta sunt docuerunt, quis cunctari potest, quin sese amet, qui amator est Dei?... Te autem ipsum salubriter diligis, si plus quam te diligis Deum. Quod ergo agis tecum, id agendum cum proximo est; hoc est, ut ipse etiam perfecto amore diligat Deum.

[2] E. G. Salmon, *op. cit.*, p. 74 : " Thus the ontological good in reference to the maintenance of man as rational constitutes the basis of moral goodness. But the more the intellect of man is developed the more will he be disturbed by this making of the ontological good as being, a means or a thing subordinated to him as man, even as rational. Being as being he can see as good in itself and he will tend to the perfection of being as his end. The moral good and the ontological good as ultimate end coincide. "

[3] D. von Hildebrand, *op. cit.*, p. 327.

[4] Augustine, *De Lib. Arb.*, II, 13, 37; PL 32, 1261 : Hæc est libertas nostra, cum isti subdimur veritati.

[5] F. J. Thonnard, " Caractères Platoniciens de l'Ontologie Augustinienne, " p. 324 : " Le bien apparaît donc comme une propriété transcendentale qui appartient à tout être en tant que tel, variable avec sa place dans la hiérarchie des êtres; et de plus, selon le principe platonicien de participation, toutes ses réalisations, enfermées en une mesure déterminée,

for an intellectual aristocracy; it is within the power of all, and no man can effectively interfere with such freedom.

Following after God is the desire of happiness, to reach God is happiness itself. We follow after God by loving Him; we reach Him, not by becoming entirely what He is, but by nearness to Him, and by wonderful and immaterial contact with Him, and by becoming inwardly illuminated and occupied by His truth and holiness... And then, if nothing can separate us from His love, must not this be surer as well as better than any other good? [1]

Since this response to the Good is marked by a self-abandonment that is really a self-fulfillment, it is opposed to that self-centredness that is known as egoism in all its obvious and all its subtle forms. [2] It is important to realize that by our very nature we are called to conform to the good-in-itself, and therefore " following nature " means following the objective order of love. This is an essential philosophical implication in Augustine's description of theological freedom, for it brings to light the basic natural foundation of an " engraced freedom. "

CONCLUSION

We can conclude, therefore, that if man had spiritual or moral freedom, he would almost always be able to use the faculty of free choice as a power for doing good. This implies :

découlent du Bien Suprême qui est ainsi la cause de l'univers. ' Car, dit Saint Augustin, c'est parce que Dieu est bon que nous sommes bons. ' Et il ajoute, unissant selon son habitude synthétique, l'aspect moral aux considérations métaphysiques : ' D'autre part, c'est parce qu'il est, aussi, juste, que nous ne sommes pas mauvais impunément, et dans la mesure où nous sommes mauvais, dans cette même mesure aussi nous sommes moins. Car Celui-là est souverainement et primordialement, qui est absolument immuable et qui a pu dire en toute plénitude : Je suis celui qui suis... Ainsi les autres êtres ne peuvent exister que par lui, et ils ne sont bons que dans la mesure où ils ont reçu l'être ! ' " *De Doctrina Christiana*, I, 32, 35, PL 34, 32.

[1] Augustine, *De Morib. Ecc. Cath.*, I, 11, 18; PL 32, 1319 : Secutio igitur Dei, beatitatis appetitus est : consecutio autem, ipsa beatitas. At eum sequimur diligendo, consequimur vero, non cum hoc omnino efficimur quod est ipse, sed ei proximi, eumque mirifico et intelligibili modo contingentes, ejusque veritate et sanctitate penitus illustrati atque comprehensi... Item si nulla res ab ejus charitate nos separat, quid esse non solum melius, sed etiam certius hoc bono potest?

[2] M. Blondel, *op. cit.*, p. 446 : " ...et s'il y a un exode à subir pour atteindre Dieu, c'est en sortant de nos idolâtries et de notre égoïsme pour tendre à ce qui nous est plus intime que notre intimité; car je suis le plus souvent absent de moi, et l'hôte invisible est toujours au dedans. "

1. That he knows the truth, for freedom will be in proportion to the truth of one's knowledge;

2. That he is free from wanting things that conflict with his true good as man, for freedom will be in proportion to one's adherence to the order of love. Therefore, to be spiritually free is to will according to the truth and to love what you will. This makes one healthily independent of things, of others, and even of the law, but it ratifies the metaphysical dependence of the creature as one who receives being from above. Now, in the present situation of confused knowledge and divided tendencies, how can man be assured of the truth that will make him free, the love that will detach him from all so that he may attend to the truth?

3. That faith will lead man towards freedom by providing a higher and more certain truth than man could attain by himself.

4. That charity will give man a power to love God as God loves Himself.

There is still, however, the doing of the truth in charity which represents man's free cooperation with grace. Freed from ignorance and liberated from unworthy desires, man will be personally free to attain the perfection that comes with the consent to the Good. And so with respect to theological freedom we find that grace does not destroy man's natural liberty but perfects it.

CHAPTER IX

PLOTINUS AND AUGUSTINE

Have historians overemphasized the similarities between Plotinus and Augustine? Have they too readily classified the philosophical doctrines of Augustine as Neoplatonic? To determine how far such classification is justifiable, one must examine precise doctrinal points as they are exposed in the *Enneads* of Plotinus and in the works of Augustine. This we have tried to do with regard to free choice and freedom, only to discover that similar terminology concealed a real divergence on the subject of freedom.

In *Ennead* VI, 8 the discussion of freedom in man is a prelude to the consideration of freedom in the One. According to Plotinus, to be free is to be powerful. Plotinus sees man's power curtailed by adverse fortunes, by compulsions, passions, experiences, by nature; and this makes him doubt that man can dispose of himself, that he has self-mastery. Even after tracing self-disposal to the activities of Intellectual Principle where one lives above the states of the body, he is doubtful that freedom has been found. For, if to live by Intellectual Principle and by desire to be conformed to it, is to possess freedom, and yet desire, expressing need, causes activity — does this not contradict self-disposal? But who would not prefer his own good? Therefore : " Effort is free once it is towards a fully recognized good. " [1] And when the good is not external to the agent, there is no subjection to another. In this sense freedom can be asserted of Intellectual Principle. Thus, when the individual soul has been heightened to intellectual quality, our " ...freedom is found to lie not in act but in Intellectual Principle immune from act. " [2] According to Plotinus, then, " virtue is a mode

[1] *Enn.* VI, 8, 4.
[2] *Enn.* VI, 8, 5.

of Intellectual Principle..." [1] And when he inquires why freedom is connected with will, it develops that it is "...called will because it expresses the Intellectual Principle in its willing-phase." [2] Thus, "soul becomes free when it moves without hindrance through Intellectual Principle, towards The Good;" [3] in this way it acts as the unembodied, not as the governor of its body. Obeying the law of its higher nature, the soul is intellectually determined to rise above passions and earthly experiences, a state Plotinus calls self-mastery, because the self is one with its essence, and essence is the master. One must be oneself, that is, intellectual, in order to be free. Self-knowledge is knowledge of the Good, and this is freedom. [4] The freedom attributed to man by Plotinus is one that suppresses impotence by abstraction from all activity but intellection, a spontaneous *élan* towards the Good. When the Good is attained, there is Divine freedom because the soul then possesses the principle of its own satisfaction. [5] Since the One is as He wills to be, He alone is omnipotent, and so absolute freedom in God is being "solely and essentially that One Thing..." [6] Man rises through all the stages of reality to freedom in the One, where he is freed from all dependence, from all individuality, even from the memory of it.

If Plotinus is the last great philosopher of pagan antiquity and Augustine is the first great philosopher of Christian modernity, it is not surprising that Augustine's understanding of freedom should differ from the foregoing account of Plotinian freedom. This statement needs amplification. In the first place, we can recall that philosophical science gives essential knowledge, and the chief characteristic of intelligible being, essence, is necessity. By reflection on the universe any philosopher could come to a knowledge of the dependence of the world on an invisible cause, but could he also know that there was ever a time when the world did not so depend? Could he reason

[1] *Enn.* VI, 8, 6. — [2] *Enn.* VI, 8, 6.
[3] *Enn.* VI, 8, 7. — [4] *Enn.* V, 6, 5.
[5] *Enn.* VI, 8, 13.
[6] *Enn.* VI, 8, 15.

to the non-eternity of the world? Could he deduce rationally that the world is unnecessary?

If the pagan philosophers were able to reason to the truth that the world was created in time, the history of philosophy does not reveal that ability. Considering the world eternal, Aristotle accorded to man a temporal happiness of philosophical contemplative activity, a knowledge of the First Cause from his effects; and in order that man might enjoy this earthly paradise, his free choice was to be used to restrain all vagrant passion. Plato promised to the man who by his reason would make the dialectical ascent to the Idea of the Good a re-incarnation in better bodily conditions. Plotinus, stimulated by Aristotle to see the role of reason in liberty, [1] puzzled by the Platonic wavering between the descent of the soul as a willful act of audacity *(Phædo)* and its necessary role assigned by Providence in the making and ruling of the material world *(Timaeus)*, originated a wholly new conception of liberty. He made it a property of the best in man, the *Nous,* the intuitive phase of the human soul, withdrew liberty from any but intellective activity, and accented both its necessity and its liberty which he reconciled by defining the free act solely in relation to the Good. [2] The law of its being by which the soul yields to its best is the ontological desire for the Good, the *élan* that is the return movement to the One, as necessary as was the emanation. The return to unity is the return to transcendent independence, alone with the Alone. If the One is really transcendent to the universe, this liberty would consist in a self-transcendence that enables one to lose oneself in God, with no memory of the past. If the One is immanent in all men but transcendent to many insofar as they have not remembered their dignity and by a wholly interior recollection raised themselves to that apex of the soul whence they are called by *eros* to find their Good in self-awareness, this liberty would consist in self-possession, rest and independence, because of the possession of the Good.

[1] Paul Henry, S.J., "Le Problème de Liberté chez Plotin", *Revue Néo-Scolastique de Philosophie*, 1931, Louvain, XXXIII, p. 213.

[2] *Ibid.*

In any case, can we not say that Plotinus' conception of will is far superior to that of Aristotle because he does not confine will to the lower function of keeping order in the sensible world, but he describes it in terms of its relation to the good which is God? Yet Plotinus does not remove from this *élan* a " must. " He has seen that free choice is not the essence of liberty because it includes the possibility of a wrong choice; he has seen that true liberty comes from the pursuit of and finally the attainment of the Good, but he has not brought the desire for the Good under the power of free choice, and therefore has not given to man as a person any autonomy over his nature. It seems that the Plotinian return of man to God is accomplished as necessarily as was emanation. Yet as an observant philosopher, Plotinus could not deny the fact of free choice in the world and the responsibility of men for their actions; still less could he as a man be unaware of his own personal individuality to which free choice bears witness. Father Paul Henry, S. J. has thoroughly analyzed the texts in which Plotinus affirms the fact of human liberty, but he points out that these affirmations are not demonstrations. Plotinus argues against his deterministic contemporaries, the atomists, the Stoics, the astrologists, but his conclusion is that when the soul descends to the body, while it resides in the body, and when it leaves the body, it is both free and necessitated because it is constrained by an interior law, the working out of a rational necessity that Plotinus calls Providence; but so good is the law of being that man only departs from it involuntarily.[1]

The human liberty that Plotinus the man affirmed was contradicted by Plotinus the philosopher; not otherwise could all be explained by the One. Because Plotinus did not know from revelation of the free act of creation, he did not comprehend how liberty could be divorced from necessity. With his unaided mind he did not deduce the non-necessity of the world. God's simplicity, moreover, provides no *raison d'être* for

[1] Henry, *Plotin et l'Occident*, p. 55, p. 68. The treatises Father Henry refers to are: " On Destiny, " III, 1; " Of the Descent of the Soul into the Body, " IV, 8; " Difficulties relative to the soul, " IV, 3. Also, I, 4, 8, at the end of his life, and III, 2, 3.

the willing phase in man. As the object of intellection, the Good is identified with the intelligible. The *élan* towards the Good is really a tendency towards the intellectual love of God, the spontaneus natural appetite of the intellect for the true. There is never a word to indicate that man by his will is directed towards existence. The Good is seen as the principle of freedom but it is presented as the object of intellect. Free choice is recognized as implicit in human nature, but its role is not evaluated in relation to the perfection of reaching one's end. Man is given no power over this *élan* — to ratify or to reject. He is not given personal status, and therefore his relation is to goodness for himself rather than to communion with one whom he loves.

The *élan* for goodness born of need in the Plotinian soul can be contrasted with the gift of love that marks the Augustinian soul's activity. Love between persons is the glory of the Augustinian universe. The highest kind of being is personal being. To be a person is to be related to others: to be, and so to know and to love. It is not a case of which shall it be, intellectual or voluntary? To be a person is to be both. By knowing and loving, man has his highest experience of being, but this experience involves duality and plurality. To be a person is to be part of a social unit with God and with others.

Augustine, if he had read the treatise of Plotinus on liberty, would have concurred with him that the most profound aspect of liberty is to follow the law of ontological spiritual gravity, but to do this man must make decisions. It is not sufficient to wish for one's good. Who does not? If we refer to will-as-desire, and this seems to be the Platonic understanding of will, evil is involuntary. Will represents love for the good, because it is the faculty of man who was made "towards God." But if we refer to will-as-decision, evil is voluntary. Man decides that this particular object or action is good for him, although he knows that it is not in the line of his human finality and not really, therefore, his good. This power of substituting other ends for human nature may be called an impotence, but as an activity it is a positive entity. Are there not two possibilities involved in every power-entity? Water-power can be destructive as well as constructive; likewise, fire; likewise, atomic energy. We expect that when man has control over these forces only their constructive work will be done. But does not this depend on whether man has control over his own will and is using it according to its purpose, to love the Good for its supreme value, therein finding fulfilment, rest, peace? There are natural calamities from floods, fire, accidents which bring devastation, misery, but as long as these could not be avoided by human action, as long as they are not man-made, they are not tragedies in the true meaning of that word. A tragedy is man's failure to use his will constructively by choosing his true good. If there is no free choice in the world, there is no tragedy. The misery that comes through wrong decisions is man-made. In the full daylight knowledge of all the circumstances, of what he is doing and why he is doing it, as well as what he should be doing, man can set up an end that is not his good. Of course, he must see it as good in some respect, as pleasing or satisfying some aspect of his complex nature, but it is not his true good if he cannot choose it without repudiating his love for God, to whom by his highest powers he is dynamically related.

Not only did Augustine see the inevitable risk involved in the exercise of man's quasi-creative liberty, but he appreciated the choiceworthiness of the objects making up human existence in this world. In other words, while possessing a deep realization that the will was magnetized towards God, Augustine saw God in His world and saw, therefore, the tremendous temporal role of the will that enjoys the gifts of God and tries to civilize, to beautify, and by enterprising activity to better God's good world.

We are allowed to rejoice in those true and certain goods, which gleam even in the darkness of our present path. Is not this what Scripture tells us about the conduct of Wisdom towards her lovers, when they come and seek for her: *she shall show herself to them cheerfully in the ways and shall meet them with all providence*? [1]

[1] Augustine, *De Lib. Arb.*, II, 16, 41; PL 32, 1263: Et quod istis veris et certis bonis, quamvis adhuc in hoc tenebroso itinere coruscantibus, gaudere concessum est, vide utrum

The will can find worthy and wonderful objects to appease its unlimited longing for God; the only thing that Augustine asks is that the relation of the beautiful or lovable object to God, its Creator, should not be overlooked. The relation to God is the necessary lodestone in voluntary activity. Augustine realized that although man has free choice because he is intellectual and is able to know of his spiritual and infinite end in a general way, thereby raising him above subservience to any particular thing, he only has freedom in the broad sense when the Good inspires his love and brings him to choose well. To love rightly and efficaciously through right desire for the true Good and through good choices is to become free. If man cannot do this on his own because of contrary tendencies and miseries, he can always turn to God whose desire is there before his own. God will give the efficacy to make one's choices ratify one's natural orientation to the Good. It is in the realm of free choice that man needs the help of God; [1] for all men naturally desire the Good, though not all choose it.

If Plotinus advanced the notion of freedom by recognizing Goodness to be its principle, Augustine revealed the reality of freedom when he described it as the fruit of love, Divine Love lifting man above slavery to creatures by giving him the Divine Will as the inspiration of human actions, and human love that enters the Divine intimacy through union with the Divine Will. If free choice is an inferior kind of liberty when compared with the blissful freedom of a being in possession of its end, its dignity is great if the freedom that comes from completion is unattainable without it and without the proper functioning of free choice. While Augustine and Plotinus agree that man's wrong choices reveal a powerlessness, an unenviable impotence to hold to the best, Augustine sees the positive side

hoc sit quod scriptum est de sapientia quid agat cum amatoribus suis cum ad eam veniunt, et eam quærunt : dictum est enim, '*In viis ostendet se illis hilariter, et omni providentia occurret illis.*' (Sap. VI, 17).

[1] Augustine, *Expos. Quar. Propos. ex Ep. ad Rom.*, 13; PL 35, 2066 : Gratia vero efficit ut non tantum velimus recte facere, sed etiam possimus; non viribus nostris, sed Liberatoris auxilio, qui nobis etiam perfectam pacem in resurrectione tribuet, quæ pax perfecta bonam voluntatem consequitur.

of free choice as man's unique affirmation and personal preference for the Infinite when he chooses things that are not only good in themselves but good for him as God has made him. The man of action is therefore not without communion with God, a communion effected by free choice. By his decisions man allows God to become the principle of his freedom.

Decision indicates not only that there is a judgment between a hierarchy of goods — the good of the intellect, which is truth, the good of the senses, pleasurable and perceptible objects appealing to various aspects of human nature but that there is an end, the Good, for the human person, which somehow presents itself in the various objects offered to free will, the faculty of the person. [1] This end cannot be chosen in every good thing, although all things are good insofar as they are. If the choice of anything at all were the choice of one's end, there would indeed be no reason for free choice, no particular point to decision; moreover all would be chosen in relation to oneself. On the other hand, man can by reason or faith come to a knowledge that his end is a Subject, supreme possessor of Personal Existence, infinitely superior to man, whose gift of being to man witnesses to His love for man as well as to His rights over man. When a personal God is realized to be man's end, every decision is a personal preference for Him, and that is why the flight to the Fatherland will, according to Augustine, take the form of submission to the Truth through love. This submission is shown when very good things, that is, ontologically good, are not chosen by man because in choosing them man would have to decide against God's wishes, as expressed in the finality of human nature known by reason, or in His revealed laws. While love for the End ought to be the deciding factor in human free choice, the various goods offered to man may quite definitely engage his love. The sensible can well be the object of human choice, for in Augustine's view the sensible as such is not an obstacle to man's attainment of his end.

[1] Augustine, *De Duab. Anim. contra Manich.*, XII, 17; PL 42, 107; *Retract.*, II, 9-10; PL 32, 634; *De Spirit. et Litt.*, XXXIV, 60; PL 44, 240, 241; *De Pecc. Mer. et Rem.*, I, 35, 65; PL 44, 147, 148; *De Natura et Gratia*, XXXIV, 39; PL 44, 266.

For Plotinus, free will is exercised by interior recollection, by identifying as far as possible the self with Intellectual Principle, by a conformity of the mind to the Good, an interior intellectual disposition. In practical action in a world of cosmic consequences, we should not expect anything to depend on us. Therefore, human liberty for Plotinus is an intellectual tendency towards the Good, and that is why he defines virtue as a mode of Intellectual Principle. Quite other is the position of Augustine: " I think that a short and true definition of virtue is: it is the order of love. "[1] Augustine realized that the contemplation of the One could not take place merely because of the natural appetite of the Intellect for its good, that is, for truth, when so many other natural appetites in human nature clamored with greater insistence for their goods. If man were to withdraw himself from other things, it would have to be because he loved something else more than these.[2] The choice of the will, allied with man's natural *élan* towards Goodness, would have the power to withdraw attention from all counter-claims.

Augustine shows us that attachment is the solution to the problem of detachment. What is perhaps more important, he faces the problem of attachment as Plotinus did not. It is a personal call and response, a dialogue before it is a decision. Because attachment is not merely evaluation, the intellect is insufficient; there must also be appreciation, which implies a willingness to pay the price entailed by surrender to the value. For this surrender the will is needed, and if the price is to be paid, the will must be master. It is " love " which gives to the will this mastery. " My love is my weight; by it I am carried wherever I am carried. "[3] As weight gravitates a body towards its natural position, so love moves the will and with it the human person.

[1] Augustine, *De Civ. Dei*, XV, 22; PL 41, 467: Unde mihi videtur, quod definitio brevis et vera virtutis, ordo est amoris.

[2] Augustine, *Sol.*, I, 14, 24; PL 32, 882: Non enim puto posse mihi hæc in summum venire contemptum, nisi videro illud in cujus comparatione ista sordescant. *De Div. Quæst. 83*, I, 66, 7; PL 40, 66: Subditur enim nobis quod inferius nostrum est, quod propterea non subdebatur, quia superiorem nobis deserueramus Deum.

[3] Augustine, *Confess.*, XIII, 9, 10; PL 32, 849: Pondus meum, amor meus; eo feror quocumque feror.

In the light of this we better understand why God has revealed himself as Love. Because God is Love He can beget love in man and move men towards Him, their End, through their love — this is in truth the omnipotence of God. God is powerful not merely over irrational beings who cannot resist His laws but over free beings whom He moves by love. Because of the Divine Simplicity, the Will of God is never found apart from His Love.

Fearful to speak of the freedom of the One lest this imply duality, Plotinus nevertheless speaks of a will in God lest silence on this subject should imply a natural necessity that would detract from the Divine Omnipotence. To preclude duality, Plotinus immediately identifies the will with the One. Now, this mention of will and even of love has led some to consider that Plotinus has witnessed to the Personality of the One. Yet the cosmos emanates forth from the One by the necessity of nature without any dimunition of the One [1] and without knowledge or desire for its return on the part of the One. Does not this bespeak a dynamism rather than a person? Contrast this notion with Augustine's God : freely creative, not dynamically through processive necessity, but lovingly, through generosity : a completely free gift of Divine Love whose proper effect is being. The transcendence of God was not jeopardized by His love for the world; the hierarchical order of true values is safeguarded; the distinction between the infinite and the finite is clear. " The Will of God is the Cause of heaven and earth and that is why it is superior to heaven and earth. " [2] Hence, the human soul returns to God by means of its will and freely. The return will be accomplished with God's knowledge and with His help, through grace. Yet even when man shares the life of God by grace, human love will always bear the mark of the infinite distance between Creator and creature. Therefore, Augustine says : " The mind returns to God by love which presses it not to equate itself with God but to submit to Him. " [3]

[1] *Enn.* II, 2, 2.

[2] Augustine, *De Genesi contra Manich.*, I, 2, 4; PL 34, 175 : Voluntas enim Dei causa est cœli et terræ, et ideo major est voluntas Dei quam cœlum et terra.

[3] Augustine, *De Moribus Ecc. Cath.*, I, 12, 21; PL 32, 1320 : Dilectione igitur redit in Deum qua se illi non componere, sed supponere affectat.

With freedom absent at the origin of the Plotinian universe, one is not surprised at its absence in the means of return to the One. Plotinus says : " ... the soul other than God but sprung of Him must needs love. " [1] We have seen that for Plotinus this love is an *élan* of intellection. The means suggested by Plotinus for those who wish to " become like unto God," is to become as intellectual as possible. [2] This " becoming like to God" *(similem Deo fieri)* sums up the moral teaching of Plato and Plotinus. It is mentioned in *Ennead* I, 6, the treatise " On the Beautiful," where we learn that escape from the outer world produces this likeness. " What then is our course, what the manner of our flight? This is not a journey for the feet; the feet bring us only from land to land; nor need you think of coach, or ship, to carry you away; all this order of things you must set aside and refuse to see : you must close the eyes and call instead upon another vision which is to be waked within you, a vision, the birth-right of all, which few turn to use. " [3] " ...Now call up all your confidence, strike forward yet a step — you need a guide no longer — strain, and see... To any vision must be brought an eye adapted to what is to be seen, and having some likeness to it... Therefore, first, let each become godlike... " [4]

Now we know that Augustine had this treatise before his eyes because in his explanation of Psalm 149, he said : " ...we enter not by ships, or chariots or feet..., " but " ...by Charity. " " ...Let them lay hold on the two wings of love. What are the two wings of love? The love of God and of our neighbor. " [5] This addition transforms the meaning. The way to enter into Beauty, into the Fatherland, is not by running away but by running forward, not by escape but by love. Augustine states in the *Confessions* that the *will* is the im-

[1] *Enn.* VI, 9, 9. " Other than " here refers not to nature but to condition.
[2] *Enn.* VI, 9, 3 and 7 and 9; IV, 7, 10.
[3] *Enn.* I, 6, 8.
[4] *Enn.* I, 6, 9.
[5] Augustine, *Enarr. in Ps.* CXLIX, 5; PL 37, 1952 : Qui ergo in hac vita gemunt et desiderant illam patriam, currant dilectione, non pedibus corporis; non quærant naves sed pennas; duas alas charitatis apprehendant. Quæ sunt duæ alæ charitatis? Dilectio Dei, et proximi.

portant way to the state of similarity; to reach that state "...was simply to will to go — but to will resolutely and thoroughly; not to turn and toss, this way and that, a maimed and half-divided will, struggling, with one part sinking as another arises." [1] Augustine recognizes that the natural foundation for the attainment of a personal end is a resolute will. As a realist he admits the wounded condition of the will; as a philosopher he knows the absolute transcendence of God; as a believer he came to understand that only the mercy of God has bridged the infinite spaces between man and God; as a convert he has reached that bridge by the humble prayer of his contrite heart. Do these facts not account for the difference between *Ennead* I, 6, 9 as quoted above and Augustine's tale in *Confessions*, VII, 10: "I entered into my inward self, Thou being my guide, and able I was, for Thou wert become my helper." [2] If God really is the end of man, He must also be the way. Only if man is God can he do without the help of God. The world was to return to God as it had come forth by the free action of God, but with this difference: man must consent. If man did not refuse to accept his being from God, why should he refuse to accept his perfection from God? In the gift of being, man was not consulted; in the gift of perfection through grace, man's consent is needed. Augustine sees life as a choice between efficacy in doing the good by way of humility, and impotence by way of pride. Augustine himself, guided by Simplicianus, pointed out the *lacuna* of the Plotinian philosophy with its high pretensions when he said: "For where was that charity, building upon the foundation of humility, which is Christ Jesus? or when would these books teach it to me?" [3]

Thus the expression, *similem Deo fieri,* has with Plotinus and with Augustine a different meaning. That is why a collection

[1] Augustine, *Confess.*, VIII, 8; PL 32, 758: Nam non solum ire, verum etiam pervenire illuc, nihil erat aliud quam velle ire, sed velle fortiter et integre; non semisauciam hac atque hac versare et jactare voluntatem, parte assurgente cum alia parte cadente luctantem.

[2] Augustine, *Confess.*, VII, 10; PL 32, 742: Et inde admonitus redire ad memetipsum intravi in intima mea, duce te; et potui, quoniam factus es adjutor meus.

[3] Augustine, *Confess.*, VII, 20; PL 32, 747: Ubi enim erat illa ædificans charitas a fundamento humilitatis, quod est Christus Jesus? Aut quando illi libri docerent me eam?

of parallel passages between the two authors, although it has its importance for determining the literary dependence of one author upon another [1] does not conclude to a similarity of doctrine. An identity of vocabulary and similarity of structure might serve only to accentuate their difference in spirit. It is, as Jean Guitton [2] has remarked, the spirit that specifies the character of philosophies and religions. The spirit of an author is more important than his words. By the spirit we mean the informing principle, the implicit thought that is not set down in thesis-form but which circulates everywhere, creating the atmosphere for the words that are used in order that they may connote the desired meaning. The spirit of an author regulates the use he makes of the materials at his disposal and the order he establishes among them. In the *Enneads,* for example, there circulates a spirit of intellectualism, and the words previously quoted from *Ennead* I, 6 are saturated with this atmosphere. In the works of Augustine there is a spirit of wisdom, and the Augustinian description of the return of the soul to God through a loving and free will is in harmony with such a spirit.

If in the Augustinian synthesis similarity to God is wrought by good choices, inspired by a love for God that God Himself makes actual, it is not surprising to discover that Augustine attributes man's entrance into the "land of unlikeness" to sin that has the human will as its sole cause. This marks a divergence from Plotinus. Because in the system of Plotinus the contingent has no place, the reality of free choice cannot be philosophically recognized. The result is that Plotinus does not distinguish

[1] This literary dependence of Augustine on Plotinus has been set forth by Paul Henry, S.J. in his scholarly work : *Plotin et l'Occident*, Louvain, 1943, pp. 105-145 :

De Civ. Dei, X, 16 — *Enn.* I, 6, 7, 30-39.
De Civ. Dei, IX, 17 — *Enn.* I, 6, 8, 16-27.
Conf., VII, X, 16 — *Enn.* I, 6.
De Civ. Dei, X, 14 — *Enn.* III, 2, 13, 18-29.
De Civ. Dei, IX, 10 — *Enn.* IV, 3, 12.
De Civ. Dei, X, 30 — *Enn.* IV, 3, 12.
De Civ. Dei, X, 23 — *Enn.* V, 1.
De Civ. Dei, X, 2 — *Enn.* V, 1 and 6.

[2] Jean Guitton, *Le Temps et l'Eternité chez Plotin et Saint Augustin*, Paris, Boivin, 1933.

moral evil from metaphysical evil. He does try to point a difference insofar as he admits that man is responsible for evil — but this evil always seems unduly linked with matter, an over-attention or absorption with material things. To fly from evil is to fly from matter. [1] This has some embarrassing consequences. If matter is evil, it either derives from the One and evil is essential, or matter is non-being, absolute nothingness. [2] Augustine did say that he had learned from "a certain philosopher" that evil was negative. Yet did he notice that Plotinus had designated matter as evil? If Augustine did not accept this position, could it not be that he did not get his first illumination about evil directly from the *Enneads*? In any case, the position of Augustine and of Plotinus on the origin of moral evil is another focal point of contrast intimately connected with their respective doctrines of free will and freedom. For Augustine, matter is not evil, [3] and matter is not non-being [4]. Nor is evil in any way necessary, since the universe is the work of a free will infinitely good and wise. [5] Augustine had to be delivered from the Manichaean doctrine that placed evil outside the evildoer as the work of a bad principle; but could he ever have been delivered from this error by the Plotinian doctrine of evil: evil an inexplicable scandal, a cosmic necessity, an enigma, inherent in matter

[1] Philippus Villiers Pistorius, *Plotinus and Neoplatonism*, Cambridge, Bowes & Bowes, 1952. This interpreter disagrees with all preceding commentators on Plotinus when he asserts that the three Hypostases are only three aspects of One God.

[2] *Enn.* I, 8, 7; cf. H. Armstrong, "Spiritual or intelligible matter in Plotinus and St. Augustine," p. 277, *Augustinus Magister*, I.

[3] Augustine, *De Natura Boni*, XVIII; PL 42, 556.

[4] Augustine, *De Quantitate Animæ*, XXXIII, 76; PL 32, 1076.
Cf. *Sermo* 241; PL 38, 1137, 1138. Here he contrasts the teaching of Porphyry on flight from the body with the teaching of Christ on the resurrection of the body. When in *Confess*: VII, 9 Augustine *ends* his account of how much knowledge of God he received and did not receive from Platonic books, he begins in VII, 10 to tell what *he* realized with God's help. 1) that the infinite truth (affirmed by Plotinus) was God and so, Being — for in his heart Augustine heard God identifying Himself with Truth by saying "I am Who Am"; 2) that God is also incorruptible Goodness, and by reflection on this he saw that things are and are good "in as much as they are from You." 3) Then we read: "My own experience had shown me..." (*Confess.* VII, 16), and "So that when I now asked what is iniquity, I realized that it was not a substance but a swerving of the *will* which is turned towards lower things *and* away from You, O God..."

[5] Augustine, *De Libero Arbitrio*, III, 9, 24-25; PL 32, 1283.

which emanates from the One, or else a supreme illusion of the senses, not really existing at all?

This conception of evil is one of the tensions in the Plotinian system. It stems from Plotinus' original conception of conversion based on the theory that there is no difference of nature but only a difference of degree between time and eternity. Plotinus' intuition that the metaphysical problem of the origin of things and the moral problem of the salvation of souls are two faces of the one problem [1] does find ultimate justification in the fact that the Absolute is both the Ontological Good and the Moral Good identified. But to understand the relation of these two aspects of the Good on the finite plane one would need an adequate understanding of human nature and a correct metaphysical knowledge of the world's origin and end. In a metaphysics of necessary and natural emanation, where there is no real difference between the finite and the infinite, the moral good and the ontological good must be identified, and the ontologically best will be the fitting object of man's natural *élan* towards Goodness. To be his best self by forsaking all that is inferior will be man's moral program. Plotinus was trying to do justice to the soul conceived as an organizing force of the body and the soul as the seat of destiny. His efforts leave unanswered the question of whether the contact of the soul with the body results from its normal functioning or whether it results from the soul's vices.

Bréhier [2] says that this interior contradiction represents the meeting in Plotinus of different traditions concerning the soul. There is the Pythagorean conception as set forth in the *Phaedo* whereby the body is a punishment, the pride and audacity of the soul having plunged it into matter; there is the later Platonic conception of the body as good, a view that can be found in the *Timaeus* and the *Laws*. [3] This is however but the particular expression of a larger conflict in the thought of Plotinus,

[1] Emile Bréhier, *La Philosophie de Plotin*, Paris, Boivin, p. 23.

[2] *Ibid.*, chapter 5.

[3] *Enn.* IV, 8, 5; *Enn.* V, 1, 2.

between the representation of the universe as a rational order and the representation of the universe as a place of destiny. [1] This tension accounts for the inconsistency that arises when Plotinus speaks of personal responsibility. Some readers of the *Enneads* have considered that by these remarks Plotinus made a place for individual human freedom. We recall the detailed analysis of such passages by Père Henry, S. J. and his conclusion that Plotinus affirmed individual human freedom but did not admit in into his system. If Plotinus asserts the reality of free choice without explaining it, is not this an indication of his seeing more truth than he could fit into his system? [2] In similar strain he has affirmed the absolute transcendence of the One to the cosmic system, approachable only mystically and by gift from above, while he has explained the world as a hierarchy of reality necessarily knit to the First Principle from which it emanates; therefore by ascending this hierarchy of the spiritual life to become *Nous,* man prepares himself for the return to Unity. [3]

All this makes for a great optimism in Plotinian philosophy and moral life, explicable perhaps by the implicit assumption of the divine quality of the universe, the best of all possible worlds. If the philosophical system of Plotinus did not include human freedom, the religious thought of Plotinus did. If this created a thought-tension with regard to the nature of man, it is not unlikely that we will find it reflected in the Plotinian description of the One. The return of the soul to universality in the Divine Mind is valued above the preservation of personal individuality, and the One is said to be beyond being, beyond thought, beyond love.

In studying the relations of God with the world, Augustine came to see man as the image of God. God had freely created the universe, attaching it to Himself by love. He knew the

[1] Bréhier, *Phil. de Plot.*, p. 24.

[2] A. H. Armstrong, *An Introduction to Ancient Philosophy*, Westminster, Maryland, Newman Press, 1949, p. 175.

[3] *Ibid.*, p. 185.

world and loved it into existence. Thus man can come through visible things to a knowledge of God and attach himself to God through love. [1] But it is God's desire that is activating without necessitating the soul's return to Him. As creation is the expression of the free love of God, so grace is the expression of that love still active to effect man's return to Him. Likeness to God, according to Augustine, is found in love. The autonomy of man is best signified by the ability of the person to go out of himself in love for others. This is the mark of the Supreme Personal Being in His relations with the universe. When man images the generous love of God in his relations with others, he is really like unto God. When such love is the principle of human activity, man is free to respond to God more intensely and extensively because he is freed from the narrow confines of one portion of finite being which can never satisfy the infinite thirst for being that belongs to man.

But if so early in his career Augustine was convinced that love makes the soul like God and gives to man a freedom for the Good, and if he very early wrote a treatise on free choice in which he stated that man's free will is the cause of evil, and if these facts are contrary to the Plotinian and the Manichaean doctrines, — whence have they come? Against the internal evidence of the very real divergence between Plotinus and Augustine that we have noted exists on the topic of freedom, it is the opinion of Prosper Alfaric that Augustine's doctrine is thoroughly Neoplatonic. In the pages he devotes to an analogy between the *De Libero Arbitrio* of Augustine and the *Enneads* of Plotinus, Prosper Alfaric [2] has taken from each author isolated statements that say the same thing but which, when replaced in their native context, have a different meaning. A certain literal confrontation of independent statements without similar vocabulary does not even argue to a literary dependence, and in this case not to a doctrinal dependence, because the meaning of the term freedom is not taken by Plotinus

[1] Augustine, *De Morib. Eccles. Cath.*, I, 14, 24; PL 32, 1321.

[2] Prosper Alfaric, *L'Evolution Intellectuelle de Saint Augustin*, Paris, Nourry, 1918, pp. 476-506.

and Augustine in the same sense. The very fact that Augustine chooses as the title of his philosophical investigation of human freedom *De Libero Arbitrio,* and not *De Libertate* is significant. It is true that Augustine concludes at the end of Book I that we cannot understand human liberty unless we see it in God from whom it comes. But to understand free choice from the vantage point of its goal, the end towards which it is orientated, is not to dismiss its reality nor its importance. Plotinus merely said that he would examine free will in man to see whether such a combination of power and impotence could be found in the Supreme. Augustine, enamoured of the Divine Freedom that can choose only the good, sees free choice as man's only way to reach this state. And so he concludes that free will, the deficient cause of sin, nevertheless comes from God, and is therefore able to image the Divine choice of the good when it allows itself to be moved by Love. One can only conclude that P. Alfaric's opinion is not founded on the context of the statements he has isolated. We do not know for certain that Augustine read *Ennead* VI, 8, and if he did, was it around the period of his conversion or after writing the *De Libero Arbitrio*? [1]

If Augustine did not obtain his philosophical education directly from Plotinus, what was the source of those Augustinian doctrines which, though somewhat Neoplatonic in expression, yet differ utterly in spirit and meaning from the Plotinian doctrine of freedom? If Augustine followed Plotinus in the elucidation of his doctrine of free will and freedom as closely as P. Alfaric has assumed, did not Augustine in the *Confessions* falsely minimize the intellectual influence upon him of the Neoplatonic writings? Moreover, if Ambrose had no intellectual influence over Augustine, would not Augustine's continual affirmation of the Ambrosian influence in the *Confessions* be a fraud? On the contrary, if Augustine discovered in the sermons of Ambrose a Christian Neoplatonism, his references in the *Confessions* to the wealth and the poverty of the Neoplatonic books becomes

[1] Cf. E. Benz, *Marius Victorinus und die Entwicklung des Abendlandischen Willensbegriffs von Plotin bis Augustin*, Stuttgart, W. Kohlhammer, 1932.

understandable. If so, there is no such question as : Was Augustine converted first to Neoplatonism and then to Catholicism, or first to Catholicism and then to Neoplatonism? With Augustine, faith and reason came together, to lead eventually to his moral conversion. Such is the considered opinion of Pierre Courcelle, whose careful analysis of all the factors in his scholarly work [1] seems to end the struggle between the traditionalists who held that it was to Catholicism and not to Neoplatonism that Augustine was first converted and the " critics " who held that the reverse was true.

Pierre Courcelle maintains that in Milan during the years that Augustine listened to the sermons of Ambrose an intellectual and religious conversion was taking place. Catholic positions and Plotinian reasons were simultaneously heard. What accounts for this? Ambrose was a close friend of Marius Victorinus who translated and perhaps paraphrased the works of Plotinus and Porphyry, as well as a friend of Simplicianus who shared with Ambrose his Plotinian culture. The hypothesis that Ambrose was the channel of Augustine's first acquaintance with Plotinus is strengthened by the evidence presented by Courcelle [2]: the sermons of Ambrose reveal parallels to passages of the *Enneads* and of the *De Regressu Animæ* of Porphyry, and when these passages are quoted by Augustine they are presented not in their Plotinian form but with the Ambrosian modifications.

In claiming that Augustine was intellectually influenced by Ambrose, it is not to be denied that he had direct access to the *Enneads* themselves, but that he read them only after much of their doctrine had been heard from Ambrose. [3] When Augustine

[1] Pierre Courcelle, *Recherches sur les Confessions de St. Augustin*, Paris, E. de Boccard, 1950.

[2] Following P. Courcelle, scholars are discovering more parallels between Ambrose and Plotinus. Aimé Solignac, S.J., " Nouveaux Parallèles entre Saint Ambroise et Plotin ", *Archives de Philosophie*, Avril, 1956 (148-156), p. 156 : " On le voit, c'est ainsi des morceaux entiers de Plotin qu'Ambroise remplie dans ses traites. Il semble difficile de nier que les textes mêmes fussent sous ses yeux au moment de la rédaction. Il est fort probable que des recherches portant sur les écrits d'Ambroise qui se situent autour de 386 (c'est-à-dire autour de l'année qui marque la conversion de saint Augustin) amèneraient encore de nouvelles preuves de l'influence plotinienne. Une autre étude de M. Hadot sur ce sujet allait paraître dans la *Revue des Etudes latines*. "

[3] In a letter written about 412 or 413, Augustine says : " If you agree, take up with me the statement of the holy man, Ambrose, which is founded, not on his authority, but on the truth

called upon Ambrose for help in understanding the reality of spiritual substance, Ambrose sent him to Manlius Theodorus who loaned him the Latin translations of the *Enneads* by Victorinus. Among the treatises read by Augustine at this time there is no mention of *Ennead* VI, 8. Professor Paul Henry, S. J. has proved by philological methods [1] that Augustine at this time read "On Beauty," and "On the Three Chief Hypostases." Pierre Courcelle speaks of the intense attention given to the treatise "On Beauty," I, 6, 8, and he accounts for this by the fact that Ambrose had made great use of this same treatise in the sermon *De Isaac* VIII, 77, 78 with modifications which are echoed in Augustine's own references to the treatise in *Enarrationes in Psalmos* CXLIX, 3; PL 37, 1952; *Confessions* I, 18, 28; PL 32, 673, 674; *De Civitate Dei*, IX, 17; PL 41, 271. But as Father Paul Henry has shown, [2] the young Augustine was interested in this subject long before he met or heard Ambrose, having written a treatise entitled "*De Pulchro et Apto*," and this explains his excitement. P. Courcelle holds that Augustine at this time also read the *De Regressu Animæ* of Porphyry [3] but this has not been conclusively shown, and Professor Henry is not convinced of it.

From Augustine's own account we learn that it was after reading these books that he had the famous ecstasy at Milan, a vain attempt to reach God philosophically. Discouraged by his dissimilitude to God which he could not change, Augustine visited Simplicianus from whom he received religious, intellectual and moral help, with advice to read the Scriptures and compare them with the *Enneads*. From Simplicianus Augustine heard the remarkable tale of the conversion

itself. My reason for liking it is not because the Lord *freed me from error by his words* and granted me the grace of saving baptism by his ministry, as if I should be too partial to the one who planted and watered me, but because, in this matter, he said what God who giveth the increase says to the soul which meditates devoutly and understands rightly. He said then: 'Even in the resurrection itself it is not easy to see God, except for those who are clean of heart...' " *Epistle* 147, 52; PL 33, 621-622 (italics mine).

[1] Paul Henry, S.J., *Plotin et l'Occident*, pp. 78-119, 128.

[2] Paul Henry, S.J., *op. cit.*, p. 117.

[3] Pierre Courcelle, *Les Lettres Grecques en Occident*, Paris, E. de Boccard, 1943, pp. 161-168.

of Victorinus, and he was stirred by it. We recall that he then received a visit from Pontitianus who vividly described three radical conversions and thereby provided the psychological motivation which led Augustine to read the message of St. Paul as a message from God to Augustine. This was the moral conversion.

But the intellectual influence of Ambrose was not yet over. According to Courcelle, after the retreat at Cassiciacum, Augustine went to Milan and was prepared for baptism by Ambrose whose homilies on Luke and Isaias he devoutly heard. Augustine testifies that they taught him " the profound designs that God has for the salvation of the human race. " [1] After the baptism, conversations with Ambrose continued until Augustine left Milan. The next great event was the vision at Ostia. This vision just before Monica's death was still quite Plotinian, as described, but it differed from the former disappointing experience of Milan by the presence of hope for the beatific vision which the possession of grace now gave to Augustine. He knew that the one moment of understanding he sighed after would be made perpetual when he at last entered into the Master's joy. Since the radical change that had taken place in Augustine, there never could be a thought, a desire or an experience in his life that would be purely Plotinian.

Pierre Courcelle has adequately shown that in the milieu of Augustine there was no opposition between Hellenism and Christianity, and he has done this by transposing the old problem of " Neoplatonism tainted with Christianity " or " Christianity tainted with Neoplatonism " from the doctrinal to the philological plane. After his scholarly and extensive findings it becomes increasingly apparent that P. Alfaric's separation of philosophical influences from religious influences, or moral influences from intellectual influences, is unfounded. [2]

[1] Augustine, *Confess.*, IX, 6, 14; PL 32, 769 : Nec satiabar illis diebus dulcedine mirabili, considerare altitudinem consilii tui super salutem generis humani.

[2] P. Alfaric, *L'Evol. Intell. de S. Aug.*, pp. 380-381, n. 1 : " Augustin a donc adopté e platonisme avant de donner son adhésion au christianisme, et il ne s'est rallié au second que

Was it then from statements of Ambrose and not from the *Enneads* that Augustine obtained his high regard for free choice, his complete conviction that freedom in the broad sense is the gift of God through grace, and not given without both human consent and human effort through the exercise of free choice? Pierre Courcelle does indicate some precise passages where Ambrose treats of free will: *Hexameron,* VI, 7, 40; *Hexameron,* I, 8, 31; *De Jacob* I, 1 and I, 10; *De Isaac,* VII, 61. [1] But is Courcelle justified in saying that this teaching on free choice was Plotinian simply because Plotinus while admitting the formula of Plato, "No one is voluntarily evil," maintains personal responsibility? [2] We have seen that an isolated statement like this runs counter to Plotinus' thorough intellectualism and his implicit pantheism. It is perhaps closer to the truth to hold that Ambrose had emphasized free choice because it is a cardinal doctrine of Christian salvation, a doctrine that could be found implicit in all the commands that Scripture records, a doctrine that was explicitly taught by Origen in *De Principiis* : Preface, 5; I, 5, 2; II, 6, 5; II, 6, 6; I, 6, 3.

But Augustine's own experience with will tended to make him doubt man's power over it; as he says : "When I was deliberating about serving the Lord my God, as I had long meant to do, it was I who willed to do it, I who was unwilling. It was I. I did not wholly will, I was not wholly unwilling." [3] But this experience of his was illuminated when Augustine read St. Paul. [4]

parce qu'il l'a, après examen, jugé conforme au premier... Même dans la suite, il a tenu quelque temps à la doctrine de Plotin bien qu'au dogme Catholique." P. 399 : "Moralement comme intellectuellement, c'est au néo-platonisme qu'il s'est converti plutôt qu'à l'Evangile." To these statements E. Gilson, reviewing the book in *Revue Philosophique*, t. LXXXVIII, 1919, p. 503, replied that if Augustine admitted free creation and the equality of the Divine Persons he is clearly Christian and not Plotinian.

[1] Courcelle, *Recherches sur les Confessions de Saint Augustin*, p. 100, note 5. Ambrose, *Hexam*. I, 8, 31 : non igitur ab *extraneis* est *nobis* quam a *nobis* ipsis maius periculum. Quorum igitur *nos* sumus domini, horum principia *extrinsecus* non requiramus nec dirivemus in *alios*, sed agnoscamus ea quæ propria nostra sunt. Quod enim possumus non facere si *nolimus*, huius electionem mali *nobis* potius debemus, quam *aliis* ascribere. Cf. *Conf.*, VII, 3, 5; PL 32, 735 : Sublevabat enim me in lucem tuam, quod tam sciebam *me* habere voluntatem, quam me vivere. Itaque cum aliquid vellem aut *nollem*, non *alium* quam *me* velle ac *nolle* certissimus eram et ibi esse causam peccati iam iamque animadvertebam.

[2] *Enn.* III, 2, 10. But Cf. *Enn.* III, 2, 11 : "Reason-Principle is the Sovereign, making all."

[3] Augustine, *Confess.*, VIII, 10, 22; PL 32, 759 : Ego eram, qui volebam, ego, qui nolebam.

[4] Augustine, *Confess.*, VII, 21, 27; PL 32, 748.

There he discovered the reason for the will's inefficacy and the remedy for it. If Plotinus spoke blissfully of the soul's desire for the good, the source of its freedom, Paul speaks of Christ as the liberator of man who makes efficacious man's desire after paying a high price for that freedom. Augustine tells us in the *Confessions* (Book VII) that he found in the epistles of St. Paul all the truth he had read in the books of the Platonists and much more, because they told him of grace which one needs to know in order to understand the whole story of man. Augustine says :

For, though a man be delighted with the law of God after the inner man, what shall he do with that other law in his members which warreth against the law of his mind, and bringeth him into captivity to the law of sin which is in his members? For Thou art righteous, O Lord, but we have sinned and committed iniquity, and have done wickedly, and Thy hand is grown heavy upon us, and we are justly delivered over unto that ancient sinner, the king of death; because he persuaded our will to be like his will whereby he abode not in Thy truth. What shall wretched man do? What shall deliver him from the body of his death, but only Thy Grace, through Jesus Christ our Lord, whom Thou hast begotten co-eternal, and formedst in the beginning of Thy ways, in whom the prince of this world found nothing worthy of death, yet killed he Him; and the handwriting which was contrary to us was blotted out? *This those writings contain not*. Those pages present not the image of this piety, the tears of confession, Thy sacrifice, a troubled spirit, a broken and contrite heart, the salvation of the people, the bridal city, the promise of the Holy Ghost, the cup of our redemption. No man sings there, " Shall not my soul be submitted unto God for of Him cometh my salvation. " ... No one hears him call, " Come unto Me, all ye that labour. " They scorn to learn of Him, because He is meek and lowly in heart...

... For it is one thing, from the mountain's shaggy top to see the land of peace, and to find no way thither; and in vain to essay through ways unpassable, opposed and beset by fugitives and deserters, under their captain the lion and the dragon : and another to keep on the way that leads thither, guarded by the host of the heavenly General... These things did wonderfully sink into my bowels, when I read that least of Thy apostles, and meditated upon Thy works, and trembled exceedingly. [1]

[1] Augustine, *Confess.*, VII, 21; PL 32, 748 (italics mine).

It was from the Scriptures, also, that Augustine became sure that man was the source of moral evil, which originates in his soul and, precisely, in his will. At last in *Confessions* X, 2, 2, Augustine expresses total conviction that all the evil of his actions belongs solely to him while all the good, by which he is freed, comes from God but is received by Augustine. As a Manichaean, Augustine had thought that sin had no relation to personality; now he sees it as an event forever impressed upon the person, if he is not freed from it. Through sin Augustine became aware of his own kind of autonomy.[1] Never could he regard sin as coming from the outside, nor could he admit the advisability of Stoic insensibility to the passions. The will gives to life its meaning, and it does this in and through the sensible. But the will is called to give personal meaning to life in and through the nature of the individual person who has been given his will with a view to an ordained end. This objectivity in willing does not detract from the unique importance of the individual person who wills, and free choice is valuable chiefly because it is the characteristic faculty of the person, bearing the mark of uniqueness and responsibility. A philosopher who does not give a proper value to the individual will never do justice to human freedom.

An essentialist philosophy belittles the individual. We should not be surprised that with Plotinus the individual who suffers in the clash and tension of the cosmic rhythm has no more right to complain than the tortoise who is trampled underfoot by the dancers as a great choral dance moves majestically to its climax.[2] How much care, how much solicitude did Augustine discover to have been showered upon him, a mere individual? In Book IX of the Confessions, he says : " For my remembrance recalls and it is pleasing to confess, O Lord, to Thee, by what inward goads Thou tamedst me; and how Thou hast evened me, lowering the mountains and hills of my high imaginations,

[1] Augustine : *Confess.*, VIII, 10, 22; PL 32, 759; VII, 3, 5; PL 32, 735; II, 6, 14; PL 32, 681; X, 32, 48; PL 32, 799; *De Civ. Dei*, XI, 23; PL 41, 336, (here he refers to Origen); XIV, 9; PL 41, 413-417.

[2] A. H. Armstrong, *Introduction to Ancient Philosophy*, Maryland, Newman Press, 1957, p. 195.

straightening my crookedness, and smoothing my rough ways." [1] Would the weak man that Augustine was have been helped by the One? Plotinus offers little hope to individuals who go astray, but he considers that having brought their misery upon themselves they have no right to expect good men or gods to put aside their own life and come down to help them. [2]

It is thus that Augustine has evaluated the dimension of freedom as something ineffable which nonetheless holds the key to the real meaning of temporal existence. Without God life is meaningless and very confusing. Life is meant to be a dialogue between the love of God and the love of man. In this dialogue God is the first speaker, and man's free will is his faculty of response to God. Through free will, man's whole being can respond. Because such response is possible, man is responsible for what he says to God and for what he does not say. This is the dialogue that brings God into time and man into eternity. Only right-ordered love can bring this successfully to pass, and that is why the love of God is the chief commandment. But the word "commandment" must not conceal the truth that this is essentially an invitation to respond to God's love for man, a love to which the creation of the world and the re-creation of man through the Incarnation bear witness. Such is the spirit of the Augustinian doctrine of freedom, a spirit that does not permeate the *Enneads* of Plotinus.

[1] Augustine, *Confess.*, IX, 4, 7; PL 32, 766.
[2] *Enn.* III, 2, 9.

PART THREE

THE NOTION OF FREEDOM AFTER AUGUSTINE

CHAPTER X

ANSELMIAN AND AUGUSTINIAN DOCTRINES OF FREEDOM COMPARED

Augustine's problem was not the existence or non-existence of free choice, but the purpose of free choice. He was interested in freedom to which right love is the key. He saw that the right use of free choice enabled man to adhere to his true end as man. " The will, then, if it clings to the unchangeable good which is common to us all, obtains the principal and important human goods, though the will itself is only a middling good. " [1] Augustine is unafraid to link this right use of free will with happiness. " The happy life itself, which consists in the disposition of the soul when it clings to the unchangeable good, is the proper and principal good for man. " [2] And yet this right will which brings happiness to man is a supernaturalized will. This is the will that Augustine calls free. Grace has given it a positive freedom by assisting it to go in the right direction.

It is significant that Augustine's use of " free " in respect to the will with which man was created is a positive use; he does not refer to freedom *from,* but to freedom *to.* Thus he speaks of a " will free to act rightly. " [3] And he makes no secret of the fact that this involves man's freedom to be happy if he wishes. " For He who has given [the will] the power to act rightly if it wishes, has also given it the power to be unhappy if it does not act rightly, and to be happy if it does. " [4] " Just as one sleeps if he is not awake, so the man who does not do what he ought to do, suffers immediately what he ought to suffer, because so great is the happiness derived from justice that to depart from it is to enter upon unhappiness. There is no alternative. " [5]

[1] Augustine, *De Lib. Arb.,* II, 19, 53; PL 32, 1269.
[2] Augustine, *De Lib. Arb.,* II, 19, 52; PL 32, 1268.
[3] Augustine, *De Lib. Arb.,* III, 18, 52; PL 32, 1296.
[4] Augustine, *De Lib. Arb.,* III, 15, 43; PL 32, 1292.
[5] Augustine, *De Lib. Arb.,* III, 15, 44; PL 32, 1292, 1293.

But it is Augustine's constant teaching even from the days of the *De Libero Arbitrio* that man cannot be happy apart from God because only by the grace of God has he the *libertas* to accomplish the salutary good. "Unless, therefore, the will itself is set free by the grace of God from that slavery by which it has been made *a servant of sin*, and unless it is given help to overcome its vices, mortal man cannot live an upright and devout life. If this gift of God, by which the will is set free, did not precede the act of the will, it would be given in accordance with the will's merits, and would not be grace which is certainly given as a free gift."[1] "I also said in another place: 'But, though man fell through his own will, he cannot rise through his own will. Therefore, let us believe firmly that God's arm, that is, Our Lord Jesus Christ, is stretched out to us from on high.'"[2] Because the good use of free will comes from God, there is nothing that is not revealed to the Divine Foreknowledge. Augustine discussed this question of God's foreknowledge in the early dialogues and again in the *City of God* and other works. This he not only reconciled with free choice but used to show why predestination in no way eliminated the natural use of free will.

In turning to Anselm we find that he likewise approaches the question of freedom from the standpoint of its purpose. He distinguishes *arbitrium,* a judgment concerning what to do, from *libertas,* a power for preserving rectitude when this is given by God's grace. Since the will was intended to have this *libertas,* we find that Anselm has chosen to call the free will *libertas arbitrii*. He discusses the will, the ways of willing, and defines free will in such a way that it can be attributed to God as well as man, although he indicates how differently this free will is found in the various grades of being. He likewise discusses whether free will can be said to be present in the unjust man and, if so, in what way. There is also a consideration of the freedom of the will in relation to outside influence — the devil,

[1] Augustine, *Retract.*, I, 9, 4; PL 32, 596.
[2] *Ibid.*, I, 9, 4; PL 32, 597; citing *De Lib. Arb.*, II, 20, 54; PL 32, 1270.

temptation, other men, God, the grace of God, foreknowledge and predestination. The Anselmian analysis, moreover, is conducted according to the Augustinian directive: Believe, that you may understand.[1] A twofold source enlightened Anselm's thinking: "The Truth shall make you free,"[2] and the fact that Satan's fall was caused by his refusal to "stand in the truth."[3] This led Anselm to hold that there is a truth of will, namely, "to will what you should,"[4] and he called this "standing in the truth," justice or rectitude of will. It is important to realize at the outset just what the term "justice" signified to Anselm. Justice is the truth of the will, that is, the will acting as it should. To love justice is to love God, and this is the purpose of the will, to which God gave at creation an inclination to justice not inseparable from the will. Anselm considers that the persecution predicted for the Christian life arises from the suffering that comes to a Christian when he strives to preserve rectitude of will, to remain in the truth, to will what he should for the sake of justice.

We shall make a survey of the doctrine of Anselm as it is expressed in: *Liber de Voluntate*, *Dialogus de Libertate Arbitrii*, *Tractatus de Concordia Præscientiæ et Prædestinationis nec non Gratiæ Dei cum Libero Arbitrio*.[5] We shall follow as far as possible the divisions suggested by Anselm himself when he referred to his dialogue on freedom of choice:

Another treatise is on Freedom of the Will, *what it is*, and *whether man always has it*, and *how many diversities of it there are* in either having or not having rightness of will, to preserve which is the prerogative of the rational creature. In this treatise I showed only

[1] Anselm, *Proslogion*, I; PL 158, 227: Credo ut intelligam; Augustine, *In Evan. Joan.*, 29, 6; PL 35, 1630: Intelligere vis? crede.

[2] John VIII, 3, 32.

[3] Augustine, *De Gen. ad Litt.*, XI, 16; PL 34, 438.

[4] Anselm, *De Veritate*, IV; PL 158, 467.

[5] Sancti Anselmi, *Opera omnia*, Migne, Patrologia Latina, tomes CLVIII, CLIX, (1841-1845). S. Anselmi, *Opera Omnia*, ed. Francis Schmitt, Edinburgh, Nelson. Vol. I: *De Libertate Arbitrii*, pp. 205-226; vol. II: *De Concordia Præscientiæ Prædestinationis et Gratiæ Dei cum Libero Arbitrio*, pp. 245-288. The Latin text is taken from this edition where possible; otherwise, it is taken from Migne. In Migne, the dialogue is called: *De Libero Arbitrio*.

the natural strength of the will for preserving rightness once it was received, and not how necessary the help of grace is to that end.[1]

THE WILL ITSELF

There are three aspects of the will, each of which goes at various times by the name of will. Will can be considered as an instrument of willing, as an affection of the instrument, or as the act of willing. The will is a power or aptitude for doing whatever has been decided upon. The aspect calling for elucidation is "affection of the will," for on this Anselm's doctrine of freedom hinges. The two chief "affections" or dispositions of the will are: an inclination toward justice (*iustitia*) and an inclination toward the useful (*commodum*).[2] The disposition to choose the useful is inseparable from the will, and under this affection is included man's invariable desire for happiness and for salvation. The disposition to will justice does not naturally belong to the will; nor is it, when it is in the will, inseparable from it. The bad angels had this and lost it; however, it is inseparable from the good angels and from the saints after their death.[3] The affections are very important because man can will nothing except through them. Volition, the third aspect of will, is the result of both the will-instrument and the affection in exercise after thought.

[1] Anselm, *De Veritate*, Prologue; PL 158, 467: Alius vero *De Libertate Arbitrii* : quid sit et utrum eam semper habeat homo, et quod sint eius diversitates in habendo vel non habendo rectitudinem voluntatis ad quam servandam est data creaturæ rationali. In quo naturalem tantum fortitudinem voluntatis ad servandam acceptam rectitudinem, non quomodo necessarium ad hoc ipsum illi sit ut gratia subsequatur ostendi.

[2] Anselm, *De Voluntate*, PL 158, 487: Voluntas instrumentum naturale est animæ. Affectiones principales duæ sunt, affectio scilicet volendi commodum et affectio volendi justitiam. Scotus later said that this "affectio iustitiæ" is the central sanctuary where freedom dwells. Bernard Vogt, "Metaphysics of Human Liberty in Duns Scotus", *Proceedings of the American Catholic Philosophical Association*, XVI, Washington (1940), p. 30: "But we possess the power to curb the promptings of mere nature. In a word we possess the power to evaluate, objectively, the right and wrong of human conduct, and to contrast the promptings of our nature with the demands of justice." 'Illa igitur affectio justitiæ, quæ est prima moderatrix affectionis commodi... illa, inquam affectio justitiæ, est libertas innata voluntati, quia ipsa est moderatrix talis (Scotus, Ox. II, d. 6, q. 2, no. 8). 'Nobilior autem est affectio justitiæ quæ est libertas ingenita.' (Scotus, Ox. III, d. 26, q. 1, no. 17). Thus the activities of the intellect combined with those of a striving will with an "affectio commodi" could only give us highly intelligent, but unfree agents..."

[3] Anselm, *De Voluntate*, PL 158, 487.

WAYS OF WILLING

The will can operate not only by willing something but by not willing it. There are three possible ways of willing something: 1) by accomplishing; 2) by approving; 3) by permitting. Accomplishment includes approving and permitting; approving includes permitting; but permitting can be considered as neither accomplishing nor approving. [1] That Anselm verified this will-diversity in man after considering it in God is evident from the context. He sees the Will of God accomplishing when it is said: "Whatever the Lord wills, He does;" [2] while the will of God approves when it is said that God wishes all men to be saved. [3] But when it is said that "whom He wills, He hardens" [4] this means that He permits the sinner to be hardened. A fourth way of willing is attributed to God in the treatise: *De Voluntate Dei,* namely, "yielding," as when God concedes marriage to men who do not choose the better. [5]

With all this diversity of willing, there remain only two basic affections through which man wills anything that he wills. Of these two affections, the utterly preferable one is the affection for willing justice, because this makes man free. These affections are not necessarily contradictory. Through the affection for justice every just man is just, but it is likewise through this same affection that a man is happy. The psychological paradox is that although a man desires happiness through his affection for the useful, "only" through the affection for willing justice "can anyone be happy." [6] The just soul would experience no misery "from the absence of some other agreeable thing, because the soul does not suffer from the need of something it does not want." [7] But if the soul uses its affection for willing the useful by reaching out for happiness without justice — the result is misery. But

[1] Anselm, *De Voluntate,* PL 158, 487.
[2] *Ps.* 113, *11.*
[3] *I Tim.* 2, 4.
[4] *Rom.* 9, 18.
[5] Anselm, *De Voluntate Dei,* PL 158, 584.
[6] Anselm, *De Voluntate,* PL 158, 488.
[7] *Ibid.*

has man any control over his affections? Yes, Anselm tells us that the will-instrument moves all other instruments, like hands, feet, pen, and so forth, as well as moving itself to its own affections. [1] This seems to mean that the will decides between the just and the useful thing when the affection for justice has not been freely relinquished by sin. The will must also decide in what way the affection for the useful is to be used. The will using its affection for the useful is not always evil — only when it consents to the concupiscence of the flesh against the spirit.

Just as Augustine realized that the will as instrument could not successfully command without getting itself to want what it commanded, [2] so Anselm insists that in order to will, man must cope with his affections or dispositions.

> I say that the instrument of willing elicits all the voluntary movements, but if we consider diligently, it is more truly said to do all that nature or the will does (which means nature and the instrument of willing) with its affections, without which the instrument does nothing. [3]

WHAT IS FREEDOM?

When Anselm tells us that all "liberty is power," [4] he is giving the genus of the definition of freedom. He immediately adds that this could not be the power of sinning and of not sinning, for then freedom of will could not be in God and the good angels. Although liberty in God and man will differ, there ought to be an essential definition of liberty which could be verified of all truly free persons. Evidently, to be able to sin does not pertain to the definition of liberty as such. [5] Moreover,

[1] Anselm, *Tractatus de Concordia*, III, 11; PL 158, 537: Voluntas quidem instrumentum movet omnia alia instrumenta quibus sponte utimur, et quæ sunt in nobis — ut manus, lingua, visus — et quæ sunt extra nos — ut stilus et securis —, et facit omnes voluntarios motus; ipsa vero se suis affectionibus movet.

[2] Augustine, *Confess.*, VIII, 9; PL 32, 758, 759.

[3] Anselm, *Tractatus de Concordia*, III, 11; PL 158, 537: Dico voluntatem instrumentum omnes voluntarios motus facere; sed si diligenter consideramus, ille verius dicitur facere omne quod facit natura aut voluntas, qui facit naturam et instrumentum volendi cum affectionibus suis, sine quibus idem instrumentum nihil facit.

[4] Anselm, *De Lib. Arb.*, III, PL 158, 494: ...libertas est potestas...

[5] Anselm, *De Lib. Arb.*, I, PL 158, 488: ...non pertinet ad definitionem libertatis arbitrii 'posse peccare'... ...Denique nec libertas nec pars libertatis est potestas peccandi...

if to have what is fitting and expedient so that it cannot be lost makes a man completely free, to be able to choose what is unfitting and inexpedient lessens liberty. Therefore, if you subtract the power to sin, you increase liberty. There is nothing freer, then, than a right will. [1] With this preliminary clarification, Anselm gives a definition of liberty applicable to God, to angels and to men : liberty of choice is the power of preserving rectitude of will on account of rectitude itself.

DIVERSITIES OF FREEDOM

The freedom that is a power of willing rectitude for the very sake of rectitude is found differently in God, in angels and in men. [2]

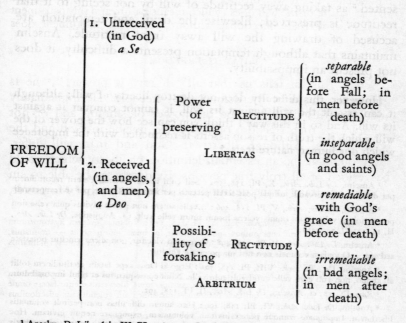

FREEDOM OF WILL

1. Unreceived (in God) *a Se*
2. Received (in angels, and men) *a Deo*
   - Power of preserving RECTITUDE — LIBERTAS
     - *separable* (in angels before Fall; in men before death)
     - *inseparable* (in good angels and saints)
   - Possibility of forsaking RECTITUDE — ARBITRIUM
     - *remediable* with God's grace (in men before death)
     - *irremediable* (in bad angels; in men after death)

[1] Anselm, *De Lib. Arb.*, IX, PL 158, 502 : Quod nihil sit liberius recta voluntate.
[2] Anselm, *De Lib. Arb.*, XIV, PL 158, 506.

LOSS OF FREEDOM

"But when the free-will forsakes rectitude, through the difficulty of preserving it, afterwards it certainly serves sin through the impossibility of recovering rectitude by itself."[1] The act of sinning never means that anyone or anything has conquered man. If choice means that something is willed, a thing cannot be willed unwillingly.[2] The "will is not conquered except by its own power."[3] God himself cannot remove rectitude of will, and temptation cannot overpower it. Anselm tells us, for instance, that although God created man and can annihilate him, he cannot separate man from rectitude. Rectitude of will makes a man just, and a just will is one that wills what God wills. God would never will man to be unjust, because this would be a self-contradiction.[4] However, God is sometimes represented[5] as taking away rectitude of will by not seeing to it that rectitude is preserved; likewise the devil and temptation are accused of drawing the will away from rectitude. Anselm maintains that although temptation presents a difficulty, it does not present an impossibility.

However, this difficulty does not destroy liberty of will; although it can assault the will against its will, it cannot conquer it against its will. And so in this way I think you can see how the power of the will which the truth of reason asserts is reconciled with the impotence which our human nature feels.[6]

[1] Anselm, *De Lib. Arb.*, X, PL 158, 502: Sed cum libera voluntas deserit rectitudinem per difficultatem servandi, utique post servit peccato per impossibilitatem per se recuperandi.

[2] Anselm, *De Lib. Arb.*, V, PL 158, 496: ...velle autem non potest invitus quia velle non potest nolens velle. Nam omnis volens ipsum suum velle vult. Cf. Augustine, *De Lib. Arb.*, II, 14, 37; PL 32, 1261.

[3] Anselm, *De Lib. Arb.*, V, PL 158, 498: Cum ergo vincitur, non aliena vincitur potestate sed sua. ...Quoniam voluntas non nisi sua potestate vincitur.

[4] Anselm, *De Lib. Arb.*, VIII, PL 158, 501: Ergo si Deus sæpe fatam rectitudinem tollit ab aliquo, non vult eum velle quod vult eum velle. Nihil consequentius et nihil impossibilius.

[5] *Rom.* IX, 18; cf. Anselm, *De Lib. Arb.*, II, PL 158, 492.

[6] Anselm, *De Lib. Arb.*, VI, PL 158, 499: Hæc autem difficultas non perimit voluntatis libertatem. Impugnare namque potest invitam voluntatem, expugnare nequit invitam. Hoc igitur modo puto te posse videre quomodo conveniant potentia voluntatis quam ratio veritatis asserit, et impotentia quam humanitas nostra sentit.

Thus, the preservation of rectitude or the loss of it can be traced only to the will itself. Unless one "should promise it something that it wishes more than that rectitude or threaten to take away what it wishes more than that rectitude, nothing, other than itself, can turn it from what it wills." [1] This is reminiscent of Augustine's statement : "It seems to me that to be truly happy a man must despise all his possessions, loving only his upright will, since that is the one thing which cannot be taken away from him without his consent." [2] The secret of freedom is to desire nothing more than a good will. This desire effectively prevents anything else from having access to one's will, because its strength or energy is dedicated to this desire. However, some other desire can grow stronger through the power of "images" or "representations." If a man lies to escape danger, it is not through lack of strength to tell the truth, but because the images surrounding the danger are more vivid than the images of the bad effects of lying.

While he can just as easily choose to tell the truth as to escape, it is safety that he prefers. But if he could see the glory of eternity, and be sure that he would enter into it immediately he had resisted the temptation; or if he could see the torments of hell and realize that immediately after his perjury he would be plunged into them; surely then he would quickly decide that he had enough strength to tell the truth. [3]

We have seen, therefore, that the preservation of rectitude for which man was given free choice is not impossible, even though it may be difficult. We have likewise seen that neither God nor the devil nor men nor things can force man to forsake

[1] Anselm, *De Lib. Arb.*, VIII, PL 158, 501 : Porro diabolus vel tentatio ideo dicitur hoc facere sive voluntatem ipsam vincere et a rectitudine quam tenet abstrahere, quoniam nisi permitteret ei aliquid aut minaretur auferre, quod magis quam ipsam rectitudinem vult, nullatenus ipsa se ab illa quam aliquatenus vult averteret.

[2] Augustine, *De Lib. Arb.*, I, 13, 28; PL 32, 1236 : Placet igitur beatum esse hominem dilectorem bonæ voluntatis suæ, et præ illa contemnentem quodcumque aliud bonum dicitur, cujus amissio potest accidere etiam cum voluntas tenendi manet.

[3] Anselm, *De Lib. Arb.*, IX, PL 158, 502 : Non enim minus fortis est ad volendum veritatem quam ad volendum salutem, sed fortius vult salutem. Nam si præsentem videret gloriam æternam quam statim post servatam veritatem assequeretur, et inferni tormenta quibus post mendacium sine mora traderetur : procul dubio mox virium sufficientiam ad servandum veritatem habere cerneretur.

rectitude. Man has the power to keep it, and the possibility of forsaking it. What does Anselm mean when he speaks of the will that has forsaken rectitude henceforth serving sin through the impossibility of recovering rectitude by itself? The fact that justice cannot be restored to the will by itself is logically inherent to the Anselmian analysis of the will. If the instrument of willing functions only through the affections, as if they were instruments, then the loss of the affection for justice prevents the effective willing of restoration of rectitude to the will. Lacking that affection, the whole energy of the will is engaged in other affections. The will-energy devoted to these affections could be drawn away by intellectual activity, and in this way the soul could be prepared to relinquish its contrary affections, but an affection for willing rectitude cannot be restored to the will by itself:

> ... because by itself it is unable to lead itself back to justice without which it is never free, since without that justice the natural liberty of the will is idle; also it becomes a handmaid of its affection, which is for the useful, because justice being removed, it can only will what that affection dictates. [1]

The point emphasized by Anselm is that man has been given rectitude of will by God with a power of preserving it. He never possessed the power of giving rectitude to himself. In no way is the will-instrument able to will justice unless God returns rectitude to man and the affection for willing rectitude. But this is the work of grace. [2] Anselm considers that God's restoration of justice to the will is a greater miracle than the raising of the dead; for people do not die through their own desire or power, whereas man sins through his own desire or power. [3]

[1] Anselm, *Tractatus de Concordia*, III, 13; PL 158, 539: ...quia per se redire nequit ad iustitiam, sine qua numquam libera est, quia naturalis libertas arbitrii sine illa otiosa est. Ancilla etiam facta est suæ affectionis, quæ ad commodum est, quia remota iustitia nihil potest velle nisi quod illa vult.

[2] Anselm, *Tract. de Concord.*, III, 13; PL 158, 540: Unde non absurde possumus dicer- affectiones eius voluntatis, quam instrumentum animæ dixi, quasi instrumenta eiusdem instrue menti esse, quia illa nihil nisi istis operatur. Perdito igitur instrumento volendi iustitiam, id est rectitudine, nullo modo — nisi per gratiam reddatur — potest voluntas instrumentum velle iustitiam.

[3] Anselm, *De Lib. Arb.*, X, PL 158, 502.

FREE CHOICE IS NEVER LOST

It is clear that Lucifer and Adam sinned through free choice, for there was nothing that could force them to sin. The sin, however, was done through choice, not through *libertas,* the positive power of preserving rectitude. [1] Choice means that the act belongs wholly to the agent. Even the sinner retains free choice because through his own power he is serving sin. But he has lost freedom which comes from having what is fitting and expedient through doing what one ought to do. With the loss of rectitude, his power of preserving rectitude is only a passive potential force. Yet it remains in man, ready to act if rectitude and the affection for willing rectitude are restored by God.

> Even if rectitude of will is absent, nevertheless rational nature has not lost what is its own... [2]

Just as when the sun is not out we yet retain the power to see the sun, so when rectitude is forsaken, we yet retain the power to preserve it. This power of using free choice for its intended purpose, to preserve rectitude, is what Anselm calls rational nature's "own." When rectitude is absent from man, however, the power of knowing it and holding to it do not avail. Man is potentially free always, but only actually free when grace enables man to love God for Himself. [3] Certain conditions must be present for the use of any power; the power of vision is useless without an object, and even with an object, it is useless without light. Free choice is a power to attain what is fitting and expedient for man when man enjoys *libertas*, right will, and possesses an affection for willing justice. Without these conditions man is only potentially free, and choice alone remains with him.

[1] Anselm, *De Lib. Arb.*, II, PL 158, 492 : Peccavit autem [Adam] per arbitrium suum quod erat liberum, sed non per hoc unde liberum erat, id est per potestatem, quia poterat non peccare et peccato non servire, sed per potestatem quam habebat peccandi, qua nec ad non peccandi libertatem iuvabatur nec ad peccandi servitutem cogebatur.

[2] Anselm, *De Lib. Arb.*, III, PL 158, 494 : Etiam si absit rectitudo voluntatis, non tamen rationalis natura minus habet quod suum est.

[3] Anselm, *De Lib. Arb.*, IX; PL 158, 501 : Potestatem autem servandi rectitudinem semper habet, et cum rectitudinem habet, et cum non habet; et ideo semper est liber.

We have no faculty, I think, which can operate all by itself. And yet, when the things we require for action are lacking, we do not on that account say that we do not have the faculty. In much the same way, no tool can operate itself. But if we do not have the things we need to operate the tool, we are still right in saying that we have the tool we need. [1]

And so Anselm, like Augustine, considers free choice to be ordered towards freedom, which can never be achieved away from truth, that is, away from God. [2]

Like Augustine, also, Anselm shows that there is no repugnance between free choice and the Divine foreknowledge, between free choice and predestination, between free choice and grace. He tells us that God's knowledge does not cause the placing of actions that He has left to the free will of man. God knows necessary acts as necessary and contingent acts as contingent. [3] The very fact that man possesses reason by which he can know what is right indicates that he is free to do right. Man has been given a true and not a pseudo-power of determining himself.

And while it is true that God has predestined man to certain good acts, he has not done it by forcing his will or by resisting it; [4] all remains within the power of the will. Like Augustine, Anselm finds the reconciliation of predestination and free choice in the divine foreknowledge. [5]

[1] Anselm, *De Lib. Arb.*, III, PL 158, 494: Nullam namque potestatem habemus, ut puto quæ sola sibi sufficiat ad actum...

[2] Anselm, *De Lib. Arb.*, III, PL 158, 494: Quapropter restat libertatem arbitrii datam esse rationali naturæ ad servandam acceptam rectitudinem voluntatis.

Cf. Augustine, *De Lib. Arb.*, II, 1, 3, PL 32, 1241: " Since, then, God punishes the sinner, what else do you think he says but: 'Why did you not use your free will for the purpose for which I gave it to you; that is, to do right?' "

[3] Anselm, *De Concordia Præscientiæ et Prædestinationis et Gratiæ Dei cum Libero Arbitrio*, I, 6; PL 158, 516: Sequitur ergo Deum velle hoc modo rectam voluntatem ad volendum recte et ad servandum eandem rectitudinem esse liberam, quæ quando potest quod vult, libere facit quod facit. Unde quoque apertissime cognosci potest aliquam esse liberam voluntatem cum actione sua, non repugnante Dei præscientia, sicut supra monstratum est.

[4] Anselm, *De Concordia*, I, 6; PL 158, 517: Nempe sola voluntas determinat ibi quid teneat, nec aliquid facit vis necessitatis, ubi operatur electio sola voluntatis. At cui non est deserendi rectitudinem voluntatis quam habet necessitas; palam est quia non deest servandi potestas sive libertas. Semper enim hæc potestas libera est. Hæc enim est libertas, quam esse dixi potestatem servandi rectitudinem voluntatis propter ipsam rectitudinem. Hac ipsa libertate rationalis naturæ et arbitrium liberum et voluntas libera dicitur...

Cf. Augustine, *De Civ. Dei*, V, 10, 2; PL 41, 153; *De Lib. Arb.*, III, 3; PL 32, 1273.

[5] Anselm, *De Concordia*, II, 3; PL 158, 52: Dubitari utique non debet quia [Dei] præscientia et prædestinatio non discordant; sed sicut præscit, ita quoque prædestinat. In quæstione de

We are also forcefully reminded of Augustine when Anselm states that the liberty of man which he calls *libertas* in the *De Libertate Arbitrii* is an actuality only by the grace of God. For liberty means preserving rectitude and no creature has rectitude of will except through the grace of God.[1] But to preserve this God-given rectitude man must truly choose it. And so grace, far from being irreconcilable with free choice, strengthens it to do what it was ordained to do without destroying the will's very real power to refuse to cooperate with grace. Rectitude does not eliminate free choice but adds to the will a union with a supernatural end; this is received freely by adults and retained freely, but always under the influx of grace.[2] It is Anselm's constant contention that grace, far from eliminating free choice, assists it. Like Augustine before him, he holds that the salvation of man is achieved not by grace alone or by free choice alone, but by both together.[3] The achievement, however, is to be imputed not so much to free choice as to grace.[4]

Like Augustine, Anselm was led by the consideration of two kinds of texts in Holy Scripture to hold firmly to his position that good could not be done without grace and without free

præscientia cognovimus aperte præsciri futura per liberum arbitrium sine omni repugnantia. Unde veritas quoque evidens et ratio docet prædestinari similiter per liberum arbitrium quædam futura absque omni inconvenientia. Nam neque præscit Deus neque prædestinat quemquam iustum futurum ex necessitate. Non enim habet iustitiam, qui eam non servat libera voluntate. Cf. Augustine, *De Grat. et Lib. Arb.*, XXIII; PL 44, 910. *De Div. Quæs. ad Simp.*, q. 11, n. 2; PL 40, 138; *De Dono Persev.*, XVII, 47; XVIIII; XIX; PL 45, 1022 ss.

[1] Anselm, *De Concordia*, III, 3; PL 158, 524: Sequitur itaque quia nulla creatura rectitudinem habet quam dixi voluntatis, nisi per Dei gratiam.

[2] Anselm, *De Concordia*, III, 3; PL 158, 524: Deo igitur largiente invenimus gratiam eius ad salvandum hominem cum libero arbitrio concordare, ita ut gratia sola hominem salvare nihil eius libero arbitrio agente — sicut fit in infantibus — et in intelligentibus ipsa semper adiuvet liberum arbitrium naturale, quod sine illa nihil valet ad salutem dando voluntati rectitudinem quam servet per liberum arbitrium. Cf. Augustine, *De Grat. et Lib. Arb.*, XV; PL 44, 899.

[3] Anselm, *De Concordia*, III, 5; PL 158, 526: ...nec sola gratia nec solum liberum arbitrium salutem hominis operetur. Cf. Augustine, *De Grat. et Lib. Arb.*, IV, 6; PL 44, 885.

[4] Anselm, *De Concordia*, III, 4; PL 158, 525: Nempe quamvis illa servetur per liberum arbitrium, non tamen est tantum imputandum libero arbitrio quantum gratiæ, cum hæc rectitudo servatur; quoniam illam liberum arbitrium non nisi per gratiam prævenientem et subsequentem habet et servat.

Cf. Augustine, *De Grat. et Lib. Arb.*, IX, 21; PL 44, 893; VIII, 20; PL 44, 892; V; PL 44, 887; *De Diver. Quæs. ad Simp.*, I, 2, 12; PL 40, 117; *Sermo* CLXIX, 1, 2; PL 38, 916.

choice. [1] And if this is the case, and Scripture is to be believed, then it is difficult to see how anyone could think that this grace, given to man for the purpose of salvation, since it cannot be had without his free cooperation, could eradicate human free choice.

Although the good that is done by man is the work of the human will helped by grace, the evil that man does comes from his will alone. It was, morever, from a will created good and just and strong for the purpose of preserving received justice (justification) that evil first entered the world. Therefore, God is not to be blamed for the evil that is present today. [2] The fault is entirely man's because he has deserted justice when he was perfectly able to preserve it. [3] One cannot help recalling Augustine's similar defence of God at the end of the *De Libero Arbitrio*, when he said:

If you refuse to turn towards Him, He loses nothing, while unless you turn to Him and give back the existence you have received from Him, you lose Him without whom you would be nothing and from whom you receive your being. If this happens, though you will not cease to exist, will you not suffer unhappiness? Everything owes to Him, first of all, its existence as a nature; secondly, the added perfection it can gain if it wills what it has received the power to will, all that it ought to be. No one is responsible for what he has not received; but he is justly responsible for not doing what he ought to do and what he has a duty to do if he has received a free will and sufficient power.

Therefore, when a man does not do what he should do, this is certainly no fault of the Creator; rather, it is a matter for praising Him that the man suffers what he ought....

But if a man is not compelled to sin either by his own nature or by that of someone else, it remains that he sins through his own will. [4]

[1] *John* XV, 5 : " Without Me you can do nothing. " *John* VI, 44 : " No one can come to Me unless My Father draws him. " *I Cor, IV, 7 :* " What have you that you have not received? " *Ps*. XXXIII, 15 : " Turn away from evil and do good; seek after peace and pursue it. " *Matt*. XI, 28 : " Come to Me, all you that labour and are burdened, and I will refresh you. "

[2] Anselm, *De Concordia*, III, 13; PL 158, 539 : Hoc igitur modo voluntas instrumentum creata bona inquantum habet esse, et iusta et fortis ad servandum acceptam iustitiam : per liberum arbitrium facta est mala, non inquantum est, sed inquantum iniusta facta est per absentiam sponte desertæ iustitiæ, quam semper habere deberet. Infirma quoque modo facta est ad volendum iustitiam desertam. Non enim per liberum arbitrium ita potest eam velle, cum illam non habet, quemadmodum valet eam servare cum habet.

[3] Anselm, *De Concordia*, III, 14; PL 158, 540 : Non est enim culpa Dei, qui creavit in eo cum libertate arbitrii voluntatem, et contulit ei iustitiam, ut nihil nisi iuste vellet; sed culpa hominis, qui iustitiam deseruit, quam servare potuit.

[4] Augustine, *De Lib. Arb.*, III, 16, 45; PL 32, 1293.

And if it is urged that our present ignorance and difficulty of doing the right thing is unjust, Augustine will recall the fact that " a man who knows what he ought to do and does not do it loses the knowledge of what is right, and the man who has refused to act rightly when he could, loses the power when he wishes to have it. " [1] And so this is an absolutely just punishment inherited by all who are descended from Adam. Man might have cause for complaint if there were no one to save him from error and from passion.

There is, however, everywhere present One who in so many ways uses His creatures to call back the servant who has abandoned Him, who teaches him when he believes, consoles him when he hopes, encourages him when he loves, helps him when he strives, and hears him when he prays. It is not counted to you as a fault that you are ignorant against your will, but that you fail to seek the knowledge you do not possess. Nor is it a fault that you do not tend your wounded members, but that you despise Him who wishes to heal them. These are your own sins. No one is prevented from knowing how valuable it is to seek the knowledge which it is useless to ignore, and from knowing the duty humbly to confess his weakness, so that when he seeks and when he confesses he may be helped by Him who neither errs when He gives help nor becomes weary of giving it. [2]

Those who have forsaken rectitude cannot, according to Anselm, restore it to their wills, but by their free choice they can admit their need of the One who can return it. With His grace they can do everything, and in a very fundamental sense God does it all. [2] But since the evil man does, which is injustice, lacks all being, God is in no sense its cause. [4]

It is to be noted that neither Augustine nor Anselm discusses free choice apart from the historical man who has been offered a supernatural end by God. Subsequent philosophers will draw a neat distinction between the natural and the supernatural will. When Anselm considers justice, he is speaking of the justification by faith, which abounds likewise in good works. This, too,

[1] Augustine, *De Lib. Arb.*, III, 18, 52; PL 32, 1296.
[2] Augustine, *De Lib. Arb.*, III, 19, 53; PL 32, 1297.
[3] Anselm, *De Concordia*, I, 7; PL 158, 517 : Facit igitur Deus omnia...
[4] Anselm, *De Concordia*, I, 7; PL 158, 518 : malum, vero, quod est iniustitia, omni carere existentia...

was the only kind of justice that interested Augustine. He once said: " It would be absurd to say that a man possesses true virtue unless he is just. But it is absurd to say that man is truly just unless he live by faith. "[1] The ideal of human freedom for both these thinkers was freedom as a participation in divine freedom which is, of course, a power to do what is right and good and well-ordered. To be free according to Augustine is to will according to the order of love; to be free according to Anselm is to will what God wills. For both thinkers, God is the supreme object of the human will, to love Whom and to choose Whom is true freedom.

CONCLUSION

Anselm's doctrine of free choice and freedom is established in the treatises we have studied. It emerges in the stark lines of a formal exposition. Of man's free will, God is the first efficient Cause in the order of nature; of man's freedom, God is the first efficient Cause in the order of grace. Anselm himself distinguished free choice from freedom when he referred to the dialogue *De Libertate Arbitrii,* saying: " In this treatise I showed only the natural strength of the will for preserving rightness once it was received, and not how necessary the help of grace is to that end. "[2] The man whom God created in history was the religious man in whom both free will and freedom were present without impairment of nature, without denial of grace. The potency for that freedom of fulfillment which is the perfection of free choice resides in man's spiritual nature. The actuality of freedom in the broad sense comes both from God and man, by grace and right choices. Freedom is the fruit of the unification of sense life with spirit life, of intellect with will, of the human will with the Divine Will. To exercise free choice properly, man, like the soul in the *Enneads,* must recall his dignity — not his Divine worth, but what he is worth to God

[1] Augustine, *Contra Jul. Pelag.*, IV, 3, 17; PL 44, 745: Sed absit ut sit in aliquo vera virtus nisi fuerit justus. Absit autem ut sit justus vere, nisi vivat ex fide...

[2] Anselm, *De Veritate*, Prologue; PL 158, 467.

Who freely willed him into existence and asks only for a free adherence of each human will to the Divine Will. No one can do this for another. In commiting the destiny of man to the individual choice of each man, God has given a unique value to the individual.

The distinction between free will and freedom — a distinction indispensable to a correct understanding of Augustine's teaching on freedom — is taken up and utilized by Anselm. Augustine had discovered that the key to human freedom and fulfillment is right love and had announced as a program for freedom: Love and do as you please. [1] Anselm, on the other hand, suggested as his program for human fulfillment and freedom a devotion to duty, an undeviating pursuit of what one ought to do, and declared that the purpose of free choice is the preservation of rectitude or justice, or the affection for justice for the sake of rectitude itself.

For Anselm as for Augustine, Adam was free before the fall to keep rectitude and free after the fall to acknowledge his helplessness and to accept the Divine help offered, so that he might again begin to enjoy the freedom of the children of God.

The will can cause us to fall, but it cannot raise us up again. [2]

It was by sin freely entered into that man lost the liberty which gave him the possession of justice and immortality. [3] Without the grace of God, the fallen will is radically incapable of performing any act meritorious of eternal life. Yet when man realizes he is unhappy and asks: "Who will free me?" [4] the answer has already been given by Christ. When freedom is restored to man by baptism, it must be cherished and cultivated so that it may develop; for there are degrees of freedom. All Christian life is actually a growth in freedom. [5]

[1] Augustine, *In Epist. Joan.*, VII, 8: PL 35, 2033; Dilige, et quod vis fac; cf. *De Trin.*, VIII, 7; PL 42, 956.

[2] Augustine, *Retract.*, I, 9, 6; PL 32, 598.

[3] Augustine, *Contra Duas Epist. Pelag.*, I, 2, 5; PL 44, 552.

[4] *Rom.*, VII, 24.

[5] A great educator once noted that she could watch the children passing through four stages of liberty which she called: 1. The bad-glad stage; 2. The bad-sad stage; 3. The good-sad stage; 4. The good-glad stage.

The reward of a created will that participates in the Divine Will is to communicate with God in friendship. The will of God acts from the fullness of good, from perfection, from pure love. United to God's will, the human will ushers into the world the glorious reality of generosity. The union of God and man is accomplished by God's omnipotent love, through which He can enter into the inviolable intimacy of the human heart. Through experience of the generous love of God man can attain some insight into the reality of personal being. Generosity is the truest way that man can image God. There is, however, a condition for the use of the divine largesse, a condition that Anselm and Augustine both insist upon : man must admit that he is drawing on the goodness of God.

"For no holy being rejoices in his own power, but in His from Whom he has the power which he fitly can have; and he knows it to be more a mark of power to be united to the Omnipotent by a pious will than to be able by his own power and will, to do what they may tremble at who are not able to do such things."[1]

[1] Augustine, *De Trinitate,* VIII, 7; PL 42, 957 : Non enim sanctus quisquam potestate sua gaudet, sed ejus a quo habet posse quidquid congruenter potest : et novit potentius esse conjungi Omnipotenti pia voluntate, quam propria potestate et voluntate posse, quod contremiscant qui talia non possunt.

CHAPTER XI

DEVELOPMENT OF THE AUGUSTINIAN NOTION OF FREEDOM BY ST. THOMAS AQUINAS

To explore the texts of St. Thomas on free choice and on the free man is to discover that the Thomist doctrine ratifies, develops and metaphysically justifies the Augustinian conception of freedom. St Augustine summed up the radical indetermination of the human will before any finite object proposed by the intellect when he said: " Thou hast made us towards Thyself, O Lord, and our hearts are restless until they rest in Thee. "[1] St. Thomas reveals that the human will's natural orientation towards unlimited goodness accounts for this human restlessness.[2] And he teaches that the reason for the will's natural ordination to the total good is the intellectuality of man.[3] In holding that free choice is for the sake of attaining a greater freedom — a spontaneous tending towards one's true end, St. Thomas is in agreement with Augustine. Although man cannot achieve such freedom without the help of God, man always has the power to ask for the help needed. All men possess the power of free choice because it is rooted in rational nature. Not all men possess the freedom of fulfillment which comes from a strong, positive adherence to one's true end, because such freedom is attained by the individual's use of free choice which includes the acceptance of grace. Insofar as a man by disobeying the natural law misuses free choice, he frustrates his nature, and so in a true sense each man is for himself the only serious enemy. Man makes right choices when he evaluates things as they are in reality and in relation to the end he should reach. By such choices man is fulfilled as a person. Frustration or fulfillment — the risk and the glory involved in the possession

[1] Augustine, *Confess.*, I, 1; PL 32, 661: ...quia fecisti nos ad te, et inquietum est cor nostrum donec requiescet in te.

[2] Thomas Aquinas, *Summa Theologica*, I-II, q. 2, a. 8.

[3] *Ibid.*, I, q. 59, a. 3.

of free choice! Here we glimpse the profound significance of free will. Free will is not merely the power to act or not to act, to choose this or that, to choose what is really good or only apparently good — it is the power of self-creation. Because he has the power of free choice, man is able to determine his very being, to become what he wants to be. Only when he wants to be what he should be is man fulfilled as a person and, consequently, happy. The Augustinian definition of happiness as having what you want and wanting the right thing [1] can be transposed into the Thomistic metaphysics of the will as "being" what you want and what God wants you to be. To show how this determination of personal being is utterly within the power of the person, we shall turn to St. Thomas' teaching on the will.

HUMAN WILL IN ACT

St. Thomas tells us that the human will is by nature pre-determined to the "good as good," namely, the total good. This is because the will is an appetitive power deriving from intellect. [2] In the apprehension of any good, the intellect implicitly perceives the good, and since will is intellectual appetite, it is inclined by the First Cause to love necessarily the good-in-general. Actuated by its First Cause to tend to the indeterminate good, [3] the will moves itself to all particular goods. The good-in-general, apprehended by the intellect, is the formal object of the will, and since a faculty is moved by necessity only when confronted with its formal object, we can see why the will is free before any particular good. [4] But what is meant by good apprehended by intellect? Is not truth the object of intellect?

Being is the object of intellect, but being as related to intellect is called true, and being as related to will is called good. Does

[1] Augustine, *De Beata Vita*, II, 10; PL 32, 964.

[2] Aristotle, *De Anima*, III, 9; quoted by St. Thomas, *De Veritate*, q. 22, a. 10, ad 2. Q. 22, a. 11, ad 1: "Augustine takes reason and intelligence for the whole intellective part, which includes both the apprehension of the intellect and the appetite of the will..."

[3] The negated determination pertains to subject, content, matter, not to form.

[4] Freedom derives from superdetermination, an excess of causal power.

the human intellect then have direct contact with being? Through the senses man comes in contact with existing material things, and when by the abstractive power of his intellect he knows the natures of things, he knows them as natures of existing things, because human knowledge is both intellectual and sensible. Gradually by an ever more refined reflection he may realize that the whole perfection of things comes from their act of existence, because, as St. Thomas says, this is the ultimate act of all things, even of forms. [1] If things are intelligible to man's rational intellect in their forms, intentionally present, it is by the act of existing that they have their forms. While the intellect is directly related to being as true, man is intellectually aware that his intellectual appetite is related to the actuality and perfection of things as they exist in themselves. The will tends to the perfection of being as to an end. [2] The end in the intentional order is in the intellect. But if man tends towards things only through a representation, he nevertheless is seeking the good apprehended and not the representation of the good. And so the end of the will is the good in the real order. The will is dynamically desirous of being as existing in all fullness — but the intellect apprehends only the good-in-general. The formal object of the will is not then a subsistent thing. Hence the will is said to be naturally necessitated or predetermined to an indeterminate object. It is impossible for a man not to desire this total indeterminate good as his end. Anything man lingers over is loved because it is good in some way, and when man finally chooses any particular good he does so in virtue of this natural desire for the total good. [3]

ANALYSIS OF CHOICE

The structure for the complete act of choice, which is a making or doing, includes both the activity of the speculative intel-

[1] Thomas Aquinas, *De Potentia Dei,* VII, 2, ad 9.

[2] Thomas Aquinas, *De Veritate*, q. 21, a. 1, c. "Inasmuch as one being by reason of its act of existing is such as to perfect and complete another, it stands to that other as an end."

[3] Thomas Aquinas, *De Veritate*, q. 22, a. 2, c.; q. 24, a. 1, ad 18; *Summa Theologica*, I-II, q. 8, a. 2, c.; a. 3, c. and ad 2.

lect [1] and the activity of the practical intellect. By intellect man tends naturally to being-as-good, but this always occurs under a certain expression of being-as-*a*-good. [2] Therefore, choice originates in the speculative intellect. Since the will is not determined to *a* being, but only to the total good, the love awakened by any epiphany of being is already a certain preference; it is, one may say, an incipient choice. Since the will is the inclination to an apprehended good, the first requirement for human love is an intellectual apprehension of a being, a good. This may, of course, be either a sensible or a spiritual good. There may arise in the will an indeliberate complacence in the good proposed, a mere wish or contentment with the good present to the mind. Man by will may efficaciously desire the good in question and move the intellect to judge whether the loved good is attainable. If so, the will intends [3] the good as an end and directs the practical intellect to seek ways and means of realizing the good. [4] The will as intending is the principle of the will as choosing. Among the ways proposed, the practical intellect *under the influence of the will,* judges finally that *this* good is choiceworthy here and now. The will's election continues the inclination of the will intending the end. Man infallibly follows this practical judgment which he by will has caused to be, and directs the proper powers to attain the existing good.

What must be underlined is the fact that man is following a judgment that was determined by the will [5]. Why could the

[1] St. Thomas continually states that there is nothing willed that is not first known. Also cf. Augustine, *De Trinitate*, X, 1, 2; PL 42, 973. Cf. Thomas Aquinas, *Contra Gentiles*, II, 48: "Only those beings move themselves to judge which apprehend the all embracing essence of the good or the fitting."

[2] Thomas Aquinas, *Summa Theologica*, I-II, q. 9, a. 1, c. ad 2. Cf. *Contra Gentiles*, II, 48.

[3] Thomas Aquinas, *De Veritate*, q. 22, a. 13, ad 16: "Intention is an act of the will in subordination to reason as it directs to an end the means thereto. Choice is an act of the will in subordination to reason as it compares among themselves the means to an end." Cf. q. 22, a. 15, c.

[4] Aristotle, *De Anima*, 433 a, 14-17: "...by extension the speculative intellect becomes practical."

[5] R. A. Gauthier, O. P., "Saint Maxime le Confesseur et la Psychologie de l'Acte Humain," *Recherches de Théologie Ancienne et Médiévale*, t. XXI, 1954, p. 51: "C'est incontestablement à saint Augustin que saint Thomas comme ses prédécesseurs est redevable de sa

practical judgment not be formed without the will? Since the practical intellect is moved by the will-in-pursuit-of-the-good, it is no longer merely concerned with being as true, but also with being as good. Value is related both to intellect and to appetite. Being as related to the will is valuable, but this value is always revealed by the mind. The practical intellect will therefore judge all things in relation to the will's end — the total good. But the practical intellect can never judge : "It is true that this particular thing is the total good." And yet such a judgment is the only kind that can determine the will to act. For, a faculty is only necessitated to act when moved by its formal object. Therefore, the decision that any particular good is a fitting object for man's will must come from the will. [1]

This is why man is not intellectually determined, but self-determining. Motivation is not a sufficient reason for choice when no motive is absolutely sufficient. Man can always perceive the difference between any good thing and the reason for desiring it. The formal object of the human will is an indeterminate object, the good-in-general, and since man acts in view of this end, this is the final cause of human activity. The formal cause of every human act is a judgment, but one that is considered insufficient to move a will athirst for the fullness of being. The efficient cause of every human act is the will which for no infallibly sufficient reason identifies this good proposed by the intellect with the total good to which the will is naturally ordered.

When a man swings the weight of his finalized energy to fix a choice, the act is human, personal, free — utterly his own. When the practical intellect judges : " it is true that this is good, " the will has already desired this to be true. [2] The fact that any practical judgment becomes final, thereby legislating that this particular good thing is choiceworthy here and now, is the decision of the person. [3]

notion du *consensus* [consent], et Mgr. Wittmann a reconnu à bon droit dans le *consensus* augustinien la [assent]..... stoicienne. " Cf. Wittmann, *Die Ethic des hl. Thomas von Aquin*, Munich, 1933, p. 153.

[1] Cf. Augustine, *De Civ. Dei*, XII, 6; PL 41, 353-355.
[2] Thomas Aquinas, *Summa Theologica*, I-II, q. 13, a. 1, c, a. 6, ad 3.
[3] Thomas Aquinas, *Summa Theologica*, I, q. 83, a. 1, c, ad 5; q. 82, a. 4, c.

In the light of the vastness of the will's yearning, derived from its being an intellectual appetite with a formal object as wide as that of the intellect, namely, being as being, there is no way of predicting how a man will choose. [1] No detailed, intimate knowledge of the man or of the value of the object proposed to him, no awareness of the circumstances, the dispositions of the man, his past choices, can lead us to know what choice he will make now or whether he will choose at all. A choice is unknown until born. It is often a revelation of the man to himself. The fact that something was chosen before by the same man in the same dispositions and circumstances does not insure that it will now be chosen. There is an infinite distance between any finite thing and the proper object of the will, and only the will's formal object, the total good, can infallibly move the will. The will is in relation to the intellect what natural dynamism is in relation to the natural form, and since intellectual knowledge provides an infinite form, the will is an infinite tendency. [2] The infinite distance is spanned only when man equates a finite thing with the good. The nature of any human act is specified by the intellect, but the reason why this act exists at all—that is the secret of the will.

St. Thomas explains free choice philosophically by accepting the Aristotelian suggestion : causes are causes of each other in different orders. The total good apprehended by intellect acts as final cause, and the partial good apprehended by intellect acts as formal cause specifying the will which, as efficient cause, moves the practical intellect to a decision which the will then elects. There is, of course, a priority of knowledge in the speculative order giving rise to love of an apprehended being, but when truth is related to action, the practical judgment is formed under the influence of the will. This is because the will is the faculty for attaining the end of man, and this is attained in the order of action or finality. The will moves the other powers insofar as they are concerned with the order of action. That

[1] Insofar as the will is shaped by habits and virtues, the limits of free choice are such as to make for prediction within limits.

[2] Thomas, Aquinas, *In I Sent.*, d. 27, q. 1, a. 4.

is why the practical intellect proposes the formal cause under the influx of the will as efficient cause in pursuit of its end.[1]

The metaphysical basis for the radical indetermination of the practical judgment and the active domination of the will before all partial goods is the incommensurability of any finite being to the totality of being. The intellect recognizes that any particular good has some aspect of non-being. If a thing is good insofar as it is, a finite object will lack total goodness because it lacks the fullness of being. Wherever there are many beings, there will be a potential principle to account for the multiplicity. In apprehending any good thing, the intellect is aware of the good according to the *ratio* of the good, and simultaneously aware of its concomitant non-good aspect. And so it judges that this finite thing is not the formal object of the will. The question now arises : given such indetermination on the part of the judgment and on the part of the will — how does choice ever take place?

MAN THE MAKER OF DECISIONS

Left to itself, the practical intellect remains undetermined to a final judgment. Acting as a formal cause, revealing the *ratio* of this good thing both in itself and in relation to end, thereby channeling the influx of the final cause, the intellect can be determined to judge conclusively that this act should here and now be done only when the will acting as efficient cause, with the dynamism that belongs to it by its ordination to the end, freely identifies this good with man's good. No finite thing can fulfil the infinite capacity of the will for good. No motive is absolutely, infallibly sufficient to actuate the will. If it becomes sufficient, the will has made it so. No finite object has an ontological right to be chosen. Only God can know future free actions, because the truth of them is not verified until the present act of choice is made. The chooser does not know what his choice will be and God knows such actions in His eternal present.

[1] Thomas Aquinas, *De Veritate*, q. 24, a. 1. For St. Thomas, free choice means a "free judgment about acting or not acting." cf. *Contra Gentiles*, II, 48.

It is not the mind that fixes choice. [1] Choice is a free response arising from an infinite well of desire that no particular good can fill. Man, the master of his judgments in the practical order, makes an object choiceworthy. Thus the desirability of an object largely depends on the person who is the agent. "According as a man is, such does the end seem to him." [2]

If free choice is the act of the individual person, we can understand where the mystery in human choice lies. The individual is intellectually unknown to us; the will with its capacity for the universal, resides in the individual and cannot but be profoundly affected by such residence. We know the factors that modify an individual — knowledge, passions, habits, virtues, vices, all greatly influenced by heredity, environment, education and experience. The individual, moreover, is intellectually unknown to himself. That is why a choice is often a self-revelation. But all the possible intrinsic or extrinsic influences cannot determine the will, because it is a transcendent power. And so even though "as a man is, so his end appears to him," only man himself by his personal power of saying "yes" and "no" can account for his being what he is.

CONCLUSION CONCERNING FREE CHOICE

Aristotle had said that choice is either intellect influenced by appetite or appetite influenced by intellect. [3] St. Thomas showed that choice is both appetite influenced by intellect and intellect influenced by appetite. Choice occurs through the reciprocal influence of the judgment as formal cause, the good-in-general as final cause, and principally by the free will as efficient cause, which is reduced from potency to act by the unmoved First Mover Who moves the human will to be free by moving it towards a super-determining end — being as good. [4]

[1] Thomas Aquinas, *Summa Theologica*, I, q. 83, a. 3.

[2] Aristotle, *Eth. Nic.*, III, 5; quoted by St. Thomas, *Sum. Theol.*, I-II, q. 9, a. 2, c.

[3] Aristotle quoted by St. Thomas, *Sum. Theol.*, I-II, q. 13, a. 1, c.

[4] Thomas Aquinas, *De Malo*, q. 6; also, *De Veritate*, q. 22, a. 9, c.: "There is one (object) to which the natural inclination of the will is determined with necessity. This object is implanted in the will and proposed to it by the Creator, who gave it its natural inclination to this."

Cf. *De Veritate*, q. 24, a. 1, ad 18; *Sum. Theol.*, I-II, q. 8, a. 2, c.; q. 9, a. 6. c; q, 10, a. 2, c.

The immateriality of the speculative intellect is the root of liberty; the consequent indetermination of the practical judgment is the proximate cause of free human acts; and the immediate explanation of the free choice is the active domination of the free will whose formal object is never proposed to it for choice in the natural order. [1] "God made man from the beginning, and left him in the hand of his own counsel (Ecclus. XV, 14)." [2] St. Thomas formulated a metaphysical explanation of free will and a psychological analysis of the free act which marks a peak of philosophical precision in the development of the notion of freedom.

FREEDOM IN THE BROAD SENSE

Although man naturally desires the total good as the ultimate end to which he is super-determined, he himself has to fill in this vague outline by determining what will be his good, the good-for-him. His ordination to the total good intellectually apprehended is indeed the metaphysical root of his free choice. But this freedom imposes upon man the obligation of choosing some aspect of the good that will orientate his actions. [3] Animals cannot choose their reason for action; man can. Although the human desire for happiness is not free, man must freely choose in what his happiness will consist. When the content has been decided upon, this aspect of the good becomes the principle of his choices.

Because everything is ontologically good, anything can be chosen as man's end, but reflection upon the specific capacities of man brings awareness that there is an ordained end for him, an end he should reach. His proper powers, by whose

[1] Thomas Aquinas, *De Veritate*, q. 22, a. 4, c. : "And so a rational nature's inclination is not determined for it by anything else but by itself."

[2] Thomas Aquinas, *De Veritate*, q. 22, a. 4; q. 24, a. 2, ad 4 : "Not only Damascene but also Gregory and Augustine assign reason as the cause of free choice." Cf. Augustine *De Lib. Arb.* II, chaps. 6, 18.

[3] Thomas Aquinas, *De Veritate*, q. 22, a. 7, c. : "But man has implanted in him an appetite for his last end in general, so that he naturally desires to be complete in goodness. But just what that completeness consists of, whether virtues or knowledge or pleasure or anything else of the sort, has not been determined for him by nature."

activities a being is generally perfected, are of their very nature directed to others. They are, moreover, capacities for infinite being, so that when a man by metaphysical analysis of contingent being arrives at the knowledge of Necessary Being, Who is consequently infinite and unique, he knows that this Being is lovable as the Supreme Value. Ontologically, God is worthy of being loved for His intrinsic Goodness, loved more than man loves himself or others.[1]

God's supremacy in being is the foundation of man's obligation to love Him above all things. That God is that End in which man finds completion in goodness or fulfillment follows from the fact that it is the nature of the good to be perfective of those who participate in its being through knowledge and love. But to love another is also to enter into the will of the other, wanting what the other wants. And so the will of God as expressed in rational nature is for the lover of God not only a law that he must obey, but the desire of God that man wants to fulfil. An action that conforms to right reason and therefore to God's Eternal Will or choice is objectively good. It is likewise good for man because it leads to the end he should reach — voluntary union with God.

This human good by which man is completed in goodness is called the moral good. The moral good is not a transcendental. It signifies that which is good in the order of fulfillment of the human being. The moral good is the ontological good in relation to what man is made to be. When human action is what it should be, we say it is morally good. But the important point is that when man's actions are morally good, he becomes good. The moral good is then the principle of human fulfillment in goodness and, therefore, in being. It is because God wants man to be, and to be ever more completely, that He wants him to be morally good.

[1] In his early writings St. Augustine was intent upon showing that human happiness came from loving the right thing : *De Beata Vita*, PL 32, 959-976. Although he had first approached human destiny from this psychological viewpoint, he soon asserted that things were to be loved according to their hierarchical order : *De Ordine*, PL 32, 977-1020; *De Morib. eccles. Ca* PL 32, 1310-1344; *De Doctrina Christiana*, PL 34, 15-122.

The norm for judging what ought to be done is a true knowledge of man's nature in relation to its ultimate end. Out of the speculative intellect's true knowledge of human being, the will's tendency to the good as perfective of man, and the practical intellect's judgment in accord with right appetite — the moral good is born. It is in this sense that the moral good is constituted of existential relations. When something is chosen because it is morally good, that is, because it ought to be, there is in the choice at least an implicit love of the Subsistent Good as ultimate end, and subordinately, a desire for happiness.

Although the infinite Goodness of God obliges man to love Him for Himself, the power to fulfil this obligation comes from the dynamism of man's natural ordination to his end. Maritain says that the decision to do something purely and simply because it is good, morally good, is the choice of man's true good as his good; he calls this the beginning of moral life and an implicit choice of God. [1] It is an entering into His Will. The choice of a moral good makes man more completely existent and it is God's Will that man should be and be perfect. And so if by good moral acts man becomes perfect, this is the way to freedom of fulfillment. Man thus continues the creation of the person begun by God. By the right ordering of his love, man increases his resemblance to God in the order of being.

There is, however, no right ordering of human love when the will is divorced from truth. [2] St. Thomas' well-known emphasis upon prudence, right knowledge about things to be done, reveals that he shares Augustine's appreciation of the role of truth in the making of man's personal perfection. St. Thomas likewise emphasizes the moral virtues because through temperance, fortitude and justice the will is disposed

[1] Maritain, *Neuf Leçons sur les Notions Premières de la Philosophie Morale*, Paris, Tequi, pp. 120, 121. St. Thomas holds that God wishes man to choose Him explicitly. Cf. *De Veritate*, q. 22, a. 2, c.: "Only a rational creature can trace secondary ends back to God by an analytic procedure so as to seek God Himself explicitly."

[2] Thomas Aquinas, *De Veritate*, q. 22, a. 11, ad 5: "The intellect rules the will, not by nclining it to that to which it tends, but by showing it that to which it should tend."

to act reasonably. If the practical intellect is undecided before a good with both desirable and undesirable aspects, the person must "make up his mind." An integrated and mature human personality is one that interposes in favor of the true value, the goodness, the plenitude of being in the object proposed as this is revealed by an impartial intellect.

If man uses his will apart from the guidance of intellect, declaring his independence of being, he will not achieve freedom in the broad sense. Nor will man become free if he merely possesses an intellectual love of the good. Good ideas in themselves do not make good men. An idea exercises influence only when applied to action, because by action man perfects his being. Although the human individual has supremacy over all external and internal influences in the order of secondary moral causality, there is a more fundamental priority : the cosmic priority of being. The will as appetite of reason is meant to enter into dependence on the intellect, which itself is a power for consent to being. It is an attitude in human action that verifies man's dependent state as participator in being. When man freely chooses to incarnate the truth in his actions, he is moving towards freedom.

And so we can say that *choice* is free because its determination in both the orders of exercise and of specification is dependent on the will itself *(negatio determinationis ad unum)*. But *man* is free when he assents to the truth of things, to the natural law that expresses the eternal choice of God. *Choice* is free when man judges freely. But *man* is free when man judges truly. This does not mean that man should choose all things under their moral aspect only. Naturally, things make their appeal to man under various aspects and for various reasons which include the education, the tastes, the temperament of the chooser. The point is that although a thing may be chosen because of its special appeal to some human yearning, it should not be chosen if it conflicts with the eternal law legible in human nature. Man is free to act as an individual and seek satisfaction from various aspects of the ontological good in material conditions, but as a person he belongs to the moral order and, therefore, right reason should inform his complex activity.

St. Thomas considers that every full-fledged human act is a moral action in the sense that it has an implicit direction to or away from the true end of man. If in the concrete there is no such thing as an indifferent act, then every human act is facing in the right or the wrong direction. To make progress is to advance in the right direction and become what one ought to be. Freedom in the broad sense is the absence of constraint in becoming a perfect person. Thus, freedom of fulfillment is another name for the plenitude of personal being.

OBSTACLES TO FREEDOM

Though St. Thomas and St. Augustine are in agreement that the efficacious love for man's true good characterizes the ascent to freedom, both are aware of the present distracted will in man. Man seems inclined to seek things in relation to himself, and not always to the best in himself. In itself the force of desire tends naturally to sensible pleasure; since it is human, it does this according to the order of reason, and consequently, to act in an unbridled manner is not natural to this force because not human; it is, rather, contrary to nature. [1] The disorder visible in human acts seems to point to some original deordination that has affected all men. From revelation St. Thomas knows that the substitution of self for God as man's end was the sin of Adam. St. Thomas speaks of the effect sin has had upon the intellect, [2] and of the necessity of remedying this by faith. He speaks, too, of the will deprived of union with its end, [3] and of the will's incapacity for any prolonged and steady performance of duty. He shows that free will has itself caused its own disorder by a choice, and that "...sin takes away nothing from free will, but adds a union with a perverse end." [4] That human nature

[1] Thomas Aquinas, *Summa Theologica*, I-II, q. 82, a. 3, ad 1.
[2] Thomas Aquinas, *Summa Theologica*, I, 8 . 94, a. 1; II-II, q. 2, a. 7, c. 1; q. 7, a. 2. c.
[3] Thomas Aquinas, *De Veritate*, q. 24, a. 12, ad 2.
[4] Thomas Aquinas, *De Veritate*, q. 24, a. 10, ad 14.

has not been wholly vitiated is indicated by the fact that acts implicitly contradicting the wrongly chosen end can occasionally be done, such isolated acts as defending one's country, saving a drowning child, and so forth.[1]

THEOLOGICAL FREEDOM

Because of man's inherited union with a perverse end and because of every man's mental darkness and weakness of will, caused by actual evil choice in the first man, St. Augustine concluded that the human will was radically impotent to do anything to merit eternal life.[2] Man had lost rectitude of will, union with God as End, and this could be restored only by God through the gift of grace. St. Thomas also spoke of the inadequacy of the natural man who would be able to love God as the beginning and end of natural good but who could not enjoy a spiritual fellowship with God.[3]

For God to offer Himself to man not only as an object to be known, but as a subject to be loved, He has to give man supernatural powers of knowing and loving. What is not possible to men by themselves becomes possible to them with God. God offers to the free acceptance of all men His Gift of Faith. Faith opens to man the First Cause, the Source of all truth in the speculative order, and the Last End, the Principle of all activity in the practical order. Faith widens the horizons that are natural to reason. Dogma, held by Faith, is not really an enemy to human freedom. It frees man from ignorance in matters too difficult for the natural intellect to penetrate, or too important to wait upon the slow acquisition of natural knowledge.

But Faith, working through love, does more than open man's mind. It strengthens, steadies, secures his will to his true, concrete End, so that man is able to do the truth. Grace does not take away man's free choice or introduce him

[1] Thomas Aquinas, *De Veritate*, q. 24, a. 11, ad 3, ad 6; a. 12, ad 14, ad 19.

[2] Second Council of Orange, can. 7: The will is powerless to lift itself to "...bonum aliquid, quod ad salutem pertinet vitæ æternæ." Denzinger, n. 180.

[3] Thomas Aquinas, *Summa Theologica*, I-II, q. 109, a. 3, ad 1.

immediately into unlimited divine freedom. It adds a union with man's true End, but moral obligation will appear at first as a constraint to reason, because man's fallen nature makes him rebellious to reason. In so far as grace heals nature, the constraint will vanish, and man will do the morally right thing with increasing spontaneity.

Great is the freedom of that man whose perfection enables him nearly always to choose his true good without hesitation. Though habit lessens freedom of choice by reducing deliberation, we must be mindful that free choice is given not for its own sake but rather for the sake of union with man's End. Although grace transforms, heals, strengthens, perfects, elevates human powers, it neither destroys them nor eliminates the need to use them. Man is still at the helm. He alone can retain his Faith because he wants to, in response to God's desire that he should have Faith in Him.

Nor is man, simply because he has Faith, infallible in his choice of the good. He must still think and then make his choice of ontological good in relation to an end he should reach. By means of the theological virtues, however, man sees his obligation as a responsibility to God not only as Creator but also as Friend. The kind of freedom that is born of man's communication with God as a Friend we have called theological. [1] St. Thomas speaks of this perfect freedom in grace. [2] He sees it as the mystery of the Divine economy of salvation — the human creature's cooperation in his own salvation by his free response to the invitation of grace, the great mystery so greatly defended by Augustine against Manichaeans and Pelagians.

Accordingly, when the Holy Ghost by love inclines the will to the true good to which it is naturally directed, He removes both the servitude whereby a man, the slave of passion and sin, acts against the order of the will, and the servitude whereby a man acts against the inclination of his will, and in obedience to the law. Wherefore, the Apostle says (2 Cor. III, 17): ' Where the Spirit of the Lord is,

[1] Thomas Aquinas, *Contra Gentiles,* IV, 22 : "... it is proper to friendship to consent to a friend in what he wills."

[2] Thomas Aquinas, *Summa Theologica,* I-II, 10, 4; I-II, 112, 3; *Contra Gentiles,* III, 148.

there is liberty, ' and (Gal. V, 18): ' If you are led by the Spirit, you are not under the law. ' [1]

Man does not relinquish free choice when he freely passes from freedom of choice between good and evil to freedom to choose the good in the majority of instances. Such freedom increases man's resemblance to the Divine Being Who can do only good. But it also presupposes the transformation of man by grace and love. With grace man does not immediately experience the joy and spontaneity of one perfectly free. There are stages in the ascent to freedom. [2] Nor is the ascent accomplished without human effort. Love, however, generates the generosity that makes effort desirable. Where faith is lively, response to Divine Love replaces the norm of conformity to reason. Man then does what he ought to do because he wants to; he is " ...a law unto himself, because love inclines him in the manner of a law, and makes him act as a man who is free. " [3]

CONCLUSION

Unlike Plotinus and Aristotle, both St. Augustine and St. Thomas recognize the tremendous dignity and power of love. [4] Through love man undergoes the attraction of being in its aspect of perfection, and the profound reason for this is that God is Being. There is, therefore, a natural inclination to love God above things. The role given by St. Augustine to charity [5] finds its metaphysical foundation in man's real relation to being, viewed primarily as perfection, only secondarily as perfective. To be a person, is, after all, to be in communication with others and, above all, with God. If it is true that by his proper activities of knowing and loving, man is brought to perfection, is not the purpose of these activities to bring a person into dynamic

[1] Thomas Aquinas, *Contra Gentiles*, IV, 22; *Summa Theologica*, I-II, 93, 6.

[2] Thomas Aquinas, *Contra Gentiles*, IV, 22.

[3] Thomas Aquinas, *Contra Gentiles*, III, 28.

[4] Because they had a true understanding of human love, their moral philosophy cannot justly be called a pure eudaimonism.

[5] Augustine, *De Doctrina Christiana*, III, 10; PL 34, 72 : Charitatem voco motum anim ad fruendum Deo propter ipsum...

relation with other subjects? Loving is "...not simply an actuation of the will, but the giving of being to being, the dynamic adhesion of being to itself."[1] If such direct and generous attachment is characteristic of personal love, man's very perfection is related to his generosity. The desire to perfect one's nature, however, is a natural desire and if chosen as a means of communing better with God and one's neighbor, it is perfectly legitimate.

The Augustinian emphasis on charity and interiority finds justification in Thomistic metaphysics.[2] "The original call to love is made by God, present in us by participation. It is a call to generosity, to the direct love of value in all its plenitude. And a love that restricts its horizons to the narrow limits of the *I,* that loves one finite *self* to the exclusion of other *selves,* is a love that never attains this plenitude."[3] By His gift of being to man, God solicits man's love. He wants man to be and to be ever more fully. Man's expansion in being comes from resembling God in personal love — willing others to be and to be more fully.[4] Although persons may approach each other through need as man often approaches God, knowledge of another person should lead to direct love. As a unique participation in the plenitude of Being, each person is lovable. Thus, every friend is a new revelation of God.[5]

[1] Robert Johann, S.J., *The Meaning of Love,* Westminster, Maryland, Newman Press, 1955 p. 66.

[2] *Ibid.,* p. 68.

[3] *Ibid.,* p. 42.

[4] *Ibid.,* p. 71. Cf. Augustine, *In Epist. Joan.,* VIII, 5; PL 35, 2038; *Sermo* 368, 4; PL 39, 1654; *De Cat. Rud.,* IV, 7; PL 40, 314, 315; *De Fide Rer.,* II, 4; PL 40, 173, 174; *De Trin.,* VIII, 10, 14; PL 42, 960; *Confess.,* IV, 6, 11; IX, 12, 30; PL 32, 697, 698, 776.

[5] Joseph de Finance, *Etre et Agir,* Paris, Beauchesne, 1945, pp. 303-304: "The metaphysics of the will and the metaphysics of the intellect have in St. Thomas a very close solidarity with an 'existential' metaphysics. If the will is characterized by its relation to the thing *prout est in se,* its value and role will necessarily depend upon the value given to the concrete. Where being is reduced to its pure ideal determinations, spiritual activity is reabsorbed in the dynamism of the intellect in search of adequate knowledge. In a metaphysics of essence, in which opposition between concrete and abstract is the same as that between immersed form and pure form, the will insofar as it differentiates itself from the lucid progress of thought, belongs to those inferior forms of activity that philosophy need not justify. For it represents the lowering of pure spiritual activity to sensible contingencies. That is why a metaphysics strictly idealistic will fail to understand the originality of moral values. In order that the will should be made to distinguish itself from both organic tendencies and the dynamism proper

By St. Thomas, therefore, love is placed within a metaphysics of personal *esse*[5] whose being is God's presence by immanence, bidding man to be attentive to the significance of being. The human will is correctly understood only in relation to love and therefore to being. We have seen that the act of free choice is born of the reciprocal causality of intellect and will as related to transcendental being. St. Thomas concurs with Augustine in holding that the communication with Absolute Good, Subsistent Love, by Charity is the only foundation for the enjoyment of freedom in the broad sense, the freedom to adhere to one's true end — since the true historical end of man is a supernatural union with God as Friend. This theological freedom is the image of the divine liberty that Christ enjoyed while never foregoing his human free choice. By nature and by grace man can image the liberty of Christ in nearly always doing the things that please God. Love for God makes what is pleasing to God desirable to man. It is well to recall that it is because beings below God are analogous to Him that men love particular goods at all. The two aspects of being, truth and goodness, are in God identified. Through grace man's awareness of the relation between good things and God can grow ever stronger, so that all choices, besides perfecting man, can be primarily acts of communication with God. By the spontaneous loving of God known by faith, man is prepared to enter into the fullness of Being, the Source of all freedom. And that is eternal life.

to the intelligence, existence must be an act,f reely elicited by a divine decree, to which I must conform myself freely. The Thomistic metaphysics of *esse*, by justifying speculatively the doctrine of creation, conjures away the danger always threatening for any intellectualism of not appreciating the proper value of ' good will '." This helps to show why an adequate understanding of the role of the will was missing with the ancient philosophers; they spoke of will and free choice, but they were just *there*, as existence was.

CHAPTER XII

TWENTIETH CENTURY VIEWS ON FREEDOM

No one would ever claim that freedom has lost its charm for the twentieth century man. The very word has magical power to win assent to the most undeserving causes. It is the word most flagrantly abused in popular parlance. It is invoked to undo the power of the law court. It is a focal point in modern philosophy. But if freedom has retained its attraction for all men, has it retained its meaning for all men? This may prove a fruitful question.

One cannot discuss current opinions on freedom without considering the rich and varied contributions of the existentialists. Nor should the variety among these existentialists ever be overlooked. With the increasing number of scholarly studies pointing the differences among the current philosophers influenced by Kierkegaard and Nietzche and Husserl, we are less likely to think of existentialism as synonymous with atheism. [1] Among today's major existentialists — Sartre, Camus, Merleau-Ponty, Jaspers, Marcel and Heidegger — there is little agreement upon God. Divergent in their attitudes towards God in philosophy, these existential thinkers are united in taking man as a focal point for their philosophizing. It is thus that they reveal their common ancestor to be Kierkegaard, who reacted to Hegelian rationalism by reaffirming the importance of the individual man. It is because they see the individual man as dynamically involved in existence that they all concern themselves with freedom. Their conceptions of man will differ

[1] James Collins, *The Mind of Kierkegaard*, Chicago, Henry Regnery Company, 1953; Jean Wahl, *Esquisse pour une Histoire de l'Existentialisme*, Paris, L'Arche, 1949; James Collins, *The Existentialists*, Chicago, Henry Regnery Company, 1952; Regis Jolivet, *Les Doctrines Existentialistes*, Fontenelle, 1948; Emmanuel Mounier, *Introduction aux Existentalismes*, Paris, De Noel, 1947.

according to whether or not they have consented to bury God, and if God is affirmed, according to His relation with the human person.

If Kierkegaard rediscovered the individual, however, he did so by seeking the true significance of free choice. He viewed reality from the standpoint of the human vocation to ascend the three stages of existence — the aesthetic, the ethical, and the religious. Kierkegaard was close to Augustine in realizing that the power and the confidence to mount from one stage of life to another, to transcend self, comes from God Who unifies and uplifts man. But in his repudiation of reason he is unlike Augustine. Moreover, his existential descendants have fastened upon man's uniqueness in moulding the self without reference to the principle and the end of that development. Jaspers, however, sees in the direction of the free act towards the Transcendent a certain guarantee of the existence of that One whom he calls Wholly Other; but because there is no analogy between God and man, the Transcendent cannot be known philosophically. Jaspers considers the transcendent attitude in man to be the basis of his freedom, but because he does not recognize the immanence of God through His presence as constant efficient cause of being, human freedom lacks definite orientation.

This philosophical faith in a transcendent God at a discreet distance is Jaspers' way of insuring complete autonomy to man. Marcel has recognized, however, the intimate tie between free will and being, between freedom and dependence. God is seen not as the enemy of human freedom but as the friend of freedom. A free man is one who receives his being with humility, and Marcel is Augustinian in realizing that the more perfect man becomes by free activity ordered to the true end of man, the more he participates in being, and therefore the more dependent he is on God. The greater the dependence on God, the greater the being, the greater the freedom. Free will is seen as the faculty of personal communion, with the consequence of personal perfection. By love the self is enlarged to enter into other selves.

Although Heidegger is primarily interested in being, he enters into the experience of being through the human individual. It is the call to being with the ability to resist that Heidegger considers the challenge to freedom. The major responsibility of man is to mature himself by opening up to the truth of being. Not the individual who reads his own meaning into being is free, but the spokesman for being. Although Heidegger considers the philosophical method inadequate for the approach to God, his ontology does not exclude God. It may be that when he comes to know the meaning of the being he affirms, he will see in it the implication of God, whose proper effect it is.

The fact that many of Heidegger's analyses of conscience and of freedom derive from his careful reading of Augustine, as he himself notes, may eventually bring him to the Augustinian position that the fullest participation in being is through inter-personal communion with God as the recognized bond of friendship. Heidegger admits both an intrinsic value in every human being as human and the unique irreplaceablity of the personal being moulded by each man. Both Marcel and Heidegger recognize a link between freedom and being and value, and because they do not make of man the Absolute, they admit the limitations of human freedom without loss of hope for its self-transcendent power. As Heidegger's insight into being increases, or as he makes the meaning of being more explicit, both to himself and to us, his understanding of freedom will deepen.

When we turn to the atheistic existentialists we are not surprised to find a conception of freedom that is wholly other than that of Augustine. As a representative of those who have buried God to make man absolutely free, we shall for the present consider Sartre. Jean Paul Sartre is so entranced with freedom that he has equated it with man. In setting forth his doctrine of freedom Sartre declares that he is opposing the Christian notion of freedom. Yet Sartre, on the one hand, is really reacting against a notion of free will wherein human choice would be determined by nature, pinned down by passion, coerced by circumstances, harassed by heredity, the present merely flowing from the past; but this is not the Christian notion of free will any more than it is the real state of free will in man. On the other hand, he is more fundamentally reacting against a power of free choice that acts in relation to a nature with a preordained end, and so he is in radical opposition to all philosophers — ancient, medieval, modern — who admit that every given aspect of being contains a value or inherent meaning.

In a very deep way the Christian philosophers built upon the insights into " nature " provided by their Greek predecessors for the elaboration of the conception of freedom in creatures. To read the inherent meaning of a being is to discover the whole being — what it is to be — in relation to its end. A nature is a principle of improvement, and its fulfillment is nothing else than its good end. Although in impersonal beings this good end is imposed, man as a person can ratify or reject it. But he cannot change the established end of his nature, which is obtained by following the law of that nature as read in the hierarchy of tendencies.

While the negation of any natural tendency is an evil, only that negation which frustrates the nature of man is moral evil. As a person man can act as an individual but he is responsible for the fulfillment or frustration of his nature; what Christian philosophy adds to this is the dialogue with God as the author of nature. The responsibility read in the nature of things is written there by God, and man's personal response to it is not merely the fulfillment or the frustration of that nature, but of the individual person who submits to or rebels against God.

Man alone is able to embrace his end and advance towards it in an utterly original way. If the Author of nature necessarily wishes the fulfillment rather than the frustration of nature, then human freedom is rightly understood as the power of making good choices. There is therefore a distinction between acts in man, the human act and the good human act. An act of man that occurs without intellectual deliberation is not different from the spontaneous acts of animals; hence it is not free. A human act may be orientated towards an end that man proposes to himself, but one contrary to the established end of his nature — the total good as related to his highest powers; such an act is freely done, but since it is not a good act, it is against the best interests of man and has an enslaving character. In the Augustinian conception of freedom as the capacity to interiorize one's end by self-realization in response to the true good of man, a bad choice is the sign of the mixed perfection that human freedom is, but that is the risk involved in being free with respect to one's good end.

If all things are intended to image God by their goodness, the bad use of free choice is not only never an absolute freedom, but its very aping of absolute autonomy prevents the similitude to God that man may legitimately possess. Like the free choice of God, human free choice is man's opportunity to give unique expression to the transcendent values of truth, goodness and beauty. The field of choice is great but it is morally limited by its relation to truth and goodness.

This is creaturely freedom, the only kind open to man. Because Sartre considers existence as merely " there, " without inherent meaning or value, a mass of stuff which man organizes and endows with meaning, he is metaphysically prevented from attaining the notion of ordained freedom, of freedom as functioning within an order of being. Where he departs most widely from all philosophical tradition is in failing to see *good ends*. In eradicating value, he has dismissed good ends and thus the subjects who choose are impersonal centers of activity. Then every act of man is value-creative, and all human acts are good when they are done for an end that originates with the agent.

The lack of any standard, criterion, or guide is what Sartre understands by total responsibility. The act is inspired only by self-will. Man is the complete and sole cause of his action. Man, moreover, is the only one to be considered in acting. That is why Sartre thinks of hell as " other people. " His theory of freedom cannot but produce hostility and selfishness. In the traditional conception of free action, for an action to be right, it must not simply be directed towards the good of the agent but towards the good of all affected by this action. That is why Christian morality as blueprinted by Augustine was permeated by love and resulted in peace. Love makes a person one with others, and then the good of the other is sought as one's own; love for God makes one eager to do what God wants. This is efficacious moral transcendence, when one does completely unselfish things for God and for others with complete self-contentment.

For Augustine, love is the synthesis of obligation and happiness. Obligation, however, implies a created nature, as love implies a personal preference, and so responsibility and response only make sense within the order of received being, the true metaphysical status of the human person. Because total responsibility in the Sartrian sense eliminates God as the giver of being which bears a message from Him, it is a self-contradictory term. That is why Sartre contends that man is condemned to freedom and loneliness and to the ultimate frustration of attempting the impossible — Divinity.

In a Christian metaphysics, being is the source of meaning made known to man through the intellection of essence. By grasping the essence of man we become aware that freedom is inherent to him, and his value cannot therefore be divorced from his very real responsibility. His human vocation is to image God, not to substitute himself for God. With the help of God, man can grow not merely physically but spiritually. As man allows himself to be possessed by truth and by goodness, he perfects his spiritual dignity, but this he does through the medium of material things.

Freedom is possible because man has spiritual subsistence and because as a person he transcends his nature; the human will does not, therefore, follow the blind forces of nature. Free will is natural to man, but the person possessing human nature is responsible for the functioning of that nature. The human person is able to perceive the purposes of nature and to adopt them freely. Man is then responsible for his actions as well as his passions. He is free in and through his nature to control his passions indirectly, and should his passions grow stronger than he, there always remains the moral power to disavow or to sanction them.

And so man is neither condemned to a slavery to his nature nor to his passions. The person is the possessor, the user, the master of the nature. But because of the reality of that nature with its inherent value, there is a direction for his will, and rules for the use of free will. Only in such a case can there be any question of responsibility at all. It is difficult not to conclude that Sartre's description of total responsibility [1] which he fears to lose for man is in reality a description of radical irresponsibility.

Sartre's other fear is that without an absolute freedom man would be just another object among many, like a stone or a table; and so by conferring on man a subjectivity [2] that makes man nothing other than what he makes himself, Sartre wishes to confer on him a greater dignity. Yet the nature of man, endowed as it is with free will, already confers on man a self-mastery that raises him completely above material objects in dignity, for the root of free will, as we have seen, is spirituality.

Moreover, man's subjectivity, according to Sartre, is surpassed by the fact that he becomes by his action the maker of other men, since a man's acts, by creating man as he himself wishes to be, likewise create an image of man as he deems he ought to be. For, to choose anything is to affirm its value, to create it as valuable, and so in choosing myself I choose all men. According to Sartre, we are in the same creative condition as the artist who constructs a work of art and thereby creates new values. This activity of man without any attempt at conformity to pre-established values is the cornerstone of man's absolute freedom. Sartre concludes that if man creates values — he is the Absolute.

And therefore his existentialism is truly seen when it is seen as an attempt to deduce all the consequences of a coherent atheistic position. Existentialism, like many modern systems of thought, has adopted the scientific method of hypothetical

[1] J. P. Sartre, *L'Existentialisme est un Humanisme*, Paris, Nagel, 1946, p. 60.
[2] J. P. Sartre, *L'Existentialisme est un Humanisme*, Paris, Nagel, 1946, p. 22.

reasoning. The hypothesis underlying existentialism is : If there is no human nature, then there need be no God to conceive it. But the "*Cogito, ergo sum*" witnesses to an existence preceding essence. Then the only reality is action, and since all actions are different, men are alike only in their human conditions, that is, in the world, since they work in the midst of other men, and are mortal. Anguished, forlorn, and despairing, man is truly condemned to freedom. Man alone then must save himself.

Sartre's longing for true freedom and his conviction of the fact of free will are indicative that his ideal is a corruption of the true view of man : a being endowed with free will that fully accepts responsibility for actions, for influencing others, for raising himself by the acquisition of intellectual virtues which perfect man as knowing, and the acquisition of the moral virtues which perfect man as man. It is because man has the decisive "yes" and "no" in the matter of his own completion as a person by the integration of his personality and the fulfillment of his person through union with the end that St. Augustine said : "God who created man without himself will not save him without himself." [1]

The kind of free will that Sartre longs for is a fact, but it is the consequence, not the cause of nature, and yet it is truly the cause of man's moral being, over which he has absolute mastery. In this self-mastery God shares with man something of His absolute power. But Sartre desires more than this — he wants for man an infinite freedom which he describes as freedom for the sake of freedom. The difficulty is that man is finite, and yet there is a certain infinity in his will, but only because the Infinite God, Truth and Goodness, is its object. There is something above freedom in value, and it is God, and therefore freedom is for the sake of God. For man to enjoy infinite freedom we have seen that man must become united with the utterly free God — a union that is God's gift to all whose free wills function for the sake of Truth.

[1] Augustine, *Sermo* 169, 11, 13; PL 38, 923 : *Qui ergo fecit te sine te, non te justificat sine te.*

With Sartre we return to the original temptation: Do what you please and you will be like God — infinitely free. We have witnessed the disorder that resulted from man's falling into this temptation of seeking to erase the distinction between Creator and creature, making the mere will of the subject the norm of the good. We have witnessed the order that entered into the life of Augustine when he realized that to love God was to do as he pleased. It is this order of love that is the concrete setting for peace of heart where anguish gives place to hope, and forlornness to friendship with God, and despair to courage for the making of a better world.

Sartre does not claim originality in the doctrine of freedom that he has popularized today. He tells us that Descartes saw before Heidegger that the unique foundation of being was liberty. But Sartre holds that Descartes was forced by his milieu and by his point of departure to reduce human freedom to a mere negative power of resisting any external interference with the development of nature. For Descartes distinguished human freedom, the ability to do what one can, from divine freedom, the ability to do what one wishes. Descartes identified this latter kind of freedom with power and withdrew it from man. It is this productive liberty that Sartre returns to man, a creative liberty that constructs the truth.

Why does Sartre insist on giving this sort of freedom to man? He considers that Descartes' notion of freedom is too close to Christian liberty [1] which is a false freedom because if we do not invent our Good, "...then Good will have an independent a priori existence, and if man sees it, he must do it." [2] Sartre finds no difference between this position of Descartes in which the will gives way to understanding and that of the Platonists. Sartre thinks that the Cartesian man, like the Christian man, is by this doctrine freed for evil but not for good, for error and not for truth; for this man there is only action with regard to evil, only passion with regard to good. He concludes that such freedom is negative, scarcely worth discussing, for the liberty of God

[1] Jean Paul Sartre, *Situations*, I, Paris, Librairie Gallimard, 1947, p. 330.
[2] *Ibid.*, p. 325.

on which being is founded is the necessity of man who submits to it. Sartre declares that Descartes really had intuited an affirmative, productive liberty in the "*Cogito*," but, unfaithful to this intuition because of his religious traditions, he hypostasized this limitless liberty, and it remained for his successors to deny the existence of God and to recover this "freedom" as the foundation of man's being, a power which makes man completely responsible for his being.

It is a rather common opinion that Sartre has taken the freedom proper to God and attributed it to man, but when one becomes aware that it is Cartesian voluntarism that is the point of departure for Sartre's notion of freedom, we can see that the new error of existentialism is the offspring of the old error of the Cartesian notion of Divine Freedom, wherein wisdom takes second place. Even if the "existential dialectic" of Kierkegaard gave its name to that philosophy which states that one's own existence is prior to one's essence, the promise of Cartesian divine freedom to man is the facet that gives to Sartre's existentialism its appeal. That is why this philosophy thrives only with those whom it can persuade to reject faith and reason, for it is a system of disbelief in God's existence. Ultimately, the freedom of the existentialists becomes freedom for the sake of revolution. This is because the contruction of one's individual freedom implies the destruction of the freedom of every other individual who might cross one's path.

Freedom is indeed one of the mysteries at the heart of personal existence, and only an authentic philosophy of the person can do adequate justice to the dimension of freedom. A re-evaluation of freedom is imperative for our age and may well bring about the modern man's return to God. For an understanding of freedom would demand an understanding of love, and it is the experience of true love that is needed to experience true freedom. Erroneous as is Sartre's notion of freedom when taken in its total implication, may it not be an unconscious deviation from a true notion of freedom as of immense import for man?

Freedom was not belittled nor explained away by St. Augustine, nor by St. Anselm, nor by St. Thomas Aquinas. The free act, born of intellect and will, is the act of the spirit and a participation in the creativity of the First Cause. Man directs the will that has been given to him and in so doing he gives himself his own personality. Not only because of his marvelous words on the Persons in God to be found in the *De Trinitate,* but also because of his appreciation of the personal power of free will in the making of man unto the image of God, Augustine deserves to be called the Prophet of Personality. This is the part of truth in Sartre's exorbitant exaltation of freedom. When Sartre therefore speaks of the human essence, the ensemble of qualities of the individual, as rooted in the liberty of man and varying with the use made of liberty, he is with a certain correctness speaking of personality. Yet the irrationality of the will in Sartre would prove the negation of personality, which is the perfection of a rational individual.

If, according to Augustine, free will is for the attainment of the Infinite, and one attains freedom in proportion to one's union with God, in Whom Personality is perfect, it is likewise a fact that in this process man is best personalized. And as man becomes more perfectly a person, he becomes more " *capax Dei.* " Personality is not one of life's digressions; it is not a side issue. We cannot take the attitude that the present emphasis on personality must be pagan. It is rather an outgrowth of a very old concern, as old as Christianity.

The reality of personality engaged the attention of the earliest theological thinkers. It was not a living issue when Plato and Aristotle lived. That is why in these philosophers there was always a certain opposition between man and society. It is individuality that is actually opposed to society, not the person. At the world's origin there is a society of Persons, and They are perfect. In our world, personality is present in each man imperfectly. There is an interesting parallel between the achievement of freedom and the achievement of personality. Man is born with free will and must achieve freedom, and man is born a person who must achieve personality. The glorious side of free will is then its purposefulness. There is nothing negative in this attitude toward free will.[1]

Inasmuch as the Greeks had a certain esteem for "*causa sui*" they drew near to the aspect of self-possession that characterizes the person, but this ideal could only be realized when men became truly enfranchised.

Take again the notion of Greek self-sufficiency; the closed-in naturalness that it presupposes is in point of fact only a self-betrayal. This false ideal again merely foreshadows the Christian truth that independence from others can become a reality when we enter into the freedom of the children of God. The Christian, as Anselm aptly put it, becomes free by depending completely on God. This state of freedom is a participation in the Divine Freedom by which God freely loved us into existence. Of the Christian man we can say :

> He is independent of every external constraint because he is dependent only on the Divine Causality which is in no sense stranger to him. He is self-sufficing because he has lost his own self and lives only by the life of the Divine Savior who lives in him. Far more truly than the sage of pagan thought he is all things to himself since he is now one only in Love and Spirit with the Absolute : 'two natures in one Spirit and Love.'[2]

If the free man is the fulfilled person and if human fulfillment cannot occur without God, it can be seen why both the "*causa sui*" and the "self-sufficient man" were only imperfectly realized among the pagans. Somehow or other, the pagan philosophers continued the mental error of Eve : hoping to become like God without God. In his doctrine of freedom, Augustine has radically recognized the impossibility of freedom without God. This insight, preserved through medieval days, is echoed by a modern Thomist when he says : "God being the

[1] Gerald Phelan, "Person and Liberty", *Proceedings of the American Catholic Philosophica Association*, XVI, Washington, Catholic University of America Press, 1940, p. 65 : "In a sense which few who use the expression understand, the realization of one's personality is indeed the true purpose of life. Men must grow in personality, i.e., in self-control, in the dominion over their acts, and in the mastery over, and possession of, their own being."

[2] J. Maritain, *Freedom in the Modern World*, trans. R. O'Sullivan), New York, Scribner's, 1936, p. 37.

perfection of personal existence and man being also, though precariously, a person, the mystery of the achievement of freedom is contained in the relation of these two persons." [1]

Augustine realized that the root of freedom is spirituality, which is also the root of personality. This casts light on why Augustine, knowing the Aristotelian definition of man as a being of matter and form, [2] constantly spoke of man as spiritual, thereby following Plato, although for reasons other than those of Plato. This he did without offering supporting metaphysical reasons; yet the metaphysical reason becomes more apparent as the philosophy of personality becomes more penetrating. As Father Phelan says:

> Even man's body exists by an *esse* which is spiritual. For this reason all the acts performed by men as men (all human acts) are spiritual acts even though they be performed through bodily powers. Human life, whole and entire, insofar as it is truly human, is spiritual. [3]

It is not surprising then that in the history of philosophy the Christian thinker most famous for defending the human soul should be both the prophet of personality and a pioneer philosopher of freedom.

If the authentic notion of liberty is absent today, cannot we trace this to the loss of its presuppositions: the meaning of personality, and the true position of the human person in the universe? Until lately the history of philosophy was marked by a great gap between the Greeks and Descartes. Pushed aside as inconsequential was the thinking and philosophizing done by theologians. There was an implicit assumption among history-compilers that the theological cancelled out the human in the man; they did not realize that superior knowledge was a fruitful atmosphere for philosophical thinking. This *lacuna* resulted in a certain impoverishment of intellectual life, one that is only now slowly being remedied. Thus in saying that despite the vast literature on the subject of freedom, there is something yet to

[1] *Ibid.*, p. 36.

[2] Augustine, *Confess.*, IV, 16, 29; PL 32, 705; *De Quantitate Animæ*, I, 2; PL 32, 1036; *De Immortalitate Animæ*, XV, 24; XVI, 25; PL 32, 1033-1034.

[3] Phelan, "Person and Liberty," p. 64.

be said, Maurice Cranston [1] is calling attention to the poverty of the present notion of freedom as well as exposing the current denial of freedom.

There is a connection between these two facts. People who understand freedom do not deny it. We do not go to textbooks to understand it, but to the experience of personal relationships and responsibilities in the context of time and history. It was this contextual evaluation of freedom that Augustine bequeathed to the world by the basic implications of his philosophy of history contained in the *City of God.* There Augustine upheld the ideal of a holy and balanced order of society which all social orders must seek to embody. This Augustinian view of history springs from the conviction that God created and preserves the universe with man as His co-worker in the building of human society. But this

> ...involves man in choice and so in freedom... sharing in the achievements, culpable of the failures, carrying the grandeur and the servitude of responsibility. No longer absorbed blindly in the social process, he had reason and conscience to guide his judgments and his actions. [2]

The building of God's City was the "terrible yet magnificent vocation of a son of God." [3] This, we must admit, is a far cry from that view of history where repetition, not progress, is presented as the reality, symbolized by the revolving wheel of recurrent birth and death characterizing the determinism and pessimism of the ancient civilizations. From this there could only be generated a philosophy of melancholy which

> ... echoes in the words of the greatest disciple of Greek Stoic philosophy, the Roman Emperor Marcus Aurelius, who declared: 'Up and down, to and fro, round and round: this is the monotonous and meaningless rhythm of the universe. A man of ordinary mental powers who has reached the age of 40 has experienced everything that has been and is to come.' [4]

[1] Maurice Cranston, *Freedom*, London, Longmans Green, 1953.
[2] Barbara Ward, *Faith and Freedom*, New York, W.W. Norton and Company, 1954, p. 13.
[3] Ward, *Faith and Freedom*, p. 25.
[4] Ward, *Faith and Freedom*, p. 21.

By contrasting Augustine's vision of man in time with this conclusion of Marcus Aurelius we are helped to see that our own western society is founded on the Augustinian conception of the destiny of man with its implications for time and freedom, rather than upon the Stoic acceptance of a universal determinism.

Nevertheless, the absence of agreement upon the nature of freedom and the travesty that has been made of freedom by 20th century existentialists would seem indicative in our civilization both of the loss of the meaning of freedom and the longing to understand and enjoy this reality. Now if we recall that it was in an atmosphere of faith that the Augustinian notion of freedom flourished, we come to see that our present secularism is not a congenial climate for the comprehension and the enjoyment of freedom. The separation of God from man, of religion from life, is contrary to the order of reality. Could it be that the loss of faith in our day is the signpost of an impending loss of freedom?

It seems, no doubt, a far cry from the earth gods and fertility rites of ancient Sumeria and the melancholy determinism of archaic philosophy to our modern rationalism with its picture of a closed material universe or to modern Marxism with its single economically conditioned historical process. Yet it may be that our supposedly modern ideas have more in common with the submerged civilizations than with the two or three thousand years of human history which lie in between. It may be when we examine modern determinism more closely, that it will appear something of a throwback to ancient ways of thought, a relapse into earlier intuitions and the relinquishing of a significant part of mankind's intellectual and moral heritage.[1]

It is not without significance that this brilliant thinker of our day, Barbara Ward, recognized the 19th century as the turning point in our civilization, a point of turning back to the dark clouds of determinism that had been banished by the spirit of truth. By means of the 18th century theory of a "hidden law" regulating economic life, determinism began its re-incarnation. Thus, some important parts of human life were removed from proper human control when man was advised to act solely

[1] Ward, *Faith and Freedom*, p. 21.

according to the pressure of his material interests. It was not long before man himself was removed from the freedom of rational control and set within a universe of material conditioning. Feuerbach, Darwin, Freud, and Watson showed the great power wielded over man by the physical, the temporal, the psychological, the environmental stimuli. Their propaganda has had effect.

The belief that material events alone are real and condition everything else — in other words, determinism — is the stuff of so much modern, popular thinking that it must be counted the most widespread belief of our day. For at least a third of the human race — in Russia and China — it is not only widespread but obligatory. Far beyond the totalitarian frontier, however, popular determinism has its hold. In their personal lives, for instance, men believe that environment and heredity make them precisely what they are — the former in the shape of class or race and the latter in the shape of genes, chromosomes, drives and instincts. In social life the struggle for survival, class interest, and racial antagonism, are held to be the very 'web of history.'[1]

We are then well warned; modern determinism's likeness to archaic fatalism should alert us to what it asks us to forego — our highest values of freedom, responsibility, the quest for goodness, law, and representative government. In a conditioned universe the struggle for goodness is meaningless and so, freedom, initial or terminal, being unreal, has lost its meaning. Yet there are islands of freedom today pushing their way above the sea of inevitability. Determinism has not the unchallenged sway it knew before the coming of Christ.

However rigorously a Marxist or a rationalist seeks to accept his own completely fatalistic version of society, he lives today after centuries of belief in liberty and choice and responsibility, and in a spiritual order of life. Freedom, like Dr. Johnson's cheerfulness, will keep breaking through, even if it has no place in the system. The determinism of ancient society was more thorough because it was not recognized as determinism at all. The unity of all experience, which has to be proclaimed now as a dogma, was then simply accepted as reality itself.[2]

[1] Ward, *Faith and Freedom*, p. 12.
[2] Ward, *Faith and Freedom*, p. 24.

And so in these days of rampant determinism the longing for freedom that is evidenced in the aberrations of existentialism is a call to restore the real meaning of freedom in all its pristine splendor. Man's clamoring for freedom is not to be dismissed. For "beside the hunger for gain and the hunger for power there is a hunger for creation, for justice, for the realization of an ideal — in a word, St. Augustine's two cities co-exist in every civilization and neither Europe nor any other society can be understood unless the opposite energies of the human heart are allowed their play." [1] Man's awakening today to the achievements possible to creative love is the dawn-star of true freedom.

If faith in freedom has waned because of secularism and materialism, one way to revive that faith might be to review its philosophical foundations. Recently, some contemporary philosophers and professors of philosophy were asked to view the question of freedom from as many angles as possible. It is interesting to note that their various statements about freedom cannot conceal the Christian climate of thought in which their ideas took shape. Thus, when James J. Shotwell concludes that "...liberty will increase in proportion as society learns to make intelligence the guide to conduct," [2] he has riveted attention on a true facet of freedom. When Paul Tillich, as a Christian theologian, requires that human freedom be creative, that is, able to determine history and transform human nature through history, he only nominally echoes Augustine, because his idealism seems to dissolve the literally divine factor in history and thus to render the City of God a mere symbol. [3] John MacMurray sees "freedom and determinism as implicates, not contradictories" and recognizes freedom "as the product of right personal relations." [4] Croce agrees with Tillich in calling freedom "...the force that creates history" and he would read all history as the history of freedom. [5] But in Croce profound Augustinism is

[1] Ward, *Faith and Freedom*, p. 72.
[2] *Freedom, Its Meaning*, (ed. Ruth N. Anshen), New York, Harcourt Brace, 1940, p. 22.
[3] Anshen, *Freedom, Its Meaning*, p. 131.
[4] Anshen, *Freedom, Its Meaning*, p. 509.
[5] Anshen, *Freedom, Its Meaning*, p. 28.

absent; without the Augustinian dialectic between man and God, all similarity in the expression of thought is superficial. Croce dissolves the tension between nature and the supernatural which provides Augustine with so much of the dynamism of history.

When we read the history of today's struggle for universal democracy, we can see in it the urge to realize in history the freedom man has by nature, while the wider cosmic strife of nature and of purpose witnesses to the primacy of the spiritual which is ever being asserted by the achievement of new spiritual values. [1] Spiritual freedom is one of those values. It is highly esteemed, but this esteem exists side by side with the most flagrant disregard for man's right to basic freedom of will in many spheres of life. Where this occurs — under totalitarian regimes — the rulers are only being logical in their rejection of freedom. For they have already rejected the presuppositions of freedom — the dignity of personality, the equality of all, and brotherly love. They will admit that the so-called liberties or rights would help the welfare of man but they "deny that man's welfare is a worthy object." [2] This would suggest that the freedom-loving peoples of the world should place the attainment of world freedom upon a broader and deeper basis. Man's utter dependence on God together with the glorious height of human destiny must be pondered.

Today after almost twenty centuries of reflective thought, freedom, confirmed by the Incarnation, is more admired than understood. And yet many of our contemporaries have shown real insight into the reality of freedom. James Truslow Adams considers that the question of freedom is really a religious rather than a political one. Thus with the loss of religion today has come the loss of liberty. He says that the question of the kind of freedom desired is "...twin-brother to the old question in the Presbyterian catechism, 'What is the chief end of man?' Until we can decide that we cannot decide what type of freedom we desire." [3]

[1] E. S. Brightman, in Anshen, *Freedom, Its Meaning,* p. 499.
[2] Anshen, *op. cit.*, p. 489.
[3] Anshen, *Freedom, Its Meaning,* p. 112.

If the answer to the question of man's chief end illuminates the meaning of free will, the root of man's actual state of freedom can be located in his relation to the truth. Intellectual liberty is the first step to the achievement of human freedom. But what is intellectual liberty? Etienne Gilson tells us that "mental liberty consists in a complete liberation from our personal prejudices and in our complete submission to reality." [1] Gilson sees realism as the source of personal liberty and the guarantee of social liberty. [2]

Like Gilson, Edgar Sheffield Brightman emphasizes the connection between choice and objectivity when he speaks of freedom as the "freedom to purpose value." [3] For the deliberation involved in choice implies a "reference to value — a standard of estimation; the possibility must be regarded as worth choosing." [4]

On the other hand, Kurt Riezler sees that something else besides objectivity is necessary to insure freedom, something that comes from the subject. We are not slaves because we obey rules, nor are we free because we disregard them. "Not the rules as such but our relation to them determines whether in obeying or disobeying we are free or slaves." [5]

It is Aristotle whom Raphael Demos blames for the confusion surrounding human action, some philosophers seeing it as determined and others claiming freedom for it. It was Aristotle who defined substance as essence, thus making human choice determined. "...Unless we differentiate the self from its nature, there is no alternative to a deterministic account of human action." [6] Only when the self is distinguished from the nature is there opened up the possibility of deciding to be or not to be rational.

Finally, with Herbert W. Schneider we can agree that "...it is profitable to ask the question whether liberty is best gained

[1] Anshen, *op. cit.*, p. 168.
[2] Anshen, *op. cit.*, p. 169.
[3] Anshen, *op. cit.*, p. 489.
[4] Anshen, *op. cit.*, p. 487.
[5] Anshen, *op. cit.*, p. 544.
[6] Anshen, *op. cit.*, p. 607.

by a love of liberty and by preaching that freedom is an end in itself, as Sartre does, or by a love of truth, art, neighbor, God, in the hope that a love of liberty will be a by-product."[1]

Among the modern philosophers of freedom none more fully unites many insights of Augustine and Aquinas on the subject of freedom than does Jacques Maritain. Within the existentialist metaphysics of St. Thomas he demonstrates why free choice must belong to spiritual beings. He distinguishes with Augustine between free choice and freedom of spontaneity or fulfillment, freedom in the strict sense and freedom in the broad sense; and he concludes with Augustine that it is by grace that man is best fulfilled and enjoys the truest liberty.

Jacques Maritain recognizes in human liberty the hallmark of human nature. Early in his philosophical career, this erstwhile student of Bergson expressed disagreement with Bergson on the issue of liberty. To Bergson Maritain would ever be grateful for awakening in him a desire for metaphysics, but to other thinkers and to reality Maritain must turn to fulfill that desire. To Bergson freedom meant escape from intellectual guidance. To Maritain freedom is permeated with, secured through, and preserved by intellectuality, at least as the natural foundation for freedom. This is, as we have seen, in direct line with Thomism. After making the Thomistic philosophy of freedom his own, and after having realized the purposeful implications of freedom for human destiny, Maritain has deduced the special implications of human liberty for the terrestial and political world. He calls this platform "Integral Humanism,"[2] and shoulders the full responsibility for an outlook of charitable, universal cooperation known as "Maritainism."

Maritain, therefore, set forth his thought on free will in opposition to that of Bergson, in whose philosophy the only truly free act is the one decided upon without reason. Bergson calls that act free which springs from the personal self alone.

[1] Anshen, *Freedom, Its Meaning*, p. 671, 672.
[2] Jacques Maritain, *Humanisme Intégral*, Paris, Aubier, 1936.

He sees freedom as the "relation of the concrete self to the act which it performs."[1] Such a relation is indefinable "...because the relation of this action to the state from which it issued could not be expressed by a law, this psychic state being unique of its kind and unable ever to occur again."[2] Maritain considers that this is a confusion of freedom with spontaneity of the whole soul. He points out the metaphysical implications of such a position: the contingent would create itself, and potency would pass of itself into act.[3] Holding that Bergsonian anti-intellectualism compromises and destroys the liberty of man just as truly as does the intellectualism of Parmenides, Spinoza, Leibniz and Hegel, Maritain quotes St. Thomas as saying: "The root of all liberty is fixed in reason."[4]

Freedom is rooted in the intellectual perception of the universal, but above all in the priority of being to intellect. By abandoning being and the intellect, Bergson had abandoned freedom. It is true that Bergson's intentions are good. His recourse to unintelligibility, as Maritain sees it, is a reaction to the charges of determinism made by the scientific thinkers of his milieu. The remedy, however, is too violent; the intellect does not have to be cast out to save the indetermination of the will.

Like St. Thomas, Maritain proclaims the will to be necessitated by nature to desire the good in general; because of this, it is free in its particular choices. He looks upon free choice as a choosing between the means, because the ordination to the end remains fixed, and this end will always be at an infinite distance from any finite good. One finite thing may be better than another, but since choice is made in view of an infinite end, no practical judgment of the goodness of a finite thing can ever necessitate the will to act. Moreover, in order that

[1] Henri Bergson, *Time and Free Will*, (trans. F. L. Pogson), London, George Allen and Company, 1912, p. 219.

[2] *Ibid.*, p. 239.

[3] Jacques Maritain, *La Philosophie Bergsonienne*, Paris, Marcel Rivière, 2e éd., 1930, p. 358.

[4] *Ibid.*, Thomas Aquinas, *De Veritate*, 24, 2. Quoted by Maritain.

a practical judgment may be final for me, my will must intervene to make it so. For, in every one of its particular acts, the will acts by a motive, but one that does not necessitate it. It is indeed a motive that is constituted as a motive by the will, because the judgment in offering to the will an attractive good is acting merely as a formal extrinsic cause; the attraction is there because the good thing, apprehended by the intellect, participates in the finality of the total-good or end. But because it is only a partial good when the will chooses it, the will is the efficient cause of the very attraction it undergoes. The will

> ...triumphs, 1) over the indetermination of the object (simultaneously good and not-good, because it is not the Good Itself); 2) over the passive indetermination which characterizes itself (and which is a sign of imperfection : it is not always in act like the will of God). It triumphs over this double indetermination by exercising its active and dominating indetermination or indifference, which is the very essence of liberty. It is because many authors have not distinguished in our will this active and dominating indifference from passive indifference that they have so entirely misunderstood the Thomist doctrine of free choice. [1]

Maritain pays tribute to St. Thomas for having established free choice as being " both of intellect and of will. " [2]

Maritain follows Augustine in distinguishing the two aspects of freedom : *free will,* given with the rational nature, which is not an end in itself, but is a metaphysical root of spiritual nature which must grow and develop in the psychological and moral order; and *freedom of fulfillment,* a perfection of the spirit, a beginning of adhesion to one's last end, the perfect spontaneity of a spiritual nature in love with the Good. [3]

The will as intellectual appetite is that by which man tends towards any being apprehended by the intellect, and vaguely, towards being as such. It has a natural tendency towards the good-in-general, the total good, and consequently the will

[1] Maritain, *La Philosophie Bergsonienne*, p. 362, n. 1.

[2] Maritain, *La Philosophie Bergsonienne*, p. 365.

[3] Jacques Maritain, *Freedom in the Modern World*, (trans. R. O'Sullivan), New York, Scribner's, 1936, p. 30.

tends to rest in any being which seems good in any way. But for an actual choice to occur, man must evaluate the particular good in reference to the good-for-man. Maritain refers to the *Summa Theologica* Part I, Question 89, where St. Thomas says that we first make a decision as to our last end at the time when the life of reason and of personality comes to establish itself. This is possible because the world of nature and the world of freedom have the same Head. It is in the moral choice that the formal motive transcends the whole order of empirical convenience and desire. This is "the primary implication of the first act of freedom when it is good." [1] It is God who is chosen, and the child in this first act of freedom knows God without being aware of it.

> He knows God because by virtue of the internal dynamism of his choice of the good for the sake of the good, he wills and loves the separate Good as ultimate end of his existence. Thus his intellect has of God a vital and non-conceptual knowledge which is involved both in the practical notion (confusedly and intuitively grasped, but with its full intentional energy), of the moral good as formal motive of his first act of freedom and in the movement of his will toward this good and, all at once, toward the Good. [2]

Maritain declares that the conformity of the intellect, which is borne beyond the particular object, with this transcendent object, i. e., the separate Good, is effected by the will.

If free choice is the act of the will as a cause in the order of exercise, the intellect has its part to play in calling attention to the value of the being. It is in this order of value, the order of specification, that freedom of fulfillment or autonomy is won. When we freely recognize the right of value to impose an obligation on us, we escape the chains of egoism. By *realizing* the general truth: "Good is to be done," one enters into the free world of objectivity. [3] Freedom of fulfillment is achieved "through the operation of a good will in the secret heart of

[1] Jacques Maritain, *Range of Reason*, New York, Scribner's, 1952, p. 68.
[2] *Ibid.*
[3] Jacques Maritain, *Neuf Leçons sur les Notions Premières de la Philosophie Morale*, Paris, Tequi, n.d. pp. 122, 123.

man." [1] When the will tends towards the moral good, the intellect knows God existentially through conformity with the right will. " He that doeth the truth cometh to the light." (John III, 21). The choice of God as Ultimate End is implicit in every choice of the *bonum honestum*.

Maritain's thought on the intimate relation between the individual's freedom and the common good becomes apparent when he tells us that the society of persons is a means for the advancement of this second aspect of freedom, namely, freedom of autonomy or fulfillment.

> " A civilization... should necessarily aim at securing for the mass of its citizens conditions that are worthy of man and that will put each citizen thus equipped for the life of reason and of virtue in the way of advancing towards perfect freedom and of achieving his eternal destiny." [2]

Justice and law, in ruling men as moral agents, deal with persons, so that the relation between society and person is a relation of two wholes. Nor is society to be ignored in the pursuit of one's personal end. Although the person has been historically called to a supernatural End, Maritain sees a real temporal destiny of love for one another to be the natural implication of our eternal destiny, and to be a destiny in perfect accord with human nature. And so " ...this new humanism, having nothing in common with bourgeois humanism, and really being more human insofar as it does not adore man, but really and effectively respects human dignity and gives full scope to the integral exigencies of the person," [3] has been proposed as a positive program for the re-making of man and the modern world. The modern world needs re-making because it was made largely by non-humanists: Macchiavelli, " author of a cynical separation between politics and morality which would have shocked Aristotle;" Luther with his " egocentrism;" Descartes and his " angelism;" Rousseau, the " saint of nature."[4]

[1] Maritain, *Freedom in the Modern World*, p. 44.
[2] *Ibid.*
[3] Jacques Maritain, *Humanisme Intégral*, Paris, Aubier, 1936, p. 15.
[4] Cf. Jacques Maritain, *Three Reformers*, London, Sheed Ward, 1928.

If the world is to be re-made well, what is truly human in it must be salvaged. This calls for reinstating the world's dependence upon God by an authentic doctrine of human freedom. Maritain knows that the liberation of the human person is a supernatural work accomplished by Christ in and through His Church, in and through His living, loving members who unite their wills to the Divine Intention, but he knows also that there are good things in nature upon which all men can agree. He glimpses the fact that all men can be united in love before they are united in truth. All things, therefore, that are good and true should be united and harmonized; the remaining fragments from the Bread of Life broken for the multitude should be gathered together. The " indirect and direct impacts of the Gospel upon history, " [1] all belong together.

Maritain's aim is to rescue all that is truly human for the ultimate attainment of the divine destiny of mankind. He asks: What is the aim which Christian political action has in view as its final goal? And he answers that it is nothing less than the consecration of secular life to God in Christ, the rehabilitation of the creature in God. For the person is both within society and beyond society, at home in the universe and on his way to God. After centuries of Christian civilization, the spirit of Christ is recognizable even among non-Christians; to conserve and unite all that is true and good in the world, " the known Christ and the unknown Christ must combine to save us. " [2] This universal cooperation in the re-making of the modern world unto the image of its Maker, Jacques Maritain sees as the sublime temporal task of human free will.

The most authentic modern voice of Augustinism, however, is to be heard in the philosophical school inspired by Maurice Blondel, who lived from 1861 to 1949. It was the aim of this great French Catholic philosopher as well as of his colleagues, René Le Senne and especially Louis Lavelle, to channel the Augustinian tradition of freedom into the contemporary world.

[1] E. L. Allen, *Christian Humanism*, London, Hodder and Stoughton, 1950, p. 65.
[2] *Ibid.*

In Blondel we witness a veritable resurrection of Christian philosophy, where the spirit of Augustine moves freely as the organizing force of the best in traditional and modern thought.

In presenting a phenomenology of Christian existence, Blondel acknowledges the impossibility of entirely encompassing by thought the mystery of man. But in his attempt to understand this mystery he, like Augustine, combines, without confounding, faith and reason. Careful to affirm the supernaturally transcendent character of Revelation, Blondel is firm in holding that a logical idea of man is inadequate to encompass his transcendent vocation. He gives to reason its rightful autonomy while he explores the human conscience in the light of faith. That is why he is able to discover within the conscience of the real historical man the point of insertion for grace. This existential analysis of the mystery of human consciousness with its findings of concrete anguish and an infinity of desire is in conformity with the intuitions of Augustine and Pascal, and like these great thinkers, Blondel is careful not to make the gift of God to man as End the satisfaction of any natural exigency. The divine communication with man by grace is a gratuitous answer to an appetite that God Himself has aroused. [1]

The anguish experienced by man is the infinite distance between what man is and what he can be. The human aspiration to the totality of being, of truth, of goodness stimulates the spirit of generosity. Like Augustine, Blondel goes straight to the heart of freedom in its most profound sense. He is concerned not merely with a creative liberty orientated uniquely towards the world, but with that sublime exercise of liberty which is the free consent to the personal gift of love, above all, of Divine Love. As a consent to love, liberty is a passivity, but a passivity that is higher than any other human activity. The greatest moment in man's interior life is this consent to God, a submission which ratifies the infinite *élan* of his will. It is the beginning of a divine

[1] Maurice Blondel, *L'Action*, Paris, Alcan, 1936, vol. I, p. 200 : " Si Dieu se prête ainsi aux esprits en se cachant d'abord et presque en disparaissant sous l'enveloppe des magnificences physiques ou des obscurités de l'inconscience, c'est pour se faire chercher, c'est pour se faire trouver de ceux qu'il stimule du dedans et du dehors par l'inquiétude et par le désir, par les épreuves et les certitudes, par toute cette pédagogie de la nature et de l'âme... "

friendship which is freely and intimately begun by God. Through God's transcendent action on the soul, the will becomes more completely itself and free to love as man is called to love in a real community of God with men. [1]

Blondel successfully keeps together the human and the divine without confusing or merging them — humanism and transcendence maintain their autonomy in the supreme synthesis of Mercy. [2] Like Augustine, Blondel offers a religious humanism that brings into sharp focus the meaning of life : the freedom of man and the freedom of God meeting in the interior world of the history of salvation. Man acquires his true meaning and his personal value only in his concrete relation with a God of Charity, both transcendent and incarnate in history. Today when contemporary paganism wants liberty without God, the philosophy of Blondel can raise a prophetic voice in warning that such apparent liberty is the commencement of slavery. For the denial of God is the denial of man. Blondel's whole philosophy calls man away from servitude without God to liberty under God.

Truly Blondel has revived and made significant for our world the Augustinian notion of freedom. This is only one of the many points of contact between the total doctrine of Augustine and that of Blondel, but it would require volumes to do justice to these *rapprochements*. We shall only mention here the close similarity in their method of immanence and in their search for the real. Far from opposing action to thought, Blondel considers them as complementary functions. The will should collaborate with reason to attain what is true. That is how Blondel widens the way to truth. Besides speaking of sensible knowledge,

[1] Blondel, *L'Action*, I, pp. 200-209.

[2] Blondel recognizes the ability to do this as the great achievement of Augustine. In his article on Augustine in *Revue de Métaphysique et de Morale*, 1930, he comments on the distinction that was later made between nature and supernature when discussing man and says : " Sous ces influences convergentes, l'idée d'un surnaturel absolu telle que l'enveloppait la tradition s'opposait à un concept de nature pure, avec le risque de faire croire que ces deux ordres, légitimement distingués *in abstracto* et réellement hétérogènes, étaient effectivement extérieurs l'un à l'autre dans la donnée historique et concrète. Envisageant donc l'état actuel de l'homme, sous l'influence de cette analyse hypothétique ou omettait, au profit d'une recherche du mode de subordination réfléchie d'un ordre à l'autre, la question vitale de leur coopération profonde et de leur compénétration effective, telle qu'Augustin l'avait surtout impliquée et pratiquée. "

he speaks of two other means to attain to truth : notional knowledge which proceeds by abstract concepts; and real knowledge which by the aid of action attains the object intuitively. Real knowledge consists in an intuition of the total being, an intuition that is had by a certain connaturality which action procures. A new and higher intellectuality, a plenitude of thought is born of action when this action is the incarnation of truth already possessed. [1]

With Augustine Blondel recognizes the human drama to develop around the all-important action of man's taking a position of liberty when confronted with God. Blondel has understood that this option is the point of departure for arrival at the larger liberty of man's becoming all that God wants him to be, the ideal liberty to which God first called man. The natural basis for the enjoyment of such liberty is the infinite amplitude of the will and man's mysterious restlessness in the face of every finite good — but it is God Who has chosen to use this base to re-form man unto His own image by giving Himself to be the object of the human will.

Our search for modern viewpoints on free will and the attainment of freedom may well end with the suggestion that the development of Christian Personalism, which has been influenced so strongly by the philosophy of action of Blondel, and more remotely but just as powerfully by the spirit of St. Augustine, will effect in our time a still greater elucidation of the philosophical principles of freedom. [2] Thinkers will

[1] M. Blondel, " Le Point de Départ de la Recherche Philosophique, " in *Annales de Philosophie Chrétienne*, June 1906, 6, 54, pp. 241-242 : " Le vrai philosophe, selon l'opinion commune, ce n'est pas celui qui se contente de penser, non plus que celui qui se contente d'agir; c'est celui qui, connaissant plus, agit mieux, celui qui tire de son expérience même un surcroît de lumière et de force, sachant davantage ce qu'il fait parce qu'il a fait d'abord ce qu'il savait... Pour l'homme, ...la vie n'est pas la vie sans la pensée, pas plus que la pensée n'est la pensée sans la vie. Il faut donc savoir se servir de ce qu'on est et de ce qu'on a pour connaître, et se servir de ce qu'on connaît pour être et pour avoir davantage, sans que, dans cette propulsion alternative comme celle d'une roue qui tourne en avançant, la cycloïde puisse s'achever en cercle, c'est-à-dire sans que la réflexion spéculative et la prospection pratique se recouvrent et coïncident dès à présent. "

[2] Blondel, " L'Unité Originale et la Pensée Permanente de la Doctrine Philosophique de Saint Augustin, " *op. cit.*, pp. 432, 433 : " ...si la philosophie Chrétienne détourne d'Augustin, elle languit et se dessèche, tandis que, chaque fois qu'elle revient à lui, elle reprend flamme et vigueur. "

doubtless continue along the lines that have been drawn by Blondel, René Le Senne, Louis Lavelle, E. Mounier and others of their school, until the total reality of freedom is rendered conceptually and actually more accessible to our day.

The modern incomplete or confused concepts of freedom may come from not posing the basic question with regard to freedom. The late scholastics asked : how is man's will free? The majority of people today are asking : how can man's will be insured freedom from constraint in all spheres of life? But Augustine asked : *why* is man's will free? Without the true answer to Augustine's question there is nothing from which man has a right to be free. His answer brings to the fore the whole topic of the pre-eminence of the person in the universe and the ultimate historical destiny of man. Augustine held both that free choice exists, although we cannot achieve our own good, and that the term of our destiny is beyond our power, while sin makes salvation *by ourselves alone* all the more impossible. That is why it was imperative for faith to help Augustine to understand the purpose of free will — since man's historical destiny is supernatural. Augustine saw that true spiritual freedom is the choice of a valuable purpose and the delightful process of realizing it, and he likewise saw that there was no more valuable purpose than the purpose of the Incarnation : to restore man to the image and likeness of God by restoring his will to a union with God. The realization of this purpose requires the free will of man to be responsive to the Love of God. There is only one truth that makes men free, only one Christ, the Word of God. To find Christ is to find freedom.

CHAPTER XIII

CONCLUSION

Augustine was concerned with human freedom in the concrete. He therefore examined freedom in its existential dimensions within the whole man as man is related to God. Those dimensions are both finite and infinite. Since the human infinite is an infinite in movement, and the divine is an infinite in act, human liberty will possess the dynamism of love, the continual ascent of man towards God. Because God is the first historical Fact and man's relation to God is a historical fact which, once established, is thereafter a metaphysical necessity, the historical method of studying anything human calls forth both theological and philosophical insights. The freedom that characterizes God will not be without influence upon the freedom that Augustine will wish for man, but Augustine is never tempted to erase the distinctively human trait of desire, movement towards Being, from his conception of human freedom. To God Augustine attributes a greater autonomy than his predecessors, insofar as he recognizes that the very universe exists simply because God chose it to exist; it did not necessarily emanate from God nor exist eternally along with Him. [1]

We are not surprised then to find that Augustine gives an analogical preeminence to the human will in holding that there is nothing created above the will as efficient cause. [2] Yet in the created will he recognizes a natural tendency [3] together with a non-necessitation to good or evil. [4] While sin can destroy one's freedom to do good, the existence of free choice is never

[1] Augustine, *De Gen. cont. Manich.*, I, 2, 4; PL 34, 175; *De Diversis Quæst.* 83, q. 28; PL 40, 18; *De Civ. Dei*, V, 9, 4; PL 41, 151-152.

[2] Augustine, *De Libero Arbitrio*, III, 17, 49; PL 32, 1295.

[3] Augustine, *De Musica*, VI, 11, 29; PL 32, 1179; *Confess.*, XIII, 9, 10; PL 32, 848.

[4] Augustine, *De Correp. et Grat.*, II; PL 44, 917.

eliminated.[1] This existence is not of paramount concern to Augustine. The purpose of the will is for Augustine the important aspect of freedom in the human universe.[2] He did not consider initial freedom in the sense of free choice to be a problem. He clearly saw and stated that without free choice there could be no sin, with all the evil consequences it brings.[3] Yet these consequences are all around us. Augustine admits that all human powers are suspended from the will as from a master-power because the end of the will is the good of man.[4] To him it is clear that to resist grace is an evil that can come only from us, but not to resist grace is a positive act derived from the First Principle of Goodness, and yet by its very being the act of a creature who is free.

Without presenting proofs for the will's freedom in scholastic terminology, he describes the human will as essentially free.[5] His work *De Libero Arbitrio* is not actually concerned with the problem of free choice but with the problem of evil which was created by free choice. Yet this dialogue written between 388 and 395 already refers to that problem which Augustine was all his life to ponder : the problem of freedom or *libertas* which he translates in the *De Libero Arbitrio* as the problem of the *good will*. Only in 409 would Pelagius appear in Sicily and in Africa not till a year later, but his attribution of limitless power to the human will would serve to accentuate the Augustinian answer outlined years before in *De Libero Arbitrio*, where Augustine speaks of the positive vocation of man to use his will as a power of acting well.[6] In this early work Augustine already states that true liberty to act well is dependent upon

[1] Augustine, *Opus Imperf. cont. Jul.*, VI, 11; PL 45, 1521 : Hominis vero liberum arbitrium congenitum et omnino inamissibile.

[2] Mausbach, *Die Ethik des heilg. Aug.*, *I*, p. 174 : Und darin, daß der freie Wille die Fahigkeit zum sittlichen Rechthandeln einschließt, liegt der hohe Wert der Willensfreiheit." Cf. *De Lib. Arb.*, II, 48.

[3] Augustine, *De Lib. Arb.*, III, 18, 50; PL 32, 1295; cf. Blondel, *L'Action*, I, p. 197.

[4] Augustine, *De Lib. Arb.*, II, 19, 51; PL 32, 1268.

[5] Augustine, *De Lib. Arb.*, III, 3, 8; PL 32, 1275.

[6] Augustine, *De Lib. Arb.*, III, 15,43; PL 32, 1292; Cf. *In Joan. Evan.* XXIX, 6; XLVIII, 3; PL 35, 1631, 1741; *Enarr. in Ps*, CXXX, 1; PL 37, 1708.

truth. The truth he speaks of is not simply to be believed but to be believed in. And thus freedom is born of a sense of trust and confidence in God Who becomes the object of man's love.

Our freedom consists in submission to the truth, and it is our God Himself who frees us from death, that is, from the state of sin. For Truth itself, speaking as a man with men, says to those who believe in Him: 'If you continue in my word, you shall be my disciples, indeed, and you shall know the truth, and the truth shall make you free. (John 8, 31-32)' [1]

This Faith in God by which the will is rectified and elevated by charity is the work of God without ceasing to be the work of man. [2] Augustine insisted from the beginning on the position he would later take against the Pelagian heresy. [3] And as early as 397 in the *De Diversis Quæstionibus ad Simplicianum* Augustine was attributing to God most fully and explicitly the entire work of salvation, even its initiation. [4] But if the good desire and the good action are the fruit of divine grace, [5] the human will is nonetheless active, capable of placing obstacles in the way of grace to hinder its action, capable under grace of cooperation with grace.

True Augustinism, unlike the pseudo-Augustinianism propagated by some, calls for voluntary moral activity, an activity that does not eliminate, however, the necessity of receiving

[1] Augustine, *De Lib. Arb.*, II, 13, 37; PL 32, 1261.

[2] Augustine, *Epist.*, 157; PL 33, 675: "For the fulfilling of the Law is nothing if not love (*Rom.*, 13, 10) and certainly 'the charity of God is poured forth in our hearts', not by ourselves or by the strength of our own will, but by the Holy Ghost who is given to us. (Rom. 5, 5). Therefore, our free will is able to perform good works if it is helped from above, which happens as a result of humble petition and confession; whereas, if it is deprived of divine help, it may excel in knowledge of the Law, but it will have no solid foundation of justice, and will be puffed up with impious pride and deadly vanity."

[3] Augustine, *Retract.*, I, 9; PL 32, 598: "Thus, long before the Pelagian heresy arose, we were already debating against them. For we stated that all good things come from God — the great, the middle, and the least goods; among the middle goods is found free choice of will since we can use it wrongly, but yet it is such that we cannot live rightly without it. To use it well is at once virtue, and virtue is found among the great goods which no one can use wrongly. Because all good things... come from God, it follows that from God comes the good use of free will, which is virtue and is counted among the great goods."

[4] Augustine, *De Div. Quaest. ad Simp.*, I, 2, 6; PL 40, 111.

[5] Augustine, *De Lib. Arb.*, II, 19, 50; PL 32, 1267, 1268.

grace from above. Augustine's doctrine of grace does not defraud human nature. It enriches it from above while it satisfies the natural impulse to happiness that God has implanted in nature as the source of activity. True Augustinism, while insisting upon the divine action in the soul, is equally insistent upon man's obligation to use the natural powers received from God according to their appointed purposes within the over-all vocation of man to the End which God wishes him to reach.

If the will is not necessitated to good or evil, there is no essential guarantee in the will itself that man will make good use of it. [1] The longing for such a guarantee is the longing for liberty. Finding no such guarantee in nature, man seeks it in God. The Theological Freedom found by the gift and operation of Charity is the fulfillment and crown of the power of choice which, as we saw, has as its object what is good for man. [2] When grace enters the soul it brings a higher principle of unity to unite man with God, with himself and with others.

St. Paul had made an old Stoic concept, that the world was one large organism, actual and real when he announced that the union between Christ and men was a union between the Head and its bodily members. As members of Christ's Body, men enter into His freedom, the freedom to love the Father in spirit and in truth, the freedom to love others with

[1] Augustine, *De Div. Quæst. ad Simp.*, I, 2, 10; PL 40, 117; *Epist.*, 157, 10; PL 33, 677; *Confess.*, VIII, 9, 21; PL 32, 758.

[2] Augustine, *Epist.*, 145; PL 33, 593: "The more things to come are desirable to our love, the more things present do violence to our weakness. May those who know how to see and lament these things deserve to overcome and escape them. The human will is utterly unable to accomplish this, without the grace of God, because it cannot be called free so long as it is subject to the assaults and enslavement of the passions, for 'by whom a man is overcome, of the same also he is the slave,' (2 Peter 2, 19) and 'If the son shall make you free,' says the Son of God Himself, 'you shall be free indeed' (John 8, 36). Therefore, the Law, by teaching and commanding what cannot be performed without grace, makes known to man his own weakness, that this weakness, once made known, may seek its Saviour, through whom the will made whole can do what in its weakness it cannot do. The Law therefore, leads to faith; faith obtains the outpouring of the Spirit; the Spirit spreads charity abroad; charity fulfills the Law... 'Love is the fulfillment of the law' (Rom. 13, 10). Thus, 'the law is good for him who uses it lawfully' (I Tim. 1, 8), but he uses it lawfully who understands why it was given, and who takes refuge from its threats in the grace which sets him free."

the intensity of self-love. [1] This Body of Christ, this City of God, though mystical, is nonetheless real, and its members live in the world. As Augustine said: "We are in Christ — and also in this age." [2]

Neither do men as members of the Mystical Body of Christ lose their own bodies with their natural tendencies. But the unity between soul and body grows closer, so that ever so gradually the body is prepared for complete spiritualization in the life to come. And if the Spirit of Truth is within, human choices will more and more bring down true value-judgments into the contemporary world.

The will, all alone, cannot put itself into movement. We generally say that there must be a good, choiceworthy object. Yes, the good that attracts is needed, but to be attracted, man must somehow be adapted to the good. Man needs to receive the Holy Spirit Who will produce in him a delight and love for the Supreme Good. Before the obstacles of ignorance and difficulty man needs light to see and delight in love. All does not depend upon the condition of the object — there is also the condition of the subject to be considered. Augustine sees man modified by either the delight that is *cupiditas* or the delight that is *charitas*.

For Augustine the personal relation to God which makes freedom a reality did not imply, as in Plotinus, an isolation from men and an abstraction from current affairs. Just as Augustine refused to dichotomize the religious-moral values in the universe, so he combined the personal-social values. Human choice is best exercised when the human spirit, polarized to the divine, achieves a personal growth that results in social growth. If the world can be changed through the change in the human person, the difference in the world before and after Christ is immense and overwhelming. The attitude of Christ towards

[1] Augustine, *Epist.*, 155; PL 33, 666-673.
[2] Augustine, *In Joan. Evan.*, tract. LXXXI, 4; PL 35, 1842: Sumus in Christo... sumus adhuc in hoc sæculo.

His world is the exemplar for the Christian of every age. "Christ, by His Incarnation, prolonged in the Church, has consecrated the universe through and through, and all its human and cosmic values." [1] Man continues today the consecration of himself and of the world to God, not by static isolationism or by nervous absorption in worldly transactions, but by creating a civilization that reflects the truth of man's value-judgments and that will be a fitting atmosphere for the continued advance of human interior liberty.

If one thread more than any other is woven through the stuff of Western thinking it is that man has the power and the responsibility to mold society more closely to his heart's desire. The medieval aspiration to renew all things in Christ, the Puritan belief in work and thrift as the tools of the kingdom, the Deist and nationalist confidence in social reform and even revolution as a means of remaking society — all these philosophies are derived from the fundamental Christian roots of our society with its belief in man as a free agent, morally responsible for his neighbor and set upon earth to remold human society upon a supernatural plan. Even when, in the 19th century liberalism, all apparent theological overtones had vanished, the belief in man — in his freedom, responsibility and social duty — and in the coming of a better society by his effort still betrayed the metaphysics that had given it birth. [2]

The historical world is made by human choices. Hence the tremendous responsibility to understand the proper role of free choice. Only by the reconciliation of free will and truth shall a stable world be built. When free will is used to incarnate the truth, free will is saved from degenerating into licence, man is saved from frustration, and the world from destruction. C. N. Cochrane said of Augustine: "...if he asserts a right to freedom, it is not the freedom to say what you think and think what you like, but the freedom which consists in subjection to the truth." [3] If the world is to progress, truth cannot remain

[1] Paul Henry, S.J., "The Christian Philosophy of History," *Theological Studies*, vol. XIII, (1952), p. 422.

[2] Ward, *Faith and Freedom*, p. 179.

[3] C. N. Cochrane, *Christianity and Classical Culture*, Oxford, Clarendon Press, 1940, p. 510. Cf. also Augustine, *Epist.*, 101; PL 33, 368: "What else is to be said to those who

transcendent to it. It is the social function of the will to incarnate truth in every event of every day, in every enterprise, private and public. [1] When man forsakes truth in his actions, he forsakes freedom. In a personal universe there is no such thing as losing moral freedom; it can only be forsaken. This may indeed lead to the loss of other types of freedom. The life of illusion, with the will guided by passion or by instinct, breeds interior disorder, and when this prevails in many, the resulting social anarchy can raise up the strong hand of the dictator. The relation of free will to truth is at all times crucial. But this relation is not always correctly evaluated. The ancients failed to see that disorder does not belong to the essence of free will. The moderns do not all realize that truth is the guarantee of the freedom they cherish.

The greater the truth, the greater the freedom! How did Christianity introduce a new and higher intellectuality into the world, a new and deeper grasp of truth? Was it not because Christianity opened new roads to truth, chiefly the road of love? As Augustine said: "...we pilgrims make our way by faith and hope, and strive to reach our end by love..." [2] And the object of this love has power to draw it forth. "Indeed, the truth of the Christians is incomparably more beautiful than the Helen of the Greeks. For the former, our martyrs fought more valiantly against this Sodom than those famous heroes fought for the latter against Troy." [3]

think themselves liberally educated, however immoral and irreligious they are, but what we read in a truly liberal book: 'If the son shall make you free, you shall be free indeed'? (*John* 8, 36). By Him it is granted us to know how much of the liberal there is in those studies which are called liberal by men not called to liberty. For, they have nothing that resembles liberty unless they have something that resembles truth. Hence, the Son Himself said: 'and the truth shall make you free'. (John 8, 32)."

[1] Paul Henry, S.J., "The Christian Philosophy of History," *Theol. Studies*, 1952, p. 432: "The insertion of the Christian into the world, his duty to contribute to the march of progress, appear to me to be the logical consequence of this philosophy of history, which proclaims that Christ is the center of history, that He gives it its meaning, that He is forever working within it in the eternal present of His Incarnation continued in and through the Church."

[2] Augustine, *Epist.*, 55; PL 33, 212.

[3] Augustine, *Epist.*, 40; PL 33, 157.

If love lets man enter into God, it introduces him into a greater power, a larger liberty. It seems folly to look at obedience to God as jeopardizing one's autonomy when such obedience makes one participate in the Divine government, not only of oneself, but of the entire world. Love is, therefore, the key to the freedom and the unity and the peace of the world. St. Augustine saw that man must love well if in the practical order he is to know well, and that to love well, man must know the truth. Submission to the truth has long been recognized as the hallmark of Augustinian liberty, but its affective aspect has not always been stressed. The submission is a surrender effected by love. Love rather than knowledge is a unifying experience, and the accomplished surrender is but the prelude to a new being, a greater actuality, and when the love is that of creature for Creator it leads to an unsought supremacy.

God's love for man, which is at the origin of the world and the origin of the Redemption inspires man to love God. By inspiring this love, God frees man for the highest end open to him. The reception of grace or divine life at baptism is insufficient to accomplish this. God needs to be not only ontologically present in man, but psychologically present to him. The awareness of God's love for man comes chiefly through the Revelation of Christ and through the love experienced from His members. To the prophecy: "You shall draw waters with joy out of the Saviour's fountains," [1] St. Augustine responds: "If we thirst, let us come; and not with our feet, but with our affections; let us come, not by removing from our place but by loving." [2]

The vocation to freedom [3] through Divine love is not followed, we have noted, without a deep concern for the human

[1] *Is.* 12; 3.

[2] Augustine, *In Joan. Evan,* XXXII, 1; PL 35, 1642: Si sitimus, veniamus, et non pedibus, sed affectibus; nec migrando, sed amando veniamus.

[3] 3 *Gal.* V, 13: "For you, brethren, have been called unto liberty: only make not liberty an occasion of the flesh, but by the charity of the Spirit serve one another." Cf. Augustine, *Epist.*, 23; PL 33, 94.

community,[1] the world that must be drawn to God by the only force that it wants to experience, the impact of love. So far removed is Augustine from the viewpoint of self-perfective individualism that his degrees of liberty follow upon the degrees of love for one's neighbor. Everyone in the universe is a neighbor, and all are brothers, actually or potentially. There are, however, closer bonds with relatives and friends as well as with those in need. There are needs of the body, needs of the soul, which are fulfilled by the spiritual and corporal works of mercy.

Yet there seems to be a personal need in every man, a need to be loved by others for himself in all his uniqueness. Without such love for a person in material or mental need, there is no perfect work of mercy. The root of all teaching, of all giving should be such love. Love gives birth to mutual trust, and trust is the atmosphere indispensable for human cooperation and enduring achievement. When love translates itself into self-sacrifice, we have the highest form of love for neighbor, the highest degree of freedom.

"Here then has this charity... its beginning, to give of your temporal superfluities to him that hath need, to him that is in any distress; of your temporal abundance to deliver your brother from temporal tribulation. Here is the beginning of Charity. Having thus begun, if you will nourish it with the word of God and hope of the life to come you will come at last to such perfection, that you will be ready to lay down your life for your brethren."[2]

[1] Augustine, *Epist.*, 155; PL 33, 672: "Let us strive, then, with the greatest possible effort to bring to him those whom we love as ourselves, if we know that we love ourselves by loving Him.....There is no other love by which a man loves himself than that by which he loves God. Whoever loves himself in any other way ought to be said rather to hate himself, since he thus becomes wicked and is deprived of the light of justice, when he turns from a higher and more excellent good and is directed upon himself as to something lower and defective, and what is so truthfully written then takes place in him: 'He that loveth iniquity hateth his own soul.' (*Ps.* 10, 6). Thus, as no one loves himself except by loving God, there was no need of man being commanded to love himself, once the commandment to love God had been given."

[2] Augustine, *In Epistolam Joannis*, Homily VI, 1; PL 35, 2019: Ergo hic incipit ista charitas, fratres, ut de suis superfluis tribuat egenti, in angustiis aliquibus constituto; ex eo quod sibi abundat secundum tempus, a tribulatione temporali liberet fratrem. Hinc exordium est charitatis. Hanc ita cœptam, si verbo Dei et spe futuræ vitæ nutrieris, pervenies ad illam perfectionem, ut paratus sis animam tuam ponere pro fratribus tuis. For Augustine, charity

Such love unifies the diverse tendencies in man, unites God and man, and men with one another. Love is then the force that makes of many individual things and people a true *universe*. It constructs the City of God by healing hostilities, eradicating enmities and envies, triumphing over the natural isolation policy of the individual. Augustine sees unity as the sublime effect of Charity.[1] For the world to mirror God, it must know unity in multiplicity. The Divine love that sustains Unity in the Trinity enters our world to accomplish the miracle of making a unity out of many persons. The Eucharist is the sign of it and Heaven, the Society of the Saints, is its perfect realization. But the strength of charity to effect the unity of men depends upon its alliance with the strongest human force, the free power of human love. Such a power cannot be shut up by dams for distribution. It comes forth only from the fountains of freedom dwelling deeply, intimately and uniquely in the hearts of men. Augustine tells us that "...there is nothing, though of iron hardness, which the fire of love cannot subdue. And when the mind is carried up to God in this love, it will soar above all torture free and glorious, with wings beauteous and unhurt, on which chaste love rises to the embrace of God."[2]

As the philosopher of freedom to which right love is the key, Augustine necessarily differs from Plotinus whose ideal of freedom consisted in a self-awareness that freed man from

was not something other than love; supernatural charity made human love right, gave a supernatural power to love. Cf. Hélène Pétré, *Caritas*, Louvain, Spicilegium Sacrum Lovaniense, 1948 : "La position d'Augustin peut donc se résumer ainsi : s'il existe une tradition en vertu de laquelle les mots *amare* et *amor* sont suspects et regardés comme impropres à exprimer une notion morale et religieuse, Augustin, lui, ne partage pas cette suspicion; il tient au contraire à identifier *amor* et dilectio ou caritas. Cf. *En. in Ps.*, 125, 5; 148, 2.

[1] H. Pétré, *Caritas*; on page 339 the author notes that neither Cicero nor Seneca had used the word "unity" to speak of the unity of the human race or of social peace. Augustine in the *City of God* (XIV, 1; PL 41, 403; CSEL, 40, 11, 1, 7) says that all society must aspire to unity, symbolized by the creation of one man at the origin of the world.

[2] Augustine, *De Morib. Eccles. Cath.*, I, 22, 41; PL 32, 1329 : Nihil est tamen durum atque ferreum, quod non amoris igne vincatur. Quo cum se anima rapiet in Deum, super omnem carnificinam libera et admiranda volitabit pennis pulcherrimis et integerrimis, quibus ad Dei amplexum amor castus innititur.

exterior concerns.[1] As the theologian of that freedom which is a participation in the Divine Wisdom, freely given by God and freely received by man, Augustine necessarily differs from Plotinus who places the divinity within the nature of man, to be reached by effort alone. By intellectual power the Plotinian man becomes free; by the power of Christ, the Christian is freed from evil and made free to choose the Good. Christ has paid the price to recover for man the freedom that he freely rejected in Paradise, the freedom of choosing the meritorious good. " Bought by the blood of Our Savior we ought to attach ourselves to Him by a Charity so great that no exterior object can make us turn from Him. "[2]

Because Anselm follows Augustine in considering man and the world historically, he, too, brings to bear upon the understanding of freedom both theological and philosophical truths. Augustine and Anselm look upon sin as unnatural, and following the synthetic method, they speak of the nature of man as the work of God, including in their consideration of the natural world the presence of grace. Although St. Thomas was later to make precise distinctions between reason and faith, nature and grace, love and Charity, free will and the freedom that comes from Charity in action — these realities, though handled together by Augustine, were never confused.[3] That is why the radical Augustinism, which is the actual teaching of St. Augustine himself, is never opposed to the teaching

[1] It would seem that divergence on the subject of sin and free choice between Plotinus and Augustine is inevitable because of their opposing views on matter and ultimately on the origin of the world. Cf. *Enn.* I, 8, 2; Augustine, *De Natura Boni*, 18. For Plotinus, matter is the eternal limit of the emanative process; for Augustine, matter is a capacity " to be " and comes from God.Augustine did not exactly find the answer to Manichaeanism in the *Enneads*. Augustine sees choice as being between two goods; evil comes from man's deficient use of his own will, and not from some extrinsic " encrustment. "

[2] Augustine, *De Lib. Arb.*, III, 25, 76; PL 32, 1308 : ut prærogato nobis Christi sanguine, post labores miseriasque ineffabiles tanta charitate liberatori nostro adhæreamus, et tanta ejus in eum charitate rapiamur, ut nulla nos visa ex inferioribus a conspectu superiore detorqueant.

[3] Blondel, " L'Unité Originale et la Pensée Permanente de la Doctrine Phil. de Saint Augustin, " p. 425 : " Et si Augustin avait eu à nommer cette doctrine qu'il voulait totale par sa compréhension, universelle par son extension, pleinement satisfaisante pour l'esprit et le cœur, toute conforme aux exigences de la pensée comme aux leçons de l'expérience, aux besoins sociaux, aux vues de l'histoire, au sentiment et aux enseignements religieux, n'est-ce pas l'épithète ' catholique ' qui lui eût servi à la désigner? "

of St. Thomas. St. Thomas is indeed a most authentic interpreter of Augustine.

A seminal thinker like Augustine will have many disciples who claim him as their master, disciples both faithful and faithless. And his very adversaries keep his doctrine living, growing, triumphant. Theologically, Augustine has influenced the great medieval masters who were nourished on his doctrine; mystically and morally, Augustine has influenced the Bernards and the Gregories of all ages. Philosophically, there are today many Augustinians who follow the method of interiority, but the school that gives most promise for the perpetuation of the true and total Augustinism is that of the great French Catholic of the 19th century, Blondel and his present-day disciples who, faithful to the historical and synthetic method of Augustine, do justice to the existential world by considering it in living relation to God.

Within the cosmic perspective of a human freedom whose profound purpose is to bring man into voluntary relation with God in response to a Divine invitation expressed in a thousand ways in both the Old and the New Testaments, temporal civilization is assigned the role of ministering to that moral freedom which is made possible by the high spiritual aptitudes of man, and made actual by the Divine desire to restore to man that participation in Divine Life which frees him from self-subservience. The civilized state is intended to liberate man from the physical and the spiritual obstacles to the right use of free choice. The laws of the state attempt to secure for man the physical, economic, social, and political conditions most conducive to the best exercise of his freedom.

And if the State works to free man from exterior hindrances to the proper use of his free will, man himself through self-knowledge and self-discipline must unceasingly safeguard his interior freedom to choose the good. Not without personal effort will a man free himself from encroachments upon his interior freedom in the form of ignorance, illusions, impulses, instincts, unbridled passions, and all that can induce man to act less completely as man. Even in possession of physical liberty, social and political liberty, and psychological liberty, man longs for a more positive form of freedom, a kind that is bound up more profoundly with his metaphysical status as a person in living relation to God. Man longs not only to have a free will but to be a free man. When this yearning remains vague and unmeditated, it sometimes expresses itself in the deviationism of the pursuit of unlimited freedom. But it is the very nature of human freedom as of human nature to be defined in reference to its end. If a triangle were free to add another angle or to make its sides circular, it would cease to be a triangle. Man does not really wish for this self-destructive type of freedom. For man to be free means that he is all that he should be and can be, not apart from God but with Him, and not with repugnance, but with joy and delight.

Such is the liberty cherished by Augustine and his disciples. Because God desires such liberty for man and because man has the initial liberty of free choice, we can enjoy theological freedom. Such freedom means that man has progressed from the psychological state of responsibility to the moral state of perfection wherein he is liberated for the spontaneous and constant choice of the good through love for God. There is, therefore, a kind of freedom superior to the negative freedom more commonly discussed. We call it positive freedom. It pertains to the right exercise of free will, and becomes real when the natural power of will is perfected, strengthened, and transformed by union with a supernatural End. Because this is the historical End for all men, God offers such union to every man, but He does so freely — since human nature cannot demand it.

The following chart will draw together the various meanings associated with the word freedom. We may then more clearly draw a conclusion concerning the kind of freedom that Augustine wished for himself and for all men.

NEGATIVE FREEDOM

absence of : physical, social, psychological constraint

- *Interior* (to insure *free choice*)
  1. *Freedom from* : ignorance
  2. *Freedom from* : principles of action within man but not specifically human : passions. instincts, impulses
- *Exterior* (to insure *free action*)
  1. *Freedom from* : interference with locomotive activity
  2. *Freedom from* : interference with exercise of personal, social, political rights.

POSITIVE FREEDOM

The right use of free choice; the will guided by true value-judgments.

1. *Freedom to* be one's human self, and all that one should be (self-possession, or self-mastery);
2. *Freedom to* give oneself to others in love (friendship or gift of self)
3. *Freedom to* transform the world according to the truth (civilizing power).
4. *Freedom to* enter into the revealed desires of God for oneself and for the world (sanctity or self-surrender).

In the light of the above chart we can pinpoint more precisely the aspect of freedom which was significant and important to Augustine. [1] With his deep concern for happiness, Augustine

[1] Augustine, *De Lib. Arb.*, I, 15, 32; PL 32, 1238 : " Then there is freedom though indeed there is no true freedom except for those who are happy and cling to the eternal law. "

was psychologically incapable of considering man apart from his destiny, and destiny to Augustine meant concrete, historical destiny, not theoretical conceptions of what might have been if God and His plans did not exist. Freedom for man to be not only what his nature allowed him to be but what God wanted him to be, a child of God who imaged God by loving God — this was the reality of freedom that Augustine acknowledged to be beyond man's natural reach but fully within his grasp when given by God. When free will is used to choose God in all things chosen, there is no better, no higher exercise of freedom. It is theological in its End and theological in its means, but the *sine qua non* of such freedom is the natural power of the human will, of which man is the absolute master in the practical order.

The fact that an omnipotent God has chosen to communicate with a free being will ever keep the reality of theological freedom in the realm of mystery, [1] but this will not prevent our seeking to understand it as far as we can. Augustine was able to understand freedom more realistically than his philosophical predecessors because he studied it in the context of a created world. Augustine's own experience of existence was an experience of created existence. Self-consciousness made him aware of creatureliness. Awareness led to consideration of what God must be in relation to man.

Creation implies more than " *ab alio.* " Man not only depends on the First Cause for his being, but he grows and develops under the influx of God's creative action. The divine influence is cosmically present, implying an intimacy of God with the world that is the ontological foundation for the mystical experience without ceasing to be the true cause of all activity in the universe.

[1] The presence of human freedom in the Divine Person of Christ is equally or more of a mystery but quite as much a fact. Reginald Garrigou-Lagrange, *Our Savior and His Love for Us*, (trans. A. Bouchard), St. Louis, B. Herder, 1951, p. 172 : " The human will of Jesus possesses a very high perfection and a great mystery : His will was even here on earth impeccable and yet it was perfectly free in obeying and meriting... He was impeccable by reason of His divine personality, by reason of the immeasurable plenitude of grace and of the Beatific Vision which was His. For these three reasons He was absolutely impeccable. Yet He obeyed freely, with perfect liberty, which is not merely spontaneity but the absence of necessity in making a choice. "

The insight found in Plotinus — that there is continuity between God and man — was purified of its pantheism and saved in principle.

Truly in this sense Augustine did not abandon emanationism; neither did he accept it. Plotinus helped Augustine to see the overwhelming and interpenetrating force of a Spirit-God in the universe — a veritable cascading of Divinity. Augustine saw what Plotinus was aiming at, and concentrated on the right direction of the error rather than upon the Plotinian form it took — namely : that God is a giving God and that somehow God is in all things. (This could be saved by a doctrine of creation and the analogy of being.) And so to progress to one's real self one must progress to God's knowledge of oneself.

Aware of the created character of the world, Augustine was consumed by the realization that all good things are achieved in relation to God. If free causality is a good thing, this, too, is gained in relation to God. Since God is the cause of all being and becoming, the higher and the more independent the action, the greater reason for God to be in it as Cause. God does not run parallel to time; there is a crossing of the finite and the infinite at every moment. Therefore, Augustine had a new question to pose : what must freedom be in a universe whose First Cause is Infinite Being? He does not ask this question : if grace moves the will by supernatural activity, *how* can man be free? nor this question : if the will is moved by another, like all created things in the order of nature, *how* is any act free? For Augustine does not see any competition between God and man. The more God acts upon the human soul, the more active the soul, the more spontaneous. If He is acting upon a free will, the more voluntary is the action. God is not superadded to things; he is at the very heart of freedom.

What then is independence or freedom in a created universe? It is not found in exterior conditions — the mere absence of restraining influences. Quite possibly the Plotinian conception of reality as a subject made Augustine return to himself, to the intimacy of his interiority, marked with the signs of the creature-relationship. There he reflected upon those infinite relations to truth and goodness that make man so much more than a rational animal. In following out the direction of these relations, Augustine discovered the source of human freedom.

The discovery of man as a person in living relation to God provided Augustine with a dynamic conception of man while it simultaneously revealed the true meaning of time, of process, of history. The meaning of freedom was illuminated as a growing into unity. Just as knowledge is impossible without a vital union with God in truth, so freedom is not possible without a vital union with God in love. If Augustine's point of departure was the search for truth, he soon discovered the dual character of the quest for truth as the quest for existence. To be all that one should and can be is to be personally free. But if a person cannot develop except by means of openings into the Infinite, then independence will grow in proportion to one's communion with God. Augustine's quest for truth became a quest for freedom, the fulfillment of the individual in the widest kind of community life in God.

There are two aspects of this independence worth noting. First, its origin is interiority, but interiority is not necessarily opposed to objectivity. Secondly, the independence which comes from man's communion with God is crucial for man's relation to the whole universe. Man's growth in freedom is historical; it does not take place without God and without love. If all things are in God, to commune with God by knowing and loving is to increase one's kinship with all things. God's Love is indeed the Exemplar of world unity. As Love, God is the unity of Three Persons; likewise love will be the unity of all persons in a world that is gradually becoming one through love.

The City of God, whose Principle of Unity is the Holy Spirit, is the working out of love. In this City of God, Love is both the law and the creative force for progress. Love for God or for man or for both is at the origin of all human achievement. Where love is the law, there is order, equality, cohesion. When man's relations with others are dominated by the love of God, there is really a *universe*. Man is then under God and over the world, but there is no domination of man over man. Love for God, far from isolating man from others, regulates the world of inter-personal relations, and by entering into others, man sees things from their centers, thereby acquiring a deeper objectivity of mind.

By living in the City of God man is perfected as a person because he becomes more of an image of God. Being an image of God implies an integration by love with all humanity. (Was the Plotinian " world-soul" a symbol of the true Christian citizen in God's City where no one is excluded by God?) If man is a true image, to look at any man is to see God and all the world. By his doctrine of the image, Augustine is able to unite both Stoic and Plotinian insights. He needed these insights in order to think as a Christian, but the insights had to be brought together. The doctrine of the image opens up the way for ideas not only as transcendent but also as immanent.

The image, moreover, is historical; it is in flux. [1] Man is at best an imperfect image, and history is the accomplishing of man's imaging of God. This is accomplished through the will's submission to love. Augustine thought synthetically. He looked upon man not only as making himself by his choices, but making himself as an image. The perfect image of the Father is Christ, the embodiment of Love. Therefore, in trying to make himself, man is trying to be a Christian. Christ is the living Exemplar, the model of all human values in their proper relation with the Divine Being. As individuals conform themselves to Christ, society becomes Christian. [2] Man does not escape to the eternal to become like God; he images Christ in time, in the material world, trying to embody truth to make this world a free world.

[1] Augustine, *De Civ. Dei,* XIV, 15; PL 41, 422-424. Cf. David Cairns, *The Image of God in Man,* New York, Philosophical Library, n.d. Although one cannot agree with all in this work, the author does say : " Augustine was the first thinker to define the image as a power.... There will be few who will disagree with the opinion that our creation in the image of God is a creation by the divine love for an existence that images back God's love to Him. " p. 101.

[2] Augustine, *Sermo* 268, 2; PL 38, 1232 : Quod est spiritus noster, id est anima nostra ad membra nostra, hoc est Spiritus sanctus ad membra Christi, ad corpus Christi, quod est Ecclesia; Augustine, *Sermo* 71, 32; PL 38, 462 : Societatem Spiritus...

Early realizing the deep unity of truth and love in God,[1] Augustine taught that the way to truth was love. To understand, one must love.[2] To teach, one must love. The Incarnation of God was the Incarnation of Love. That is why people believed in Christ and believed what He taught. Because in Him the truth was associated with love and compassion, He spoke with authority. When we attempt to give the truth without compassion and love, we strip it of authority. Augustine recognized that love was likewise embodied in the Church. He perceived it, moreover, in the Christian friends he knew: in Ambrose, in Simplicianus, and above all in Monica.

If for Augustine unity was the great *desideratum,* he would naturally inquire the cause of the disunity to be seen everywhere. As we have seen, he soon discovered the human will to have disrupted the original unity. Since creation had been the beginning of an orderly development, its interruption could only have come from free will. Yet, it was never intended that free will should have this function and be, as it were, a scandal in an otherwise orderly world. Through free will every human soul was to act as a "world-soul" and project the Divine Mind forward into the universe. In this work of continuing God's creation through the incarnation of truth and love in the world, the body was to be the instrument of the soul, thereby possessing the dignity of participating in soul and ultimately being a Divine instrument. The objectivity of morality was assured in this outlook, insofar as the happy life was seen to flow not from self-satisfaction, but from thinking and choosing according to the mind of God.

A philosopher is a pioneer when he discovers some new reality or some new aspect of reality. In finding man to be not only a rational animal but an image of God, Augustine further explored the reality that is man, and in doing so he raised the human will to a greater dignity. He saw its function in the spiritual cosmos

[1] Blondel, *L'Action*, I, pp. 195, 196: "Cette cause première est aussi souveraine charité et... le nom divin de l'intelligence comme de l'intelligibilité est sagesse et générosité."

[2] Augustine, *In Evang. Joan.*, XLVI, 4; PL 35, 1729.

as the temporal faculty for communion with God. [1] But he recognized the limitations of the human situation. He came to see that the theological virtues not only gave man supernatural potencies for supernatural activity, but they helped man to be a man, since grace perfects nature. Just as faith is a perfecting power for man's understanding, so charity is a perfecting power for man's willing. In making the philosophical discovery of the role of charity, Augustine discovered the meaning of freedom. As a philosopher of freedom to which love is the key, Augustine is far removed from being a voluntarist. However high the dignity he accords the will, for him it is never an absolute. The human will is a power for loving God, self and other persons. The love of God in man is both submissive and perfective.

It was Augustine's sense of creatureliness that prevented his doctrine of will from being voluntarism. It belongs to the very essence of a created will to be a moved mover. The will must undergo the attraction of the end which supplies sufficient energy for the will to determine itself to the means. The end is the First Mover as Final Cause which impels but does not compel man towards his end. The intellectual apprehension is the formal cause, which makes known an existing good that exercises an attraction upon the will, because as a partial good it shares the attraction of the final good. The will adapts itself, and as an efficient cause it actively tends toward its object.

Love is properly concerned with ends which really exist. Therefore, it is not the intellect that exercises an efficacious action upon the will — it is the attraction of Being, the Act of all acts. This is understandable as soon as we reflect on the fact that will is always properly an intellectual appetite, and that its object will correspond to the object of intellect. If the formal object of the intellect is being, the formal object of the will is also being as related to appetite. The role of the will is metaphysical, a truly spiritual inclination to consent to being, and this consent implicitly engenders a direct love for the Absolute as the Author of Being.

[1] Augustine, *De Civ. Dei*, XIX, 26; PL 41, 656; *Sermo* 156; PL 38, 849-859; *Confess.*, I, 4, 4; PL 32, 662, 663.

Understanding the will in relation to its chief act, love, preserves one both from voluntarism and from intellectualism. The will is not an absolute; it is moved by another. That other is not really the intellect, but being seen as good. As a faculty directed to being, the will has not a subjective orientation; happiness is not its formal object. The will has a deeper, natural orientation towards value or the good. The will is, however, both the faculty by which man tends towards the good and the faculty by which man attains perfection and happiness. The formal object of the will as a metaphysical faculty is the End, Being as Good, willed in and for itself, and not willed formally *because* it perfects man. Yet, man as a creature necessarily desiring happiness cannot choose anything that he would perceive as not beneficial to himself as man.[1] The good is loved in and for itself, but this act of using the will according to its nature is perfective of man. We love God for Himself, but the act of loving God for Himself is perfective of us.

In his teaching on freedom, Augustine shows a realization of the intimate link between the end of the will and the good of the person. This fact and the perfective role of grace are the presuppositions of his whole doctrine of freedom. This explains why he has assigned to Charity, which is rooted in the will, not in free will, a chief part in making man free. If a man is free when he is all that he can be, that is, when he attains his end, then that virtue which fixes the will upon man's true end while leaving free will unimpeded in its choices, impels but does not compel the choice of true means. St. Thomas tells us that no virtue has so great an inclination to its act as does Charity, nor does any operate with such delight. While sanctifying grace restores to man the capacity for the theological freedom enjoyed by our first parents, through the operation of Charity, residing in the faculty of natural liberty, man grows in and realizes freedom.

[1] Augustine is not afraid to admit that free choice which is directed towards being as good is simultaneously an appetite for happiness; Augustine, *Opus. Imperf. contra Jul.*, VI, 11; PL 45, 1521 : Hominis vero liberum arbitrium, congenitum et omnino in amissibile si quærimus, illud est quo beati omnes esse volunt, etiam hi qui ea nolunt quæ ad beatitudinem perducunt.

As an imperfect image, as a created being, man must be moved by another. A faculty of will informed by Charity cannot reduce itself to act. The natural operation is actuated by the divine concursus, but when man chooses something meritorious for eternal life, God moves him to choose freely. This supernatural movement of the will is called actual grace. It is from God. Augustine often states that if a good will is better than an indifferent will, and the will comes from God, then God must also cause the good will. A good will is born of good acts.

Augustine has understood two things that he never relinquishes : man by sin has been deflected from his End, and that is why the will acts as *eros*, the faculty of the egoistic man, seeking the good of the individual; but man has been commanded by God to love with the love of *agape*, and this commandment, because it bears on love, cannot be observed without full freedom and voluntariness. But God never commands the impossible. What is impossible to free will alone becomes possible to the will informed by Charity and moved by grace. [1] But what becomes of free choice in this context? All of Augustine's words on this topic imply that man acting under grace retains the power to act contrary to it, but that he does not want to. The power to withdraw from the influence of God is an imperfection and is therefore not under the influence of grace. Hence, free choice is not destroyed by the strongest graces, but man himself is willing to offer no opposition to them. [2]

As a Doctor of grace, Augustine saved the supernatural character of Christianity, but as a philosopher of freedom he revealed the role of free choice in the works of love. Faith, yes, in God, in the Church and the Sacraments, but not without doing the truth in Charity. [3] Augustine simultaneously preserved

[1] Augustine, *In Epist. Joan.*, Tract. VII; PL 35, 2033; Thomas Aquinas, *Sum. Theol.*, II-II, q. 44, a. 1 ad 2.

[2] Augustine, *In Joan. Evang.*, LIII, 8; PL 35, 1777, 1778 : "Only let no one dare to defend the freedom of the will in any such way as to attempt to deprive us of the prayer that says : 'Lead us not into temptation'; and, on the other hand, let no one deny the freedom of the will, and so venture to find an excuse for sin."

[3] Augustine, *Epistle* 155; PL 33, 671-672 : "Yet, this virtue consists in nothing else but in loving what is worthy of love; it is prudence to choose this, fortitude to be turned from

the glory of God against the Pelagians and the responsibility of man against the Manichaeans.[1] But he did more than declare the reality of *free choice*. He distinguished false *freedom* from true freedom. He rejected the pseudo-notion that man attains to an autonomous and personal freedom only in proportion to his moral revolt,[2] in favor of the position that the virtuous man is the autonomous man and even enjoys the divine freedom of doing what is right because he wants to, with ease and delight. The principal feature of the will is not its independence but its love, a joyous assent to all reality and perfection.

Augustine's merit was to recognize the significant relation between human freedom and the good-for-man. Virtue was not only knowledge but a loving what is worthy of love. Among all those who ever since have seen the positive side of freedom, the metaphysical role of free will, the attainment of freedom through the good, no one more than Augustine ever had so keen an appreciation of the goodness of God and of the good appropriate to man.[3] Few men have looked at God so long

it by no obstacles, temperance to be enticed by no allurements, justice to be diverted by no pride. Why do we choose what we exclusively love, except that we find nothing better? But this is God, and if we prefer or equal anything to Him in our love, we know nothing about loving ourselves. We are made better by approaching closer to Him than whom nothing is better; we go to Him not by walking, but by loving. We will have Him more present to us in proportion as we are able to purify the love by which we draw near to Him, for He is not spread through or confined by corporeal space, He is everywhere present and everywhere wholly present, and we go to Him not by the motion of our feet but by our conduct. Conduct is not usually discerned by what one knows but by what he loves; good or bad love makes good or bad conduct. By our crookedness we are far from the uprightness of God; we are made straight by loving what is upright, that we may rightly cling to the upright One."

[1] G. B. Ladner, "Conception of The Reformation of Man", *Augustinus Magister*, II, p. 871: "Thus, St. Augustine established the balance between God's grace and man's will, between the sacraments and morality, which was to become the theological foundation of all Christian reform movements in the West for a thousand years."

[2] Augustine, *Opus Imp. Contra Jul.*, VI, 11; PL 45, 1519-1521.

[3] Cf. G. P. Vigneaux, "Références à saint Augustin chez Reinhold Niebuhr," *Augustinus Magister*, Communications, Congrès International Augustinien, Paris, 1954, vol. II, p. 1121. Augustine, *In Epist. Joan.*, VII, 8; PL 35, 2033: Dilige, et quod vis fac.

If there is wonder why Augustine is called a philosopher of freedom rather than a theologian, since man is freed by grace, we can recall the words of Maurice Blondel, "L'Unité Originale et la Pensée Permanente de la Doctrine Philosophique de Saint Augustin," *Revue de Métaphysique et de Morale*, 1930, p. 424: "Que là même où il parle en théologien et en historien, il reste toujours philosophe, que, en un sens, cet aspect philosophique de sa pensée fasse l'unité véritable de l'œuvre immense et si diverse qui se déploie en cinquante années d'incessante activité... Que, par surcroît, cette extension paradoxale (qui reste le and so lovingly and few men have attained to the self-awareness that was Augustine's. Once he realized that man was *capax Dei,* Augustine was content with nothing less then a participation in Divine freedom. If man can be freed only by Christ, as the Scriptures say, and Christ as God is transcendent, it is to be expected that the means of emancipation are supernatural. Augustine placed his own natural participation in the creative efficient causality, namely, his free will, at the disposal of the Final Cause, and allowed to his God, the End, and to Christ, the Way, full liberty in freeing him and reforming him into a clearer image of God. And God fulfilled his natural aspirations and transformed his passivity into activity, his receiving into giving. Through Augustine's experience and Augustine's teaching the notion of freedom has been illuminated. But the mystery remains.

caractère original et, pour ainsi dire, unique, de la conception augustinienne) réponde au vœu secret de l'esprit philosophique; que l'intégralité de ses perspectives rende compte d'une puissance d'assimilation et de régénération demeurée féconde et toujours actuelle en fournissant à la pensée chrétienne le principe interne et permanent de sa continuité, c'est ce que, au point de vue de la méthode et de l'histoire, nous voudrions nous borner à envisager présentement. Car, faute d'entrer d'abord en cette perspective, on a au cours des siècles, fait à Augustin bien des emprunts dénaturants, bien des critiques injustifiées."

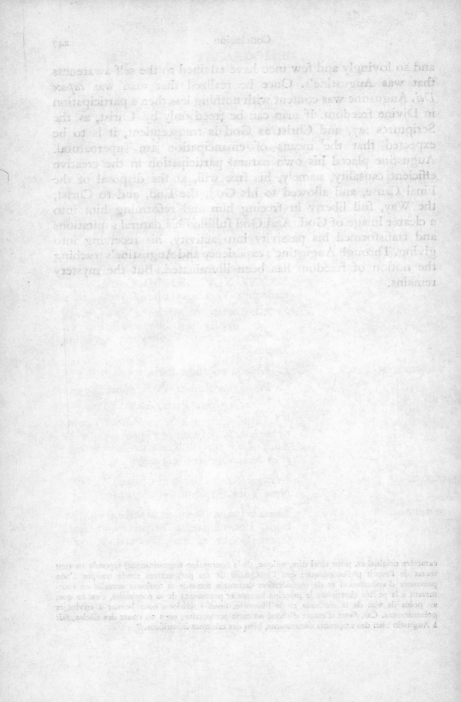

BIBLIOGRAPHY

Primary Sources :

ANSELM, Sancti Anselmi : *Opera Omnia*, Migne, *Patrologia Latina*, tomes CLVIII and CLIX, (1841-45).

Opera Omnia, (ed. Francis Schmitt), Edinburgh, Nelson. Volumes I and II.

ARISTOTLE, *Works* (trans. W. D. Ross), London, Oxford University Press, 1925.

AUGUSTINE, Sancti Aurelii Augustini : *Opera Omnia*, Migne, *Patrologia Latina*, tomes XXXII-XLVII.

Sancti Aurelii Augustini : *In Iohannis Evangelium ; De Civitate Dei*, etc. vols. XXXVI, XLVII, XLVIII, Corpus christianorum, Turnhout, Brepols, 1945, 1955.

Sancti Aurelii Augustini : Vols. 25, 35, 36, 40, 42, 43, 44, Corpus Scriptorum Ecclesiasticorum Latinorum, Vienna, Tempsky.

BLONDEL, MAURICE, *L'Action*, 2 volumes, Paris, Alcan, 1936-37.

La Pensée, 2 volumes, Paris, Alcan, 1934.

L'Etre et les êtres, Paris, Alcan, 1935.

" L'Unité Originale et la Pensée Permanente de la Doctrine Philosophique de Saint Augustin, " *Revue de Métaphysique et de Morale*, (1930), 423-469.

PLATO, *Dialogues* (trans. Benjamin Jowett), 2 vols., New York, Random House, 1937.

PLOTINUS, *Enneads* (trans. Stephen MacKenna), Chicago, Encyclopaedia Britannica (Series : Great Books of the Western World : vol. 17), 1952.

Ennéades (trans. Emile Bréhier), Paris, 1936.

Opera, Enneades I-III (ed. Paul Henry et Hans-Rudolf Schwyzer), Museum Lessianum, Desclée de Brouwer et Cie; 1951.

The Enneads (trans. Stephen MacKenna, 2nd ed. revised by B. S. Page), London, Faber and Faber, 1956.

THOMAS AQUINAS, Sancti Thomae Aquinatis : *Opera omnia, iussu impensaque Leonis XIII, P. M. edita* Romae, 1882-1900.

We cite Saint Augustine according to the first edition of Migne (1841-45), *Patrologia Latina*, tomes XXXII-XLVII. Because all of Augustine's works have not yet appeared in CSEL, it was considered best to keep the work uniform by quoting from Migne. For the key-texts on the topic of freedom, however, the CSEL was also consulted.

We utilize also the following translations of Augustine's works :

Ancient Christian Writers, Westminster, Maryland, The Newman Press, 1948.

The Fathers of the Church, (General editor : Roy Joseph Deferrari), New York, Ceina 1946 ff.

Confessions of St. Augustine (trans. Frank J. Sheed), New York, Sheed and Ward, 1947.

Confessions of St. Augustine (trans. Sir Tobie Matthew, ed. Dom Roger Hudleston), London, Burns, Oates and Washbourne, 1923.

De Libero Arbitrio (trans. F. E. Tourscher, O.S.A.), Philadelphia, Peter Reilly, 1937.

De Libero Arbitrio (trans. F. J. Thonnard), Paris, Desclée de Brouwer, 1941.

We cite St. Thomas according to the following translations : *Summa Theologica* (trans. Fathers of English Dominican Province), 3 vols., New York, Benziger Brothers, 1947; *Summa Contra Gentiles* (trans. Fathers of English Dominican Province, London, Burns, Oates, Washbourne; *Truth* (trans. from Leonine text), 3 vols., Chicago, H. Regnery Company, 1952-54.

Secondary Works :

ALFARIC, PROSPER, *L'Evolution Intellectuelle de Saint Augustin*, Paris, Nourry, 1918.

ALLEN, E. L., *Christian Humanism*, London, Hodder et Stoughton, 1950.

ARMSTRONG, A. HILARY, *An Introduction to Ancient Philosophy*, Westminster, Maryland, Newman Press, 1949.

The Greek Philosophical Background of the Psychology of St. Thomas, Oxford, Blackfriars, 1952.

Plotinus, London, George Allen and Unwin, 1953.

ARNOU, RENÉ, " L'Acte de l'Intelligence en tant qu'elle n'est pas Intelligence, " *Mélanges Joseph Maréchal*, tome II, Paris, Desclée de Brouwer, 1950.

Le Désir de Dieu dans la Philosophie de Plotin, Paris, Alcan, 1921.

" Platonisme des Pères, " *Dictionnaire de Théologie Catholique*, XII, (1934), 2258-2392.

AUTHORS, VARIOUS, *Augustinus Magister*, 3 vols., Congrès International Augustinien, Paris, September 1954.

" Etudes sur Saint Augustin. " *Archives de Philosophie*, (1930), 1-272.

Various articles on St. Augustine, *Blackfriars*, XXV (1954), 456-487.

Freedom, Its Meaning (ed. Ruth N. Anshen), New York, Harcourt Brace, 1940.

Mélanges Augustiniens, Paris, 1931.

A Monument to St. Augustine (ed. Martin D'Arcy), London, Sheed and Ward, 1930.

The Concept of Freedom (ed. St. John's University, New York), Chicago, Regnery, 1955.

The Controversy Concerning Human Freedom, San Francisco Institute for Philosophical Research, 1953.

BARDY, GUSTAVE, *Saint Augustin*, 6th edition, Paris, Desclée, 1946.

BATTENHOUSE, ROY, *A Companion to the Study of St. Augustine*, Oxford, University Press, New York, 1955

BERGSON, HENRI, *Time and Free Will*, (trans. F. L. Pogson), London, George Allen, 1912.

BERSOT, ERNEST, *Doctrine de Saint Augustin sur la Liberté et la Providence*, Paris, Joubert, 1843.

BOIGELOT, R., "Le Mot 'personne' dans les Écrits Trinitaires de S. Augustin," *Nouvelle Revue Théologique*, (1930), 5-16.

BOURKE, VERNON, *Augustine's Quest of Wisdom*. Milwaukee, Bruce, 1945.

BOYER, CHARLES, *Bulletin Augustinien*, Gregorianum, 1931, 1933.

Christianisme et Néo-platonisme dans la Formation de Saint Augustin, Paris, Beauchesne, 1920.

Essais sur la Doctrine de Saint Augustin, Paris, Beauchesne, 1932.

L'idée de Vérité dans la Philosophie de Saint Augustin, Paris, Beauchesne.

BRÉHIER, ÉMILE, *La Philosophie de Plotin*, Paris, Boivin, 1951.

"Y-a-t-il une Philosophie Chrétienne?". *Revue de Métaphysique et de Morale*, (1931).

BROGLIE, GUY DE, S. J., *De Fine Ultimo*, Paris, Beauchesne, 1947.

CAIRNS, DAVID, *The Image of God in Man*, New York, Philosophical Library, n. d.

CAYRÉ, FULBERT, *Initiation à la Philosophie de Saint Augustin*, Paris, Etudes Augustiniennes, 1947.

CHARMOT, FRANÇOIS, *L'Amour Humain*, Paris, Spes, 1940.

CHENU, MARIE DOMINIQUE, O. P., "Christian Liberty and Obligations," *Blackfriars*, XX (1939), 263-276; 332-343.

CHEVALIER, JACQUES, *La Notion du Nécessaire chez Aristote*, Paris, Alcan, 1915.

CICERO, MARCUS T., *De Fato*, (Loeb edition), Cambridge, Harvard University Press, 1942.

COCHRANE, CHARLES NORRIS, *Christianity and Classical Culture*, Oxford, Clarendon Press, 1940.

COMBES, GUSTAVE, *Saint Augustin et la Culture Classique*, Paris, 1927.

COPLESTON, FREDERICK C., *Existentialism and modern man*, Oxford, Blackfriars, 1948.

COURCELLE, PIERRE, *Les Lettres Grecques en Occident*, Paris, E. de Boccard, 1950.

Recherches sur les Confessions de Saint Augustin, Paris, E. de Boccard, 1950.

"Les Premières Confessions de Saint Augustin," *Revue des Etudes Latines*, XXII (1945), 155-174.

COLLINS, JAMES, *The Existentialists*, Chicago, Regnery, 1952.

The Mind of Kierkegaard, Chicago, Regnery 1953.

COVENTRY, JOHN, S.J., *Morals and Independence*, London, Burns Oates, 1949.

CRANSTON, MAURICE, *Freedom*, London, Longmans Green, 1953.

D'ARCY, M. C., S. J., *The Mind and Heart of Love*, New York, Holt, 1947.

DANIÉLOU, JEAN, *Platonisme et Théologie Mystique*, Paris, Aubier, 1944.

DAWSON, CHRISTOPHER, "Christian Freedom," *Dublin Review*, (1942), 1-7.

DE FINANCE, JOSEPH, *Etre et Agir*, Paris, Beauchesne, 1945.

DELASALLE, JACQUES, *Liberté et Valeur*, Louvain, Publications Universitaires, 1950.

DEMPSEY, PETER JAMES, *The Psychology of Sartre*, Maryland, Newman Press, 1950.

DIGGS, BERNARD J., *Love and Being*, New York, Vanni, 1947.

FARBER, MARVIN, *Philosophic Thought in France and the United States*, University of Buffalo, 1950.

FONSEGRIVE, GEORGE L., *Essai sur le Libre Arbitre*, Paris, Alcan, 1887.

FOREST, AIMÉ, *Consentement et Création*, Paris, Aubier, 1943.

" Le Réalisme de la Volonté, " *Revue Thomiste*, XLVI, (1946), 457-476.

FULLER, BENJAMIN, *The Problem of Evil in Plotinus*, Cambridge, University Press, 1912.

GAITH, JÉROME, La Conception de la Liberté chez Grégoire de Nysse, Paris, Vrin, 1953.

GARCIA, FELIX, *Obras de San Agustin en edición bilingue publicadas*, 2nd edition, Madrid, Biblioteca de Autores Cristianos, 1950.

GARRIGOU-LAGRANGE, REGINALD, *Our Saviour and His Love for Us* (trans. A. Bouchard), St. Louis, B. Herder, 1951.

GARVEY, MARY P., *St. Augustine, Christian or Neo-Platonist?* Milwaukee, Bruce, 1939.

GAUTHIER, RENÉ A., O. P., " Saint Maxime le Confesseur et la Psychologie de l'Acte Humain, " *Recherches de Théologie ancienne et médiévale*, Louvain, XXI, (1954), 51-100.

GEIGER, LOUIS B., O. P., *Le Problème de l'Amour chez Saint Thomas d'Aquin*, Paris, Vrin, 1952.

GILSON, ÉTIENNE, Compte rendu d'Alfaric, ' L'Évolution Intellectuelle de S. Augustin, ' *Revue Philosophique*, (1919), 497-505.

History of Christian Philosophy in the Middle Ages, New York, Random House, 1954.

Introduction à l'Étude de Saint Augustin, 2nd edition, Paris, Vrin, 1943.

Jean Duns Scot, Paris, Vrin, 1952.

La Philosophie au Moyen-Age, 4th edition, Paris, Payot, 1944.

Le *Thomisme*. 5th édition, Paris, Vrin, 1944.

" Pourquoi S. Thomas a critiqué S. Augustin, " *Archives d'Histoire Doctrinale et Littéraire du Moyen-Age*, I, (1926-1927), 5-127.

" Réflexions sur la Controverse S. Thomas-S. Augustin, " *Mélanges Mandonnet*, t. I, Paris, 372-383.
The Spirit of Medieval Philosophy, (trans. A. H. C. Downes), New York, Scribner's 1940.

GRANDGEORGE, L., *Saint Augustin et le néo-Platonisme*, Paris, E. Leroux, 1896.

GROU, JEAN, N., *Morale Tirée des Confessions de Saint Augustin*, Paris, Ruffet 1863.

GUARDINI, ROMANO, *Die Bekehrung des Aurelius Augustinus*, München, 1950.

GUITTON, JEAN, *Actualité de St. Augustin*, Dijon, Grasset, 1955.
Essay on Human Love, (trans. Melville Chaning-Peerce), New York, Philosophical Library, 1951.
Le Temps et l'Éternité chez Plotin et Saint Augustin, Paris, Boivin 1933.

HARVEY, RUDOLF, *The Metaphysical Relation between Person and Liberty*, Washington, Catholic University of America, 1942.

HEIDEGGER, MARTIN, *Existence and Being*, London, Vision, 1949.

HENRY, PAUL, S. J., *La Vision d'Ostie, sa Place dans la Vie et l'Œuvre de S. Augustin*, Paris, Vrin, 1938.
" Le Problème de la Liberté chez Plotin, " *Revue Néo-Scolastique de Philosophie*, 1931, Louvain, (50-79), (180-215), (318-339).
Plotin et l'Occident, Louvain, Spicilegium Sacrum Lovaniense, 1934.
" Augustine and Plotinus, " *Journal of Theological Studies*, XXXVIII, (1937), 1-23.
" The Christian Philosophy of History, " *Theological Studies*, XIII, (1952), 419-432.

HERTLING, GEORGE F. VON, " Augustinus-Zitate bei Thomas von Aquin, 1904, " *Historische Beitrage zur Philosophie herausg geben von Dr. J. A. Endres*, München, 1914.

HILDEBRAND, DIETRICH VON, *Christian Ethics*, New York, McKay, 1953.

HULTGREN, GUNNAR, *Le Commandement d'Amour chez Augustin*, Paris, Vrin, 1939.

JOHANN, ROBERT O., S. J., *The Meaning of Love*, Westminster, Maryland, Newman Press, 1955.

JOLIVET, RÉGIS, *Essai sur les Rapports entre la Pensée Grecque et la Pensée Chrétienne*, Paris, Vrin, 1931.

Le problème du Mal d'après Saint Augustin, Paris, Beauchesne, 1936.

Les doctrines existentialistes, Abbaye Saint Wandrille, Fontenelle, 1948.

Saint Augustin et le néo-Platonisme Chrétien, Paris, Denoel et Steele, 1932.

KONCYEWSKA, HÉLÈNE, *Contingence, Liberté et la Personnalité humaine*, Paris, Vrin, 1937.

LANGE, HERMANN, *De Gratia*, Freiburg, Herder, 1929.

LEO XIII, *Human liberty*, Encyclical Letter : *Libertas Præstantissimum*, June 20, 1888.

LÉON DUFOUR, XAVIER, S. J., " Grâce et Libre Arbitre chez Saint Augustin, " *Recherches de Science Religieuse*, XXXIII, (1946), 129-163.

LEWIS, CLIVE S., *Christian Behavior*, New York, Macmillan, 1944.

LOTTIN, ODON, *Psychologie et Morale aux XII et XIII siecles*, 3 vols., Louvain, Abbaye du Mont César, 1942.

L'UNIVERSITÉ CATHOLIQUE DE LOUVAIN, *Liberté et Vérité*, Louvain, Publications Universitaires, 1954.

LYONNET, STANISLAS, " Liberté Chrétienne et la Loi de l'Esprit selon Saint Paul, " *Christus*, nº 4 (1954), 6-27.

MARCEL, GABRIEL, *The Mystery of Being*, 2 vols., Chicago, Regnery, 1950-1951.

MARÉCHAL, JOSEPH, S. J., *Etudes sur la psychologie des mystiques*, tome I, Paris, Alcan, 1924.

MARITAIN, JACQUES, *Freedom in the Modern World* (trans. Richard O'Sullivan), London, Sheed and Ward, 1935.

Humanisme Intégral, Paris, Aubier, 1936.

La Philosophie Bergsonienne, 2e édition, Paris, Marcel Rivière, 1930.

Neuf Leçons sur les Notions Premières de la Philosophie Morale, Paris, Téqui, n. d.

"L'Idée Thomiste de Liberté," *Revue Thomiste*, (1939), 440-459.

Some Reflections on Culture and Liberty, University of Chicago Press, 1933.

Range of reason, New York, Scribner's, 1952.

MARROU, HENRI I., *Saint Augustin et la fin de la Culture Antique*, Paris, E. de Boccard, 1938.

MARTIN, JULES, *Saint Augustin*, 2nd edition, Paris, Alcan, 1923.

MAUSBACH, JOSEPH, *Die Ethik des heilg. Augustinus*, 2 vols., Freiburg, Herder, 1929.

MCALLISTER, JOSEPH B., "The Influence of Immanuel Kant's Concept of Liberty," *Proceedings of the American Catholic Philosophical Association*, XVI (1940), 38-52.

MENENDEZ, JOSEPHA, *Way of Divine Love,* Westminster, Md., Newman Press, 1950.

MERSCH, ÉMILE, "Deux Traités de la Doctrine Spirituelle de Saint Augustin," *Nouvelle Revue Théologique*, (1930), 391-410.

MONDADON, LOUIS DE, "La Modernité de S. Augustin," *Etudes*, (1930), 257-270.

MOUNIER, EMMANUEL, *Introduction aux Existentialismes*, Paris, De Noel, 1947.

MOUROUX, JEAN, *The Meaning of Man* (trans. A. H. C. Downes), New York, Sheed and Ward, 1948.

The Christian Experience, (trans. George Lamb), New York, Sheed and Ward, 1954.

MULLANEY, THOMAS, *Suarez on Human Freedom*, Baltimore, Carroll Press, 1950.

NEBREDA, EULOGIUS, *Bibliographia Augustiniana*, Rome, 1928.

NOURISSON, JEAN FÉLIX, *La Philosophie de Saint Augustin*, 2 vols. 2nd edition, Paris, Didier 1869.

NUYENS, FRANÇOIS, *L'Évolution de la Psychologie d'Aristote*, Paris, Vrin, 1948.

O'CONNELL, DAVID, O. P., *Christian Liberty*, Westminster, Maryland, Newman Press, 1952.

O'DONNELL, CHARLES, *The Ideal of a New Christendom ;* the cultural and political philosophy of Jacques Maritain, Harvard University dissertation (typed), June, 1940 (microfilm).

PAULUS, JEAN, *Henri de Gand*, Paris, J. Vrin, 1938.

PEGIS, ANTON, " Necessity and Liberty : an historical note on St. Thomas Aquinas, " *Proceedings of the American Catholic Philosophical Association*, XVI, (1940), 1-27.

PETIT, GÉRARD, *L'Homme Contemporain et le Problème Moral*, Montréal, Fides, 1943.

PÉTRÉ HÉLÈNE, *Caritas,* Louvain, Spicilegium Sacrum Lovaniense, 1948.

PHELAN, GERALD B., *Some Illustrations of the Wisdom of St. Augustine*, Chicago, Argus Press, 1946.

" Person and Liberty, " *Proceedings of the American Catholic Philosophical Association*, XVI, (1940) 53-69.

PINARD, H., " Création ," *Dictionnaire de Théologie Catholique*, III (1907), 2034-2201.

PISTORIUS, PHILIPPUS V. *Plotinus and Neoplatonism*, Cambridge, Bowes and Bowes, 1952.

PIUS XII, *Humani generis*, encyclical letter. August 12, 1950.

PLUTARCH, *Moralia*, (Loeb edition), Cambridge, Harvard University Press, 1949.

POLLOCK, ROBERT C., " Freedom and history, " *Thought*, XXVII (1952), 400-420.

PORTALIÉ, E., " Augustin ," *Dictionnaire de Théologie Catholique*, I, (1902), 2268-2472.

QUINN, EDWARD, " Free Will in the Modern World, " *Blackfriars*, XXX (1940), 459-464.

RAND, E. KENNARD, *The Founders of the Middle Ages*, Cambridge, Harvard University Press, 1928.

RICŒUR, PAUL, *Philosophie de la Volonté*, Paris, Aubier, 1951,

ROHMER, JEAN, *La finalité Morale chez les Théologiens de Saint Augustin à Duns Scot*, Paris, Vrin, 1939.

ROLAND-GOSSELIN, BERNARD, *La Morale de Saint Augustin*, Paris, Rivière, 1925.

ROMEYER, BLAISE, " S. Augustin, " *Archives de Philosophie*, VI, (1928), 603-633.

ROUSSELOT, PIERRE, S. J., " Pour l'Histoire du Problème de l'Amour au Moyen Age, " *Beitrage zur Geschichte des Philosophie des Mittelalters*, VII, 6, Munster, 1908.

RYADKIEWICZ, ARNOLD LADISLAS, *Philosophical Bases of Human Liberty according to Saint Thomas Aquinas*, Washington, Catholic University of America, 1949.

SALMON, ELIZABETH G., *The Good in Existential Metaphysics*, Milwaukee, Marquette University Press, 1953.

SIMON, YVES, " Liberty and Authority, " *Proceedings of the American Catholic Philosophical Association*, XVI (1940), 86-114.

Nature and Functions of Authority, Milwaukee, Marquette University Press, 1940.

Traité du Libre Arbitre, Liège, Sciences et Lettres, 1951.

SIMONIN, H. D., "Autour de la Solution Thomiste du Problème de l'Amour," *Archives d'histoire doctrinale et littéraire du moyen âge*, VI (Paris, 1932), 247-251.

SMITH, ENID, *The Goodness of Being in Thomistic Philosophy and its Contemporary Significance*, Washington, Catholic University of America Press, 1947.

SMITH, GERARD, "Intelligence and Liberty," *Proceedings of the American Catholic Philosophical Association*, XVI (1940), 69-85.

The Truth That Frees, Milwaukee, Marquette University Press, 1956.

STEVENS, DOM GREGORY, O. S. B., "The Disinterested Love of God according to St. Thomas and Some of his Modern Interpreters," *The Thomist*, XVI, 3, July, 1953 (307-333); XVI, 4, October, 1953 (497-541).

SWITALSKI, BRUNO, *Plotinus and the Ethics of St. Augustine*, New York, Polish Institute of Arts and Sciences, 1946.

TAYLOR, ALFRED E., *Plato*, London, Methuen and Co., 1949.

VANN, GERALD, O. P., *Morals Makyth Man*, New York, Longmans Green, 1938.

"Obedience and Freedom," *Blackfriars*, XXI (1940), 580-592.

VAN STEENBERGHEN, FERDINAND, "La philosophie de S. Augustin," *Revue Néo-Scholastique de Philosophie*, (1932), 366-387; (1933), 106-126; 230-281.

VEGA, ANGEL C., *St. Augustine - His Philosophy* (trans. Denis J. Kavanagh, O. S. A.), Philadelphia, Reilly, 1931.

VOGT, BERNARD, "Metaphysics of Human Liberty in Duns Scotus," *Proceedings of the American Catholic Philosophical Association*, XVI (1940), 27-37.

SARTRE, JEAN-PAUL, *L'Existentialisme est un Humanisme*, Paris, Nagel, 1946.

Situations I, II, Paris, Gallimard, 1947.

WAHL, JEAN, *Esquisse pour une Histoire de l'Existentialisme*, Paris, L'Arche, 1949.

WANG, TCH'ANG-TCHE, JOSEPH, S. J., *Saint Augustin et les Vertus des Païens*, Paris, Beauchesne, 1938.

WARD, BARBARA, *Faith and Freedom*, New York, Norton 1954.

WORONIECKI, H., "Pour une Bonne Définition de la Liberté Humaine," *Angelicum*, (1937).

INDEX OF PROPER NAMES

INDEX OF REFERENCES TO THE WORKS OF ST. AUGUSTINE

Printed in Belgium by DESCLÉE & Co, ÉDITEURS, S. A. Tournai — 10.317

AUGUSTINE

PHILOSOPHER OF FREEDOM

The riches of our Christian tradition need to be mined anew for each generation. Accordingly, Mother Clark's book is destined to make the treasures of Augustine's thought accessible to the student and to the average reader.

Contributing to a clearer, more complete understanding of Augustine, Mother Clark considers her subject in the light of a single, basic principle: the idea of freedom. Augustine himself is allowed in this book to speak out on a topic so appropriate to the world today. Freedom, exploited by Existentialists, denied by Totalitarians, was appreciated properly by St. Augustine.

Here is a book calculated to put in bold relief the timelessness of Augustine's genius and to explain to modern man the truths he needs most: the meaning of God and the meaning of man.